THE GETTYSBURG CAMPAIGN

THE GETTYSBURG CAMPAIGN

June and July, 1863

Albert A. Nofi

GALLERY BOOKS
An imprint of W.H. Smith Publishers Inc.
112 Madison Avenue
New York, New York 10016

Prepared by Combined Books, P.O. Box 577,
Conshohocken, PA 19428

Project Coordinator: Robert Pigeon

Produced by Wieser and Wieser, Inc.,
118 East 25th Street, New York, NY 10010.

This edition published by Gallery Books, an imprint
of W.H. Smith Publishers, Inc., 112 Madison Avenue,
New York, NY 10016.

Library of Congress Cataloging-in-Publication Data

Nofi, Albert A.
   The Gettysburg campaign: June and July, 1863.

   (Great military campaigns of history)
   1. Gettysburg Campaign, 1863. I. Title. II. Series.
E475.51.N63 1986   973.7'349   86-6561

ISBN 0-8317-3859-6

CONTENTS

From the Dustbin of History

Maps

GENERAL MAP KEY

TERRAIN FEATURES

State Line		Railroad and Incomplete Railroad
Hills and Mountains		Stream
Forest and Woods		Building
Road		Towns
Rivers and Streams		City

POSITION AND MOVEMENT SYMBOLS

UNION	CONFEDERATE
	Artillery Lines
Pickets	Pickets
Battlelines	Battlelines
Concentration	Concentration
Movement	Movement

FORMATION SIGNS

Infantry		Corps	X X X
Cavalry		Army	X X X X
Brigade	X	Reduced Unit	(−)
Division	X X	Reinforced Unit	(+)

ACKNOWLEDGMENTS

A great many people helped produce this book in one way or another. Their listing here is my limited way of offering thanks for their assistance.

Prof. John Boardman, who helped figure out the meteorological data and, with Dennis Casey, helped explore the battlefield on foot; to Matilda Virgilio Clark, who provided access to certain family records concerning the battle; to Helena Rubenstein, Daniel Scott Palter, and the staff of *West End Games*, for use of their extensive Civil War collection, and to Stephan Patejak, who helped guide me through it; to Mark Herman and Eric Smith, of *Victory Games*, who provided access to their own, and the company's extensive Civil War Collection; to Dan Kilbert of New York Compleat Strategist, who helped track down simulation materials; to Daniel David, for providing some obscure references; to Prof. Hans Trefousse, who unwittingly provided an interesting anecdote, to Bud Livingston and John Willetts of the New York Civil War Round Table, for their advice and assistance; to Dr. David G. Martin, for his advice and a copy of his and John W. Bussey's valuable volume on regimental strengths at Gettysburg; to Howard W. Hunter, who unknowingly provided some valuable material on the history of the Army of Northern Virginia; to Bob Capriotti, who provided some useful advice based on his long experience as a reenacter and to the fine people at The New York Public Library and The New York Historical Society, who patiently helped track down obscure information on arcane without knowing why.

Most of the photographs were duplicated from the extensive collections at the U.S. Army Military Institute in Carlisle, Pennsylvania. The staff at the Institute was enormously helpful as well knowledgeable, and always courteous. Without their help, I could not have gathered so many photos of just this one campaign.

The color portfolio highlights the work of several modern military artists. Their work is reproduced here by special arrangement with the American Print Gallery, 219 Steinwehr Avenue, Gettysburg, Pennsylvania 17325. Mr. Edmund Loper of the American Print Gallery was especially diligent in his efforts to secure for us these beautiful reproductions. The Eastern National Park and Monument Association was kind enough to allow us to reproduce sections of the spectacular Cyclorama at the Gettysburg National Park.

Many people helped with the thousands of details that make a book possible. Special thanks must go to Lizbeth Hoefer Nauta, Kirsten Kerr, Edward Wimble, Gary and Mary Sue Gross, and Kenneth Gallagher.

Particular thanks go to Bob Pigeon, of Combined Books, who developed the idea for *The Great Campaigns of Military History*; and to Kevin Wilkins, who made the maps from my ham-fisted sketches.

Especial thanks are due to my wife, Mary S. Nofi, who walked the field as well, and who, along with my daughter Marilyn J. Spencer, both suffered through the writing.

Albert A. Nofi
Brooklyn, N.Y.
30 October, 1985

★The Great Military Campaigns of History★

PREFACE TO THE SERIES

Jonathan Swift termed war "that mad game the world so loves to play". He had a point. Universally condemned, it has nevertheless been almost as universally practiced. For good or ill, war has played a significant role in the shaping of history. Indeed, there is hardly a human institution which has not in some fashion been influenced and molded by war, even as it helped shape and mold war in turn. Yet the study of war has been as remarkably neglected as its practice has been commonplace. With a few outstanding exceptions, the history of wars and of military operations has until quite recently been largely the province of the inspired patriot or the regimental polemicist. Only in our times have serious, detailed, and objective accounts come to be considered the norm in the treatment of military history and related matters. Yet there still remains a gap in the literature, for there are two types of military history. One type is written from a very serious, highly technical, professional perspective and presupposes that the reader is deeply familiar with background, technology, and general situation. The other is perhaps less dry, but merely lightly reviews the events with the intention of informing and entertaining the layman. The qualitative gap between the two is vast. Moreover, there are professionals in both the military and in academia whose credentials are limited to particular moments in the long, sad history of war, and there are laymen who have a more than passing understanding of the field; and then there is the concerned citizen, interested in understanding the phenomenon in an age of unusual violence and unprecedented armaments. It is to bridge the gap between the two types of military history, and to reach the professional and the serious amateur and the concerned citizen alike, that this series, *The Great Campaigns of Military History*, is designed.

The individual volumes of *The Great Campaigns of Military History* are each devoted to an intensive examination of a particularly significant military operation. The focus is not on individual battles, but on campaigns, on the relationship between movements and battles and how they fit within the overall framework of the war in question. By making use of a series of innovative techniques for the presentation of information, *The Great Campaigns of Military History* can satisfy the exacting demands of the professional and the serious amateur, while making it possible for the concerned citizen to understand the events and the conditions under which they developed. This is accomplished in a number of ways. Each volume contains a substantial, straight-forward narrative account of the campaign under study. This is supported by an extensive series of modular "sidebars". Some are devoted to particular specific technical matters, such as weaponry, logistics, organization, or tactics. These modules each contain detailed analyses of their topic, and make considerable use of "hard" data, with many charts and tables. Other modules deal with less technical matters, such as strategic analysis, anecdotes, personalities, uniforms, and politics. Each volume contains several detailed maps, supplemented by a number of clear, accurate sketchmaps, which assist the reader in understanding the course of events under consideration, and there is an extensive set of illustrations which have been selected to assist the reader still further. Finally, each volume contains materials designed to help the reader who is interested in learning more. But this "bibliography" includes not merely a short list of books and articles related to the campaign in question. It also contains information on study groups devoted to the subject, on films which deal with it, on recordings of period music, on simulation games and skirmish clubs which attempt to recreate the tactics, on museums where one can have a first-hand look at equipment, and on tours of the battlefields. The particular contents of each volume will, of course, be determined by the topic in question, but each will provide an unusually rich and varied treatment of the subject. Each volume in *The Great Campaigns of Military History* is thus not merely an account of a particular military operation, but it is a unique reference to the theory and practice of war in the period in question.

The Great Campaigns of Military History is a unique contribution to the study of war and of military history, which will remain of interest and use for many years.

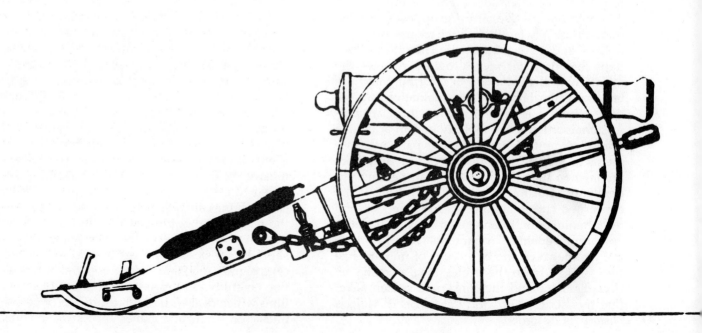

INTRODUCTION

When the Union began to come apart in late 1860 and early 1861 as the Southern states sought to create a new nation out of the fabric of the old, no one on either side of the secession issue had any firm notion of the consequences. Even as South Carolina, Mississippi, Florida, Alabama, Georgia, Louisiana, and Texas each adopted an "ordinance of secession", many believed it would not come to a clash of arms. But the questions at issue were too serious and too emotionally ladened to avoid a struggle. Neither the integrity of the Union nor slavery were matters over which men could any longer compromise. So there was war, the bloodiest and greatest in the American experience.

By the summer of 1863 the American people had suffered through two years of bloody civil war with little to show for it.

For the Union it had been a frustrating time. Great armies had repeatedly marched southwards with hopes high for a swift victory, only to be beaten back in defeat and disgrace. Some, a few, despaired, whether from conviction or political expediency, saying that it was not worth pursuing the war any further. But the spirit of the nation remained remarkably firm, sustained by the indomitable will of President Lincoln, and fueled by the Emancipation Proclamation. Despite numerous reverses, the Union remained strong. The enormous agricultural, industrial, and financial resources of the North had been mobilized and production of the munitions of war had soared. Adroit diplomacy had averted foreign recognition of the rebellious South. A powerful navy had been created to deny the use of the rivers and coasts and seas to the South. A great army of some 800,000 men had been raised, trained, and equipped, of whom some 600,000 seasoned men were ready to take the field. Able commanders were coming to the lead them in increasing numbers. All that was required for victory was time, and will.

The first two years of the war had been frustrating for the Confederacy as well. There had been many great and costly victories, but neither independence nor foreign recognition had been secured. Nevertheless, much had been accomplished. A functioning government had been set up. Whole new industries had been created. A navy had been established and commerce raiders were scouring the seas in search of Federal merchantmen. Most spectacularly, a fine army of some 500,000 men had been recruited and trained and equipped and led to victory by a remarkably talented group of generals. It was heady stuff, and Southern morale and determination remained high. To be sure, there were great dangers yet to be faced, but few in the Confederacy appear to have doubted the inevitability of victory. However, some discerning individuals had begun to realize that the ability of the South to sustain the war much longer was limited. The nature of war had changed, and changed in ways that were sometimes spectacular and sometimes barely perceptible.

What had changed the conduct of war was the Industrial Revolution. It was no longer possible for a war to be decided in one or two great, decisive battles as in the days of Napoleon. The mechanization of industry and agriculture permitted virtually limitless production of the munitions of war, while at the same time releasing enormous numbers of men to fight. Railroads and telegraphs and steamships permitted greater efficiency in the movements of men and materiél. And the increasing technical sophistication of weapons made the battlefield far bloodier and more dangerous than ever before. Nurtured on the lessons of the Napoleonic

Wars, politicians and generals were slow to see the impact of these changes; ordinary citizens had no understanding of them at all. In the new age the society with the greatest resources would win, given the will to win.

So, appearances aside, the strategic situation of the South in the Summer of 1863 was poor. The Confederacy was rapidly approaching the limits of its resources. Little more could be expected from the South's slender industrial base. Manpower was beginning to become hard to find. Foreign trade was virtually nonexistent as the Union blockade became ever more effective. Militarily, conditions were deteriorating. In the West, Grant was driving one Confederate army against the fortress of Vicksburg, while Rosecrans prepared to drive another out of Eastern Tennessee and into Georgia. And in the East, despite the reverse at Chancellorsville, the *Army of the Potomac* remained strong and game north of the Rappahannock. A significant prolongation of the war would not be favorable to the South. Thus was the stage set for the Campaign and the Battle of Gettysburg.

Gettysburg as it looked in 1863 from the west

CHAPTER I

COUNSELS OF WAR

Concerned with the overall strategic situation of the South, Confederate Gen. Robert E. Lee, commanding the Army of Northern Virginia, began to think about undertaking an offensive into Union territory during the Winter of 1863. Such a maneuver had several points in its favor. A continued defensive posture in Virginia would permanently concede the initiative to the Union, for the *Army of the Potomac* would eventually come south once again and not even Lee and the Army of Northern Virginia could win every battle. Moreover, the present position of the army, just south of the Rappahannock River, was difficult to sustain logistically, particularly as Southern resources were beginning to show the strain of war. Another winter on the Rappahannock line might well prove the ruination of the army. In the North the army would be able to carry off supplies sufficient to enable it to get through the winter in good condition. Going north would also take the pressure off war-torn Virginia for a while, which might further improve the food situation for the coming winter. On a broader strategic level, an offensive would wrest the initiative from the Union. By striking into Pennsylvania, Lee would simultaneously be in a position to threaten both Washington and Baltimore, and, indeed, at least theoretically, even Philadelphia. The *Army of the Potomac* would be unable to avoid a decisive clash and, if defeated, would be too far from the safety of Fortress Washington to readily seek shelter. Meanwhile, Union armies in the West would be forced to send troops eastwards, thereby relieving the pressure on the Confederacy along the Mississippi and in eastern Tennessee. Perhaps most importantly of all, a successful invasion of the North could have far-reaching political consequences. It would strengthen Southern morale, while dealing a severe blow to that of the

Gen. Robert E. Lee

13

These New York volunteer militiamen were among the 13,000 mustered to help defend Pennsylvania. This pose was made at Harrisburg in late June, 1863.

Union, and at the same time encourage those elements in the North who were in favor of an immediate end to the war. A successful offensive might also result in securing of diplomatic recognition from Britain and France, and possibly their intervention. In short, an offensive could well win the war.

Other Confederate leaders were thinking about an offensive as well. During the Winter of 1862–1863 President Jefferson Davis and Secretary of War James A. Seddon, had proposed that Lee transfer a portion of his army to the West. This was an idea favored by both Gen. Joe Johnston and Gen. Braxton Bragg, who commanded in the West, and by Gen. Pierre G. T. Beauregard, who was usually at odds with the President. Even Lt. Gen. James Longstreet, Lee's ablest subordinates and commander of his veteran I Corps, believed the idea was sound. The basic concept was that Lee should accompany one or more of his corps to the Western

Lt. Gen. James Longstreet

Theater, where he would assume overall command, and either conduct operations directly against Grant's armies in the Mississippi Valley, or undertake an offensive from Tennessee into Kentucky and thence across the Ohio River with the intention of cutting the Union in half. Despite the combined opinion of this distinguished company, Lee nevertheless demurred. He believed that the threat posed by the *Army of the Potomac* was too great to weaken the defense of Virginia by a transfer of part of his magnificent Army of Northern Virginia to the West. He quite accurately pointed out that Southern rail communications between the two theaters were poor, so that the Union, though operating on exterior lines, would easily be able to counter such a movement. The army was already available for an offensive in the East, where, with distances shorter, and significant objectives closer at hand, it would be more difficult for the Union to react to sudden movements. A vigorous offensive in the East by a reinforced Army of Northern Virginia would be the best way to relieve the pressure in the West. His arguments, and his enormous prestige as the most successful of the Confederacy's generals overcame all opposition. In the end, after a series of conferences held in Richmond shortly after Lee's spectacular victory at Chancellorsville, President Davis and Secretary Seddon conceded and authorized an offensive into Pennsylvania.

It is unclear when Lee began planning his offensive. As early as February he had ordered maps prepared covering much of eastern Pennsylvania. He worked in secret, as always, though he almost certainly consulted with Lt. Gen. Thomas "Stonewall" Jackson and Longstreet. The Chancellorsville Campaign briefly interrupted these preparations, but he immediately resumed planning, whilst winning support for the offensive. As he envisoned the operation, minor forces would hold the attention of the *Army of the Potomac* on the Rappahannock. Meanwhile, a dense cavalry screen would cover the movement of the Army of Northern Virginia into the Shenandoah Valley. He would then advance up the Valley, his right flank protected by the Blue Ridge and South Mountain chains. Crossing the Potomac in the vicinity of Harper's Ferry, the army would debouche into the Cumberland Valley of Pennsylvania, where it would begin to forage. By keeping his forces well in hand, Lee hoped to be able to isolate and destroy stray elements of the *Army of the Potomac*, thereby weakening the opposition. Should it become necessary to fight a general action he expected that it would be in the vicinity of either Chambersburg, York, or Gettysburg, modest agricultural and market towns with good road communications. In the event of a successful battle, Lee had a notion to fall on either Washington or Baltimore, possibly forcing a peace. If a general action did not take place by the end of the summer, he would retreat back southwards, having stripped central Pennsylvania bare. To further strengthen his plan, Lee proposed that 20,000 troops be concentrated in the old Rappahannock position under Beauregard, thereby posing an additional threat which might further weaken the *Army of the Potomac*.

Lee's plan was sound, insofar as it went. But it had some flaws. The manpower resources of the South were increasingly slender. It would be difficult enough to bring the Army of Northern Virginia up to strength after its losses at Chancellorsville, let alone find sufficient manpower to reinforce it and to create a new army along the Rappahannock. In addition, the army would be operating far from its base, in hostile territory. A defeat could lead to its complete dissolution. He would have to exercise very close control over its movements to prevent units from passing beyond mutual supporting distance, while at the same time he would have to disperse his units so that they could forage. He appears to have counted on the assumption that the *Army of the Potomac* would continue to suffer from uninspired leadership. The plan left unclear whether Lee would seek to fight a defensive or offensive action if offered the opportunity for a general battle. It also made no provision for the possibility that such a general action might result in a defeat, leaving the Army of Northern Virginia isolated in the enemy's heartland. As a result of these flaws, Lee's plan was something of a double-edged blade, able to cut in either direction. By going into Pennsylvania he might well win the war, but he could as easily lose it. Caught up in the preparations for his great offensive, Lee, a bold, pugnacious soldier saw only the great benefits which it could bring to the South.

An example of the semi-permanent structures developed by both armies during the long periods of inactivity between campaigns

WHY THEY

The political question in dispute during the American Civil War was a simple one: Did any one, or group, of the several States have the right to secede from the Union? Politically there existed a legitimate difference of opinion on the matter. The Constitution is silent on the question. Nevertheless, on both philosophical and moral grounds the existence of such a right cannot be denied. A people who find their existing political system oppressive or ineffective have a legitimate right to change that system or separate themselves from it, peacefully if possible but by force of arms if necessary. This is a course of action which has been taken throughout history by many peoples who have found themselves the subject of social, political, or economic oppression on the part of their pre-existing government, as in the case of the inhabitants of the thirteen British colonies in 1776. This is all fairly reasonable, but is subject to some problems in terms of the real world. This was certainly true in the case of the Civil War. In 1860 the matter was by no means as simple as a straight-forward issue of political preference.

Frankly, the entire question of secession might never have arisen were it not for the existence of significant social, cultural, and economic differences between the Southern states and the rest of the Union, differences which became the basis for increasing political differences and tensions. The South was essentially rural, agricultural, and aristocratic, while the rest of the country was increasingly urban, industrial, and democratic. Now these differences alone were sufficient to spawn political constituencies. The North sought higher tariffs to protect its growing industries, while the South opposed them for fear they would interfere with the export of cotton. The North and West sought government sponsored internal improvements which would further the development of a commercial society, while the South saw no point to

them. And the North and the West sought a homestead act, to provide farms and a livelihood for their land hungry citizens, while the South opposed it, rightly seeing it as incompatible with the survival of an aristocratic society. Now, since the population of the North and the West was growing at a faster rate than that of the South, the tendency was for government policies to reflect northern and western interests more than southern ones. Since the Southerners viewed the ways in which the country was being run as contrary to their interests, they expressed their opposition to many existing policies on the grounds that they violated "states' rights," the residual rights reserved to the states by the Constitution. Obviously, these issues alone were sufficient reasons for significant regional tensions. But there was more. For there was an issue so important that it ultimately lay at the root of all the other problems. That issue was slavery.

The difference between the South and the rest of the Union had a simple origin, slavery. Slavery had created the planter aristocracy of the South. Slavery, which had made the South one of the preeminent agricultural region of the world, had also hampered its further growth in an era of industrialization. Slavery also retarded the growth of the Southern population: themselves frequently fleeing aristocratic institutions in their homelands, the flood of immigrants which began washing America's shores in the 1840s settled primarily in the North and West. By the middle of the nineteenth century, though relatively few Southerners actually owned slaves, and most of those who did had but one or two, most of the white people of the South had come to view slavery as vital to the survival of Southern society. To the slaveholders, of course, the "peculiar institution" represented wealth and status. This was something to which the non-slaveholders could aspire. More-

over, the fact that slavery had a racial dimension enhanced the status of the impoverished white: whatever else he was, he was "free, white, and twenty-one" which meant something. During this same period, however, the notion that slavery was inherently wrong was spreading rapidly through Western Civilization. By mid-century the United States was the only major Western country in which slavery was still legal. Nor was there an absence of opposition to slavery.

The Abolitionist movement grew steadily through the early decades of the century, despite the indifference of many and the active opposition of some. Moreover, active resistance to slavery was remarkably widespread, among both blacks and whites, reaching right into the South itself. The Underground railroad operated in every county in the country, and involved people from all levels of society and all walks of life. Slavery came under fire in books and plays and songs, in sermons and editorials and lectures. Southerners would continously defend the institution, but slavery was indefensible, regardless of the arguments advanced. The fundamental issue was individual freedom, and the institution was inherently incompatible with the promise of America. It was true that many factory workers in the North were less well-cared for than most slaves; but the factory worker had a reasonable chance of being able to alter his status. It was also true that the slaves were dependent, innocent, and childlike; for that's the way their masters wanted them to be. Moreover, their masters also said, quite correctly, that the slaves were ignorant, shiftless, and lazy; but what opportunity or motivation did they have to be otherwise? That there were numerous laws designed for the protection of slaves was undeniable; whether they were enforced was another matter, and the point begs the question anyway. Most assuredly the character of Southern

FOUGHT

society was rooted in slavery; which justified nothing. Abolition of slavery most definitely was a blow against property rights; which presupposed that people could legitimately be property in the first place. And it was certainly true that many a New England mandarin who thundered against slavery had ancestors who had made their fortunes in the slave trade; which had little to do with point. The impact of the debate over slavery was tremendous.

Slavery was the overriding issue of the age. Not even the political polarization which rent American society during the Vietnam War approached the vehemence of the debate over slavery. Families were broken up, friendships dissolved. Every major Protestant Church in the nation split in two, one branch opposing slavery and one favoring it. While Northerners snapped up 400,000 copies of Harriet Beecher Stowe's *Uncle Tom's Cabin* within a few years of its publication in 1851, Southerners avidly read detailed rebuttals composed by pro-slavery authors. While Abolitionists and former slaves like Frederick Douglass and Harriet Tubman stumped the North pointing out the evils of slavery, pro-slavery advocates toured the South, lecturing on its importance to "civilized living." Meanwhile the South, in violation of "states rights," demanded a Fugitive Slave Law. And violence became commonplace.

Eventually it became impossible to publicly express anti-slavery views in the South, and an incipient Southern Abolitionist movement was destroyed in a series of lynchings and riots. By the late 1850s there was open war in the Kansas Territory as the debate over whether the new state should be slave or free. Proslavery groups throughout the South sent bands of thugs to overawe the largely anti-slavery settlers. Abolitionist extremists replied in kind. Much blood was shed before the army could put down the disorders. Kansas became a

free state, but in 1859 one of the revolutionary Abolitionist veterans of "Bleeding Kansas," John Brown, seized the United States arsenal at Harpers Ferry in Virginia in an attempt to spark a slave insurrection throughout the South. He failed, but he convinced the pro-slavery elements that the people of the North were determined to end slavery. Thus, the election of 1860 became a referendum on slavery. Meanwhile, in the Dred Scott decision the Supreme Court seemed to rule that no state could ban slavery, which convinced even those Northerners indifferent to the issue that the pro-slavery elements wished to make the institution universal.

It was a unique election, for there were four major candidates. The Democrat, Stephan A. Douglas, might well have won had he been supported by the South, but Douglas, who was committed to compromise on the slavery issue, had alienated the slaveholders by some relatively innocuous remarks concerning the right of individual states to abolish slavery. As a result, the South backed John C. Breckenridge, a former Vice-President with definite pro-slavery views. To complicate matters further there was a third candidate put forward as a compromise, John Bell of Tennessee. And then there was the Republican candidate, Abraham Lincoln. Lincoln was certainly not a proslavery man, but neither was he an Abolitionist. While Lincoln believed slavery was wrong, he also believed that precipitous action to abolish it would inevitably lead to disaster. He opposed the spread of slavery to new territories, but believed that where it already existed it should be permitted to continue. Although his thoughts on the subject are somewhat unclear, it appears that he believed slavery would eventually disappear. These were hardly rabid anti-slavery views. Unfortunately they were too radical for the more extreme pro-slavery elements which dominated the political life of the South. By mid-cen-

tury there had developed in the South an almost spiritual belief in the righteousness of slavery. Lincoln's relatively mild opposition to the institution was enough to spark the secession of the principal slaveholding states in the aftermath of his election.

In the generations since the Civil War, and notably with the romanticization of the Confederacy in print and film, the role of slavery in bringing the conflict about has often been obscured by reference to the social, political, and economic differences between the two sections of the country. Attempts have been made to cast the conflict as one revolving purely around the issue of states rights, with frequent references to prominent non-slaveholding Confederate leaders, like Robert E. Lee, presented in furtherance of the argument. The charge has even been made that Northern capitalists conspired to overthrow Southern society in order to secure the wealth of the South. Nevertheless, at the time, the leaders of the South themselves made no efforts to conceal the importance which slavery had in prompting their decision for secession. The Constitution of the Confederacy explicitly permitted the existence of slavery, but was silent on the question of secession. Nathan Bedford Forrest, one of the finest Confederate generals, a man who had been a slave trader before the war and went on to found the Ku Klux Klan after it, put it succinctly when he said, "If I didn't think we was fightin' to keep our niggers I'd have never gone to war." And that was why two great armies composed of American soldiers marched and fought from the Rappahannock River to Gettysburg and back again in June and July of 1863.

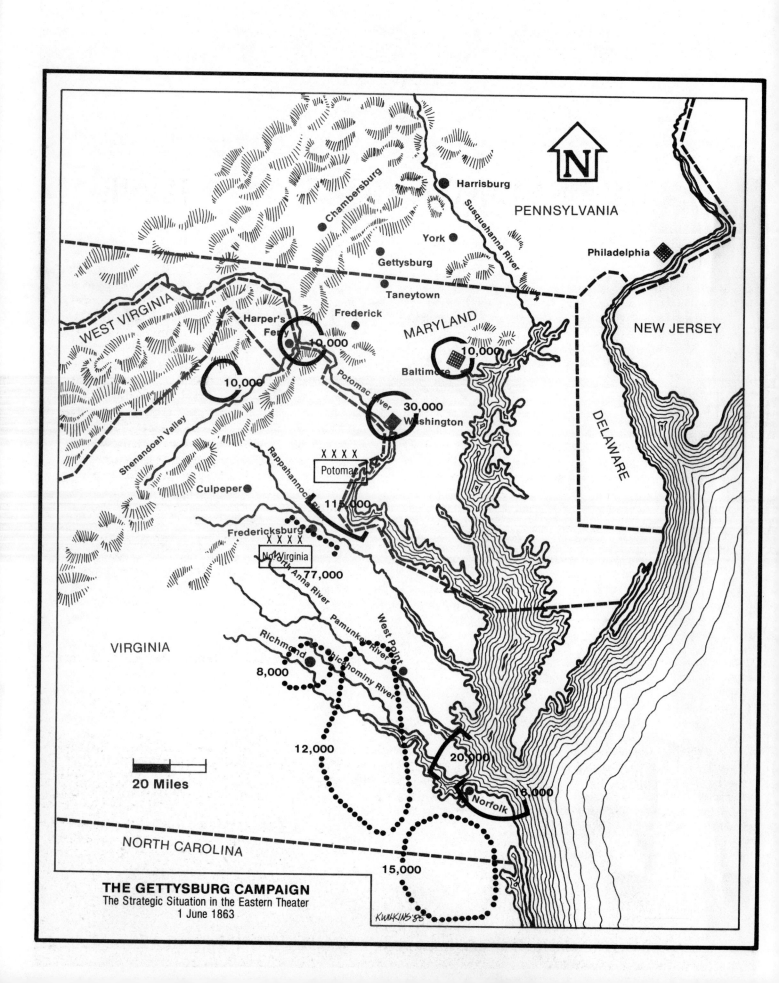

THE GETTYSBURG CAMPAIGN
The Strategic Situation in the Eastern Theater
1 June 1863

CHAPTER II

THE PRELIMINARIES, 1 – 9 JUNE

By the last week in May Union military leaders began to suspect that Lee was planning something big. Portions of the encampment of the Army of Northern Virginia at Fredricksburg were within view of Union outposts along the Rappahannock. This made it difficult for Lee to make significant preparations for a major undertaking without attracting notice. Lee had also increased his patrols, tightening security to the point where troops were no longer permitted to fraternize across the river. The number of Confederate soldiers deserting to the Union lines had risen—always a sure sign of an imminent offensive—and some of these men provided useful information. Finally, Lee had been pulling in brigades and reinforcements from all over Virginia, a fact which could not go unnoticed. On 27 May Col. George H. Sharpe, the chief intelligence officer of the *Army of the Potomac,* had issued a report in which he indicated that Lee's forces had been significantly increased, detailed the strength and location of Lee's divisions along the Rappahannock, and noted the

Army of Northern Virginia was preparing for a lengthy campaign away from rail communications. Pointing out that Lee's cavalry, under the redoubtable Maj. Gen. J.E.B. Stuart, was concentrated at Culpeper Courthouse, considerably to the west of the main encampment, Sharpe concluded that Lee planned a movement westwards and then northwards, designed to bring his army against the right flank or right rear of the *Army of the Potomac.* In the midst of restoring his army to its fighting trim and attempting to make minor improvements in its organization, Maj. Gen. Joseph Hooker, who was still in command of the *Army of the Potomac* despite Chancellorsville, was initially unconvinced. Then, on 28 May, came reports that Confederate skirmishers were reported in the vicinity of Warrenton, some 20 miles north of Culpeper, deep behind his right flank. Hooker reconsidered Sharpe's estimate of the situation.

Ambulances, wagons, drays and trucks. Each corps required such a train, demonstrating the prodigious logistical effort required to keep an army in the field.

Maj. Gen. J. E. B. Stuart

Hooker had already begun to prepare his army for operations. He ordered reinforcements to the cavalry screen covering his right, made some minor adjustments to the deployment of his forces along the middle reaches of the Rappahannock, and alerted some of his corps commanders to be ready to move. He made some tentative plans, briefly toying with the idea of falling on Richmond if Lee's movements left it uncovered. Informed of this, Lincoln rightly noted that the principal objective of the *Army of the Potomac* was the Army of Northern Virginia, an observation with which Hooker immediately concurred. Then he waited on developments.

Lee hesitated not at all. Although concerned by the presence of some 40,000 Union troops along the Virginia coast under Maj. Gen. John Dix, he concluded that the latter would pose no serious threat to his rear or to Richmond should he move northwards. He pressed his preparations, put the finishing touches on his plans, and quietly began to shift some units westwards. By calling in virtually every available spare unit in the Eastern Theater, Lee's magnificent Army of Northern Virginia numbered over 75,000 men, fell fighters all. On the morning of Wednesday, 3 June, he made his move. Two divisions of Longstreet's I Corps were the first to move out. The next day a division of one-legged Lt. Gen. Richard Ewell's II Corps marched off, followed the next morning by the other two. In the aftermath of Chancellorsville, and with the knowledge that they were on the offensive the morale of the troops was

very high, with everyone in good spirits. The men marched well, without straggling. The Army of Northern Virginia was on the march once more.

Federal balloonists alerted Hooker to the activity in the Confederate camp, on 3 June. He ordered a reconnaissance in force. Under an intense artillery barrage some 2,000 men of Maj. Gen. John Sedgwick's *VI Corps* raided across the Rappahannock at Franklin's Crossing. A brief skirmish ensued and the raiders fell back, taking with them several prisoners. Information from the raid was ambiguous, Sedgwick reporting that the entire Confederate army seemed still to be in its old position. Hooker ordered another reconnaissance on 7 June, instructing Maj. Gen. Alfred Pleasonton, commanding the *Cavalry Corps*, to take his men and some infantry and clear the Confederate cavalry out of the Culpeper area, ordering elements of Maj. Gen. George Meade's *V Corps* to support him if necessary. By this time Lee had already concentrated his I and II Corps in the vicinity of Culpeper, leaving only Lt. Gen. A. P. Hill's reduced III Corps in the old Fredericksburg position.

By the night of 8 June Pleasonton had 8,000 cavalrymen and 3,000 infantrymen with six light batteries poised along the line of the Rappahannock some eight miles east of Culpepper. Pleasonton formed his troops into two wings. The

Maj. Gen. Joseph Hooker

Lt. Gen. Richard Ewell

Maj. Gen. John Sedgewick

Maj. Gen. Alfred Pleasonton

right wing, under Brig. Gen. John Buford, comprised the *1st Cavalry Division*, the *Reserve Cavalry Brigade*, and a brigade of infantry, and was positioned at Beverly Ford, while the left wing, under Brig. Gen. David Gregg, was composed of the *2nd* and *3rd Cavalry Divisions* and a brigade of infantry, was at Kelly's Ford, six miles downstream. Buford struck under cover of a morning haze just about dawn on 9 June. The attack achieved complete surprise, although the Confederate pickets, from Brig. Gen. W. E. "Grumble" Jones' brigade, managed to maintain their cohesion and fell back in good order. Buford's wing drove on towards Brandy Station, a small railroad depot. One of the most confusing engagements of the war ensued. Fierce fighting erupted in front of Brandy Station. Maj. Gen. J.E.B. Stuart, Confederate cavalry commander, fed his brigades into the fight one after another. Wade Hampton's men came up, followed by those of W.H.F. "Rooney" Lee, second son of the general. These brigades gradually slowed Buford's advance and then, at about 1000 Hours, Hampton led them in a counter-attack. Buford, who had dismounted almost half his cavalrymen to bolster his infantry, began to fall back under the pressure. Then, at about noon, the bulk of Gregg's wing of the Union *Cavalry Corps* finally came up, having been delayed in crossing the Rappahannock by the late arrival of one division.

Gregg drove on Brandy Station from behind the Confederate right flank. As he advanced, he came under fire from a single light artillery piece on the otherwise undefended Fleetwood Hill, a long, lightly wooded ridge about a half-mile east of the town, upon which was located Stuart's camp. Gregg hesitated, uncertain as to the strength of the forces in front of him. This gave Maj. Henry B. McClellan of Stuart's staff time to call for reinforcements. The 12th Virginia Cavalry Regiment came up, supported by the 35th Virginia Cavalry Battalion, just as Gregg's troopers moved on Fleetwood Hill. Additional forces began to come up. A thoroughly chaotic melee resulted. Fleetwood Hill changed hands repeatedly, in a series of saber swinging charges and counter charges. At one point in the confused action the Union cavalrymen almost overran Stuart's artillery. Pressure on the 12th Virginia cavalry was so intense that it broke under fire. The *1st New Jersey Cavalry* made six regiment-sized charges, plus numberless smaller ones; other regiments on both sides could match its record. To counter the threat to his rear, Stuart had been forced to pull troops away from Buford's front. As a result, Buford renewed the attack. Stuart gradually fell back, fearing that he might be trapped between two hostile forces.

While the fighting raged in front of Brandy Station, Col. Alfred Duffie, commanding the Union *3rd Cavalry Division*, was engaged in a hot little fight of his own. Duffie had split off from Gregg's wing to advance on Stevensburg, some five miles south of Brandy Station, in order to cover the Union left flank. At Stevensburg, he became entangled with about 500 troopers from the 2nd South Carolina and the 4th Virginia

Brig. Gen. John Buford

Brig. Gen. Wade Hampton

Fleetwood Hill, where his slight superiority in numbers gave him a considerable advantage. Pleasonton had done all that was humanly possible. Many of his men were exhausted, his cavalry and artillery horses worn out, after nearly 14 hours of combat. When Maj. Gen. R. E. Rodes' infantry division of II Corps began to come up Pleasonton decided to pull back. Stuart's men, equally exhausted, did not pursue as Pleasonton led the *Cavalry Corps* back across the Rappahannock behind a screen of infantry skirmishers.

Brandy Station had been a tactical victory for the Confederate cavalry. They had inflicted about 935 casualties on the Union forces, about half of whom were prisoners, while losing some 525, including 200 prisoners, and the Union forces had retired from the field. But morally, Brandy Station was a major victory for the Union cavalry. It had come looking for a fight and done well. For the first time it had stood up to Stuart's vaunted cavaliers on nearly equal terms. Pleasonton's troopers had performed superbly throughout the operation, from their concentration along the Rappahannock on the night of 8 June, to their surprise crossing the next morning, in the repeated classic saber charges around Fleetwood Hill and in the hot

Cavalry Regiments. A confused, running fight resulted, at the end of which Duffie came away the victor, breaking his opponents and collecting some 200 prisoners in the bargain. But the little action prevented Duffie from marching on Brandy Station, where his presence might have been decisive.

Fighting around Brandy Station continued into the late afternoon. Stuart had managed to dismount and concentrate most of his forces on

Union cavalrymen forming a firing line. About every fourth man was detached to hold the horses.

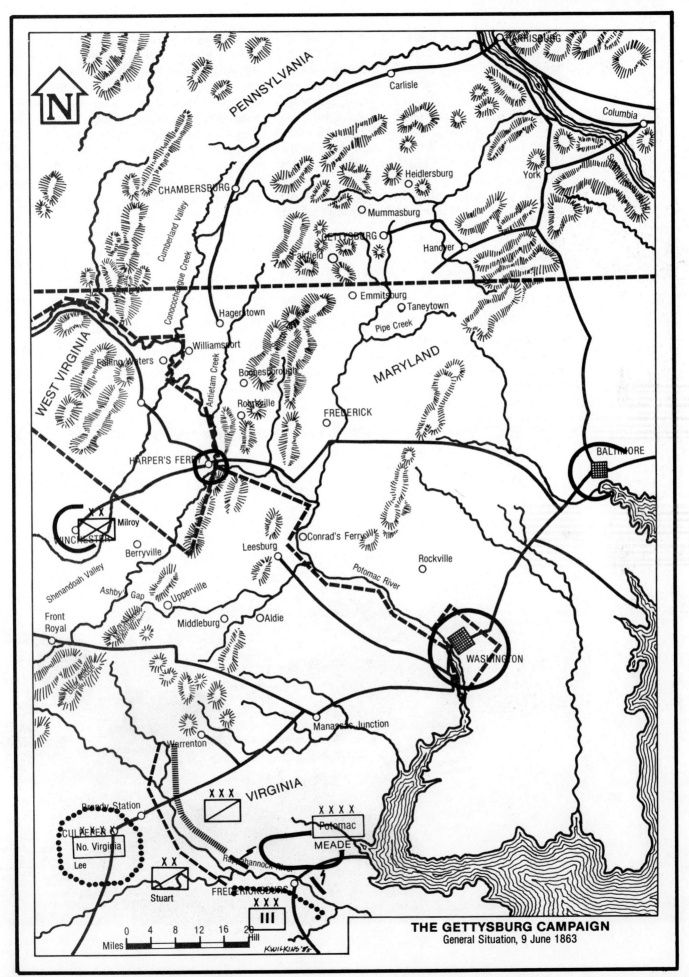

THE GETTYSBURG CAMPAIGN
General Situation, 9 June 1863

dismounted fighting that continued through the day and through to their withdrawal—all had been well executed. Stuart and the other Confederate cavalrymen would deny that they had been surprised or that they had been fought to a standstill, but the evidence was clear for all to see. Certainly Lee, who arrived on the field shortly before the end of the battle only to discover that his son had been seriously wounded, could not have been fooled as to the improvement in the quality of the Union cavalry. Stuart, who gloried in his role as a *beau sabeur*, felt his failure deeply, and the criticism of his subordinates and colleagues rankled. Of course Pleasanton had not actually accomplished his mission, which was to drive the Confederate cavalry out of the Culpeper area. The strength of the Confederate concentration around Culpeper Courthouse, and the presence of strong infantry forces in the vicinity prevented this. But his inability to do so provided substantive evidence that Lee was shifting his forces westwards, confirming that a Confederate offensive was imminent.

Part of the ebb and flow of the cavalry action around Brandy Station. Here Union troopers charge a retiring Confederate horse battery.

CHAPTER III

LEE MOVES NORTH, 10 – 24 JUNE

On 10 June Lee sent Ewell's II Corps into the Shenandoah Valley, immediately following it with a brigade of cavalry, and pressing Longstreet's I Corps behind that. Although the weather was oppressively hot and humid, the troopers marched well. Despite several small skirmishes, Ewell covered over 45 miles in two days, reaching the vicinity of Winchester on 13 June. At this point Hill's III Corps was still deployed near Fredericksburg, with the result that Lee's army was stretched over 100 miles. But it was well protected, for he had taken care to move behind a screen of cavalry and under cover of the Rappahannock River and the Blue Ridge Mountains. Meanwhile, Hooker remained uncertain as to Lee's intentions: the Army of Northern Virginia was on the move, but what was its objective? He reacted correctly, if cautiously, by shifting his base of operations from Aquia Creek on the lower Potomac, to the Orange and Alexandria Railroad coming from Washington, while juggling his army corps westwards. Maj. Gen. John Reynolds, commander of I Corps, was given charge of Hooker's right wing, comprising his own corps, plus the *III* and *XI Corps* and the *Cavalry Corps*, with the

mission of covering the Rappahannock line. A better general might have guessed at Lee's intentions. Hooker, a good corps commander but hardly fit for higher command, waited on events. On 14 June Maj. Gen. Henry Halleck, general-in-chief of the Union army, learned that Ewell was certainly in the Valley, and alerted Hooker. Soon after he was notified that Maj. Gen. Robert C. Schenck, commanding the Union forces in the Valley, had been informed that Ewell had deployed for battle in front of Winchester on the evening of 13 June. Lincoln then notified him that the prevailing opinion in Washington was that Winchester was closely invested by the enemy. Hooker still dithered, and while he did, the situation grew worse.

Union forces in the Shenandoah Valley were strong, totaling over 20,000 men. The principal formation was an infantry division of 9,000 men under Maj. Gen. Robert Milroy. The location of Milroy's division was poor. It was too far—over 20 miles—to permit it to be readily supported by the 10,000 men stationed at Harper's Ferry and the 1,200 more at Martinsburg. Most of it was at Winchester, a modest town with relatively poor natural defenses,

Lt. Gen. A. P. Hill

Maj. Gen. John Reynolds

Maj. Gen. Henry Halleck

Buford's cavalry delaying the Confederate advance upon Gettysburg

Artillery going into action

Maj. Gen. Jubal Early

while about 1,800 men were at Berryville, an even smaller town about ten miles to the east. Schenck had ignored repeated suggestions by Halleck to correct Milroy's position, but the lat-

ter had ignored him. Rather than press the issue, Halleck had let it drop. When word came that Lee was entering the Valley in strength, Schenck had ordered Milroy to fall back. Several small skirmishes had already occurred between 10 and 13 June as Milroy's outposts fell back before Ewell's advanced guards. Nevertheless Milroy procrastinated, although he did send off his trains. Then, on 13 June Ewell deployed for battle around Winchester with over 14,000 men, while sending a column to prevent reinforcement from Berryville and another northwards to seize Martinsburg. For some reason Milroy decided to hold Winchester, although he had but 7,000 men and rations were short.

Ewell struck about an hour before sunset. Twenty pieces of artillery began to batter the defenders. After 45 minutes of this, Maj. Gen. Edward Johnson's division demonstrated against the eastern and southeastern sides of the town while Maj. Gen. Jubal Early's division attacked on the west and northwest. One of Early's brigades broke into the Union position in a bayonet attack. Massively supported, the troops pressed on and succeeded in seizing a hill which dominated the defenses. Then night fell, and the fighting ended. In the darkness, the garrison of Berryville came up, having eluded the troops sent to cover them. But even with these reinforcements it was clear that the situation was hopeless. Milroy decided to retreat along several roads which his scouts reported were still open. At 0200 on 14 June his troops moved out in good order, with skirmishers covering the rear. The columns made very good time, quickly covering the four miles to Stephenson's Depot, a hamlet just north of Winchester. There they ran into a brigade which Ewell, with commendable foresight, had placed in ambush. This pinned Milroy in position long enough for additional forces to come up. Both Milroy and his men performed well, but in the confusion Milroy's rear-guard failed to support him. The situation was never in doubt. Even before dawn the command began to disintegrate, with men streaming off in all directions. Milroy managed to keep over 1,500 men together. After an extraordinarily difficult 30 mile march under almost constant harassment from Confederate skirmishers, he brought them safely to Harper's Ferry the next day, even as Lee's advanced guard, Brig. Gen. A. G. Jenkins' cavalry brigade, was crossing the Potomac. When all the stragglers finally came in the magnitude of the disaster became clear. Milroy's stand at Winchester had cost nearly half his command. The only benefit it brought was to frighten Hooker into action.

Lincoln and Halleck were becoming increasingly exasperated with Hooker. The latter found it difficult to get Hooker to listen to reasonable advice, while Hooker repeatedly complained of "interference" on the part of Halleck. Lincoln resolved the problem by putting Hooker more directly under Halleck's command. Halleck then "advised" Hooker that he should concentrate at Leesburg on the Upper Potomac, so as to be in a position to strike in any of several directions. In addition, he was to keep his cavalry as far out as possible in order to discover what the enemy was doing. Hooker therefore ordered his army northwards toward Manassas Junction, moving under the cover of the Bull Run Mountains, while instructing his cavalry to locate Lee's main body. Numerous small cavalry skirmishes had been occurring with considerable frequency for several days as Union outposts clashed with Confederate outriders. Now Pleasonton ordered his troopers to press harder, seeking information. A series of larger, hotter

clashes resulted, scattered all across the broad valley between the Blue Ridge Mountains, west of which was the Army of Northern Virginia, and the Bull Run chain, east of which was the *Army of the Potomac.* By 17 June J. E. B. Stuart had five brigades covering Lee's right, two along the Rappahannock and three along the gaps in the Blue Ridge Mountains. On that morning, Pleasonton dispatched three brigades under Brig. Gen. David Gregg to reconnoiter towards Aldie, a small town within easy reach of three of the principal gaps in the Blue Ridge Mountains.

Aldie was defended by a single Confederate cavalry brigade, that of Brig. Gen. Fitzhugh Lee, temporarily under Col. Thomas T. Munford. A hot little fight ensued, with dismounted cavalrymen trading shots all afternoon. After giving the poorly handled Union troopers a rough time of it for several hours, the defenders pulled out, heading for Middleburg, four miles further west. At Middleburg Munford ran into about 275 Union cavalrymen under Col. Alfred Duffie. Duffie's *1st Rhode Island Cavalry Regiment,* had just seized the village from a small detachment

A Union horse battery deploying for action

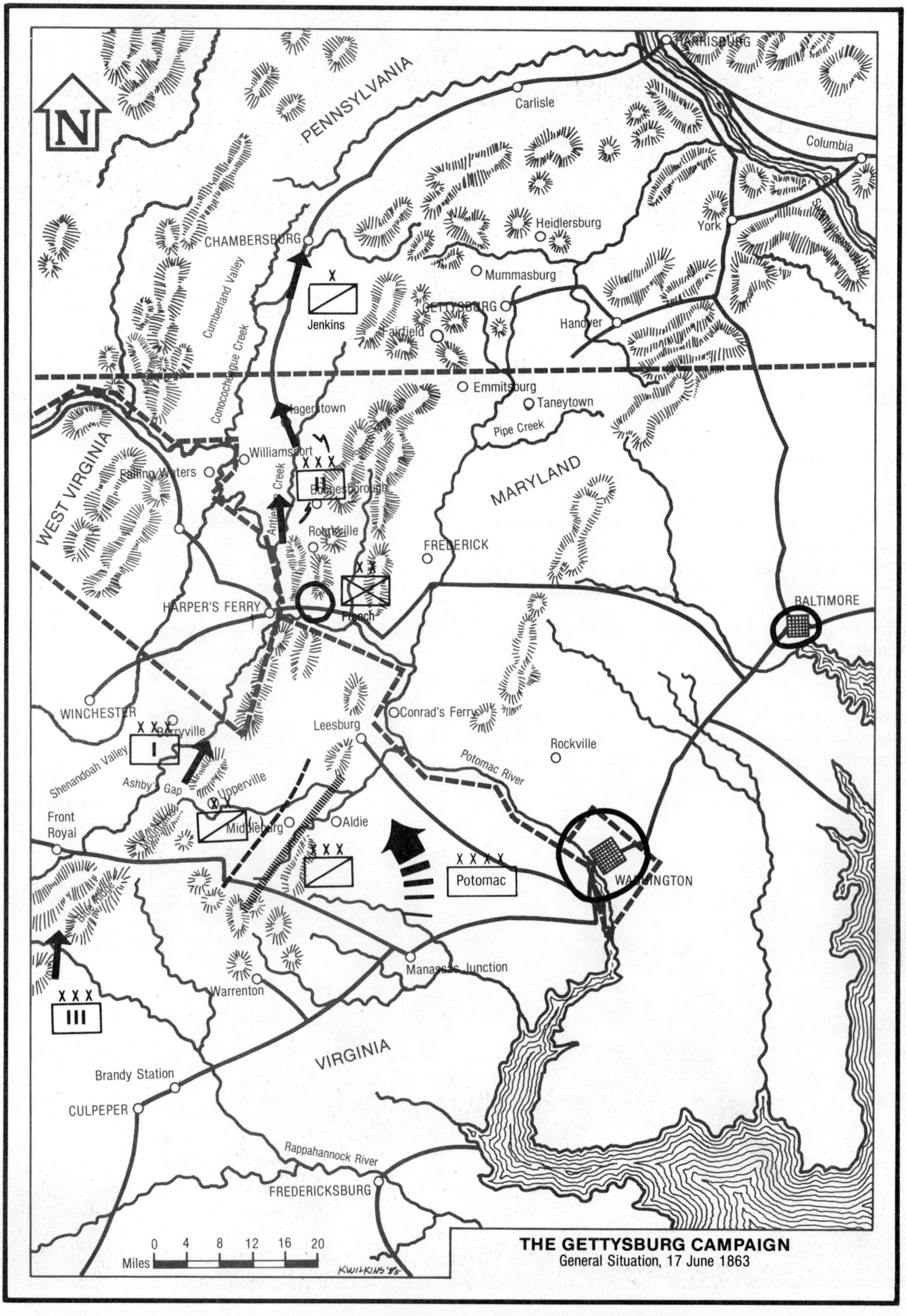

HARRISBURG

PENNSYLVANIA

Carlisle

Columbia

CHAMBERSBURG

Heidlersburg

York

Mummasburg

X
Jenkins

GETTYSBURG

Hanover

Fairfield

Cumberland Valley

Conococheague Creek

Hagerstown

Emmitsburg

Taneytown

WEST VIRGINIA

Williamsport

XXX

Pipe Creek

MARYLAND

Falling Waters

Antietam Creek

Boonesborough

Rohrersville

FREDERICK

HARPER'S FERRY

XX
French

BALTIMORE

WINCHESTER

Berryville

Conrad's Ferry

Leesburg

Rockville

I

Potomac River

Shenandoah Valley

Ashby's Gap

Upperville

Front
Royal

X
Middleburg

Aldie

WASHINGTON

XXX

Blue Ridge

XXXX
Potomac

Manassas Junction

XXX
III

Warrenton

Brandy Station

VIRGINIA

CULPEPER

Rappahannock River

FREDERICKSBURG

| 0 | 4 | 8 | 12 | 16 | 20 |

Miles

K.WILKINS '75

THE GETTYSBURG CAMPAIGN
General Situation, 17 June 1863

Union cavalry scouting for the Rebel advance

of Confederate troops, when Munford came up. In the face of greatly superior forces, Duffie dismounted most of his command and put up a spirited defense, while dispatching a messenger to Gregg. Additional Confederate forces were committed. Having held successfully for several hours, Duffie retreated after nightfall. At dawn he discovered himself surrounded. Refusing to surrender, he ordered his men to cut their way out. About 100 succeeded in doing so. That afternoon, in belated response to Duffie's call for assistance, a strong force of Union cavalry drove the Confederates out of Middleburg, and then fell back on Aldie once more. On 21 June, under prodding from Hooker, Pleasonton swept westwards from Aldie with five cavalry brigades and some supporting infantry. Deploying his men in two columns, he quickly pushed the Confederates westwards, fighting a major skirmish at Middleburg and another at Upperville, and drove them on into Ashby's Gap. There Pleasonton stopped, when he ought to have pressed on, seeking more information. Despite this, the four days of cavalry fighting between 17 and 21 June were useful to the Union cause. The Union cavalrymen had again proven capable of standing up to the best the South had to offer. Pleasonton had inflicted some 770 casualties on the enemy, including some 250 prisoners, and had taken two guns, at a cost to his own forces of perhaps 880, nearly 200 of whom had been with Duffie. Moreover, he had definitely ascertained that Lee's entire army was strung-out in the Valley, west of the Blue Ridge Mountains and moving northwards. At the same time he had totally prevented Stuart from reconnoitering eastwards

The Confederate road column

Master scouts of the Army of the Potomac pose sometime after the Battle of Gettysburg.

to the Bull Run Mountains. As a result, Lee was even less well-informed about Hooker's movements, than the latter was about Lee's. The Confederate advanced guard was well into Pennsylvania, while Hill's III Corps was still at the southern end of the Valley. Hooker had kept the *Army of the Potomac* well in hand as it moved and it was now concentrated in northern Virginia, at Manassas Junction and Chantilly, about 20 miles southwest of Washington. A better general than Hooker might well have taken advantage of the situation, driving westwards across the Blue Ridge and cutting Lee in two, as suggested by many, including Lincoln. But Hooker remained cautious. Despite the fact that he was granted considerable authority over all Union forces in the Valley area and Maryland, with detailed instructions, he became involved in petty squabbles over the limits of his authority. Believing

himself outnumbered by the enemy, he made repeated demands for reinforcements while denigrating the number and quality of those which he did receive, amounting to seven infantry brigades and two of cavalry, a total of 15,000 field troops, which virtually stripped the Washington garrison of veterans. Hooker nevertheless still felt unready.

Whatever its commander's feeling, the *Army of the Potomac* was ready. Hooker was a good manager. Supplies were plentiful. Morale was good, despite the necessity of marching in a heat wave. Officers were pressing the men hard, but being careful to prevent heat exhaustion and to treat those who succumbed to it. The *Army of the Potomac* was now closer to Richmond than the Army of Northern Virginia. Hooker's cautious maneuvering had managed to keep the *Army of the Potomac* between Lee and Wash-

Confederate soldiers prepare to cross a ford on the approach to Gettysburg.

ington at all times. By advancing in multiple columns along a series of parallel routes he had kept the army fairly well-concentrated even while on the move. On 24 June the advanced guard of the army was in the vicinity of Leesburg, with *XI Corps* already crossing the Potomac at Edward's Ferry and *XII Corps* preparing to cross a few miles upstream at Conrad's Ferry. Covered by Pleasonton's cavalry on its left flank, the balance of the army was moving up rapidly, with the rear guard less than 20 miles to the south. The Army of Northern Virginia was ready too. By 24 June, save for three cavalry brigades, Lee had brought virtually all of his elated troops across the Potomac. Ewell's corps was well inside Pennsylvania, already foraging heavily in the vicinity of Chambersburg, while Longstreet was resting at Hagerstown in Maryland, and Hill's corps was on the march across the old Antietam battlefield. Nevertheless, Lee was uneasy. The week of cavalry skirmishing had brought in little information and he had no idea of the location of Hooker and the *Army of the Potomac*. On 22 June he had instructed Stuart to leave two brigades guarding the passes into the Valley and to shift the balance of his cavalry to the head of the army as quickly as possible and by the most direct route. Unfortunately the orders were somewhat vague. Stuart chose to interpret these orders as permitting him to ride completely around the Union army, rather than as a directive to interpose himself between the two armies. He had performed this feat before, to his greater glory but with little profit to the Army of Northern Virginia. As a result, on 24 June Stuart vanished, taking with him three brigades of cavalry and a battery of horse artillery. Even as he did, Lee developed his plans further. Over the next few days Lee intended to spread his troops widely over the rich farms and industrious villages of central Pennsylvania, reaping a

rich harvest.

Pennsylvania was virtually bare of defenders. Concern had been rising for some days. A home guard had been organized with the help of the War Department, and Governor Andrew G. Curtin had called upon the men of the state to enlist. Maj. Gen. Darius N. Couch, who had ably led a corps in the *Army of the Potomac* for over a year until Hooker's performance at Chancellorsville led him to request a transfer, was appointed commander for the eastern half of the state, the *Department of the Susquehanna*. Recruiting for this home guard proved difficult, for many of Pennsylvania's finest young men were already in the field. Then too, time was short, there were many technical problems, and there was considerable war weariness as well. Moreover, there were many pacifistic Quakers and Mennonites in the state. As a result, on 15 June Lincoln issued a proclamation calling for 100,000 volunteer militia from Pennsylvania, Maryland, West Virginia, and Ohio to serve during the emergency. On 16 June all Northern governors were requested to provide special limited-service volunteers as well. Only New York and Rhode Island responded, the former with an immediate offer of 10,000 three–months militia from New York City. Couch was ordered to enroll and equip these men as soon as they reached Pennsylvania. Meanwhile he arranged for the fortification of the eastern side of the Susquehanna and of the bridgeheads at Harrisburg. The troops began to move. By 24 June perhaps 15,000 militiamen were concentrated in the central portion of the state, notably about Harrisburg, though many more enrolled as the scale of the Confederate incursion became in-

A mobile smithy of the type attached to cavalry regiments

creasingly obvious. They were not the best troops in the world, but they would fight if they had too, and Couch would do what he could with them. Panic began to spread as Lee's advanced guards moved across the state.

Rank and Service in the Civil War

Officers' ranks during the Civil War were rather confusing. One can best understand this by looking at the Union forces. It was possible for an officer to have as many as four different ranks simultaneously. A person could hold one rank in the *militia*, another rank in the *regulars*, yet another in the *volunteers*, and still another in the *state* troops.

The militia, of course, were the part-time forces which each state could muster from its own population. A rank in the militia did not necessarily have any value outside the borders of one's own state, though in emergencies the militia of one state was known to serve in another, such as the 13,000 New York militiamen who helped hold the line of the Susquehanna during the Gettysburg Campaign. The regular army was the permanent land force maintained by the Federal government. Normally the regulars and the militia were responsible for the defense of the country. However, militia terms of service were rather short, and the militia served under state control. As a result, there was also the volunteer army. The volunteer army was recruited by states, often drawing men from the militia, but served under Federal terms of enlistment. Some states over-filled their volunteer quotas and chose to retain the surplus troops at their own expense as permanent, standing forces for territorial defense. These were the state troops, maintained by several states, the most notable of which were the famed *Pennsylvania Reserves*. Militia and state regiments might sometimes volunteer for Federal service, so regiments sometimes had two designations, such as the *83rd New York Volunteers* which was also the *9th New York Militia*. In general, when a regiment is cited merely by its number and state, a volunteer infantry outfit is intended; while if the citation lacks a state designation, the regiment was from the regular army. This plethora of branches of the service complicated the rank structure.

Now, a man might be a colonel in the Maine militia, serving as a captain in a volunteer regiment. Or he might be a major in the regular army, and a brigadier general in the volunteers. Or a lieutenant in the regular army, a major in the volunteers, and a colonel in the state troops. Only one's regular army rank counted towards permanent time-in-grade for purposes of post-war retention and promotion in the regular army. As if this were not confusing enough, there was also *brevet* rank.

A brevet was an honorary promotion, awarded for distinguished service. Thus, a captain of volunteers might also have a brevet as a colonel of volunteers. Brevet rank conferred some prestige on an officer and did make him technically senior to another officer of equal rank, but brought few other benefits. And, of course, one could hold several brevets, for example in both the volunteers and the regulars. As a result, it was at least theoretically possible for a Union officer to have eight ranks, one substantive rank and one brevet in each rank of the service, the militia, the regulars, the volunteers, and the state troops, although this does not actually ever seemed to have occurred.

The situation in the Confederacy was somewhat simpler. To begin with, save for a list of mostly senior officers, there was very little in the way of a regular army. As a result, the volunteer army, known as the "Provisional Army", was practically speaking the entirety of the Confederate forces, supplemented by the militia and state troops. An officer might be, as in Union service, a captain in the regular army and a colonel in the provisional army but the former rank was of little importance. In addition, the Confederacy was rather more generous with rank than the Union, giving out the real thing to deserving officers rather than brevets.

During the Gettysburg Campaign the highest rank in the *Army of the Potomac* was major general of volunteers, which was shared by fifteen officers, including the army commander, George G. Meade, the chief of Staff and of Engineering, eight corps commanders, and four division commanders. Brigadier generals commanded 18 divisions, including three of cavalry. Of 50 infantry brigades, half were led by brigadier generals and half by colonels, which was also the case for the six cavalry brigades. The situation in the artillery was even worse. Of fifteen artillery brigades—which were actually battalions but chief of artillery Brig. Gen. Henry Hunt didn't like that word—two were commanded by colonels, one by a lieutenant colonel, one by a major, ten by captains, and one by a lowly lieutenant. In contrast, the Army of Northern Virginia had one full general, Robert E. Lee, commanding, plus three lieutenant generals, one for each corps. There were eleven major generals, one for each division, including the cavalry, plus one spare at headquarters. Of 37 infantry brigades, brigadier generals commanded all but six, which were led by colonels, while in the cavalry there were six brigadier generals leading brigades and only one colonel. In the artillery the situation was even better, for each corps had a colonel as chief of artillery, and of fourteen battalions, two were led by colonels, three by lieutenant colonels, and the balance by majors.

CHAPTER IV

THE ARMIES CLOSE, 24 – 30 JUNE

Lee concentrated his army in the vicinity of Chambersburg. From there, he moved detachments all over Pennsylvania between North Mountain and the Susquehanna River. Many of the citizens had already fled, carrying their goods with them. Those who could not, or would not, were forced to deal with the Confederate quartermasters. The spirit of the people was sullen. There was little overt resistance, but little willing cooperation. The primary motivating force was fear and it was particularly evident among the black people of Pennsylvania. Over 10,000 blacks lived in the invaded portions of the state. Many were long-term residents, freemen from birth. Others were recent fugitives from slavery. Most joined the flood of refugees fleeing before the advancing Confederate forces. Their fear had just cause. Several Confederate commanders, including Longstreet, had given orders that their troops were to apprehend fugitive slaves and return them to their owners. Not a slaveholder himself, Lee nevertheless made no attempts to counteract these instructions. Some unfortunates were seized and sent south, despite efforts of some local citizens to conceal them. Meanwhile the Army of Northern Virginia proceeded to plunder Pennsylvania, favored by unseasonably mild temperatures.

Forage was good and Lee issued careful instructions as to its collection in order to gain the maximum benefit for the Army of Northern Virginia. Private citizens were not to be molested. Specific officers were assigned to levy requisitions on each town, hamlet, and farm, detailing specific quantities of particular products which were to be taken under penalty of retribution. An enormous amount of material was seized, including foodstuffs, cattle, medicine, clothing, horse furniture, and other supplies. No horses were permitted to slip from the quartermaster's grasp, and literally thousands

were seized. All goods taken were paid for in Confederate currency. Those refusing to cooperate or concealing goods, found their goods seized, in return for a claim receipt against the Confederate government. In practical terms there was little difference, as both the money and the receipts were worthless paper in Pennsylvania, and not much more valuable in the Confederacy. Officially, care was to be taken to see that no place was actually left to starve, but the requisitions amounted to confiscation, and hardship for some was inevitable, for most towns were visited more than once and the seizure of horses would hamper the gathering of the harvest. Confederate behavior was largely correct and polite, if forceful. Morale was good, and got better. The troops were generally kept well in hand. There was, to be sure, some casual looting, and some citizens were mistreated by individual Confederate soldiers. Moreover, some Confederate officers ignored orders and sought to punish the Yankees. In this fashion, in complete disregard for Lee's instructions, Jubal Early improperly put to the torch an iron

Carlisle, Pa., anticipating the arrival of Stuart's cavalry

foundry belonging to Representative Thaddeus Stevens, one of the most vehement abolitionists in the House, who happened to make his home in the small town of Gettysburg. As the looting of Pennsylvania proceeded, the armies began to converge.

By 28 June the Army of Northern Virginia was dispersed in an arc stretching some 72 miles northeastwards from Chambersburg, with sizeable contingents at Carlisle and York and with cavalry posted along the line of the Susquehanna and westwards from Chambersburg. A number of small skirmishes had taken place over the last few days, but nothing to indicate the presence of the bulk of the Union forces. Few of the militia units in the area put up any resistance, wisely choosing to withdraw rather than confront Lee's seasoned veterans. Lee realized that his army was dangerously overstretched. He was still completely out of touch with Stuart's cavalry and was very much in the dark as to the movements of the *Army of the Potomac*.

Hooker had brought the *Army of the Potomac* across the river whose name it bore by 28 June, and had concentrated it in central Maryland, in an area stretching about 20 miles westwards from Frederick. He had conducted his movements carefully, keeping his cavalry well out in front, to prevent the enemy from receiving any intelligence while seeking maximum information. His new position was excellent, for he could cover all of Lee's optional movements simultaneously, whether the latter chose to retreat up the Shenandoah Valley back to Virginia, or to fall on Washington or Baltimore. However, Hooker's movements were timid. An enemy army was plundering the heart of Pennsylvania and his army was posing no direct threat to it. A fine administrator, a good strategist, and an able corps commander, Hooker was unsuited for independent command and was beginning to lose his nerve again. His corps commanders had lost confidence in him. In the last few days of the campaign a galaxy of generals had passed through Washington, honestly if insubordinately expressing their reservations about Hooker. He alienated Halleck, with whom he had never been on friendly terms, by refusing to inform him of his plans. He exacerbated relations with Halleck further by demanding yet more reinforcements, although already in command of over 100,000 field troops. When informed that there were no more troops to be had, he urged the evacuation of Maj. Gen. William Henry French and the 11,000 men garrisoning Maryland Heights, a strong, well-fortified position which dominated Harper's Ferry and stood athwart part of Lee's line of retreat. Halleck once more turned him down. On 27 June he offered his resignation, believing that this would force Lincoln to give him a freer hand. But Lincoln had by now lost confidence in him as well. Aware that a great battle was immi-

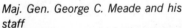
Maj. Gen. George C. Meade and his staff

Maj. Gen. George Sykes

Capt. George A. Custer

Capt. Elon Farnsworth

Brig. Gen. Hugh Kilpatrick

nent, he realized that Hooker was not the man for the job. The resignation was accepted. Early on the morning of 28 June Maj. Gen. George G. Meade, comanding *V Corps*, was roused from his bed by one of Halleck's staff officers, who handed him a presidential order giving him command of the *Army of the Potomac*. Meade's reaction was "Well, I've been tried and condemned without a hearing, and I supposed I shall have to go to execution." Then he set about assuming command. Time was short, for it was clear a great battle was in the offing. That very day *The New York Times* had observed that "the return game between the *Army of the Potomac* and the Army of [Northern] Virginia may be played this week."

Meade was a good officer, with a solid, if unspectacular reputation. He had done well with a division at Antietam and Fredericksburg, and had led his corps ably at Chancellorsville. The other corps commanders in the army liked and respected him, and appear to have formed a cabal with the intention of securing the command for him, though the rank-and-file found him unimpressive. Neither as flamboyant nor as brilliant as Hooker, he was a careful, determined, conscientious, loyal, and courageous commander, of whom Lee would remark, " . . . Meade will commit no blunder in front, and if I make one, he will make haste to take advantage of it." He had other qualities which made him attractive to Lincoln: born in Spain, he was considered technically disqualified from running for President, and he made his home in Pennsylvania, and as Lincoln put it, "Meade will fight well on his own dung hill." Meade's instructions were clear: all troops in the area of operations were to come under his command and, save that he had to maintain the army in a position to cover both Washington and Baltimore from the enemy, he was given a free hand, even to the extent of replacing any officer in the army. Meade took charge immediately and with notable efficiency. He spent his first few hours in command reviewing the strategic situation and conferring with Hooker. He formally took command at about 0700 hours, retaining most of Hooker's staff. Even while he was doing all of this, he had begun making plans, wanting to get the *Army of the Potomac* on the road once more. He worked fast, telegraphing a tentative plan to Washington along with his acceptance of command. It was a simple plan. He would advance northwards towards the Susquehanna, keeping Lee away from Washington and Baltimore, to concentrate along Pipe Creek, a highly defensible stream about five miles south of Mason and Dixon's Line, and then to seek a general action at the earliest opportunity.

Orders began to flow. Outlying contingents of the army were ordered to concentrate on Frederick. Maj. Gen. George Sykes was en-

trusted with *V Corps*. After consulting with Pleasonton, the *Cavalry Corps* was reorganized, with additional manpower and more horse artillery, and captains George A. Custer, Elon Farnsworth, and Wesley Merritt were jumped to one-star rank and given cavalry brigades. Some of the cavalry was then told to chase Stuart, who was then about ten miles northwest of Washington. After long and careful thought he ordered Maj. Gen. French, commanding at Maryland Heights above Harper's Ferry to pull his men back to Frederick, in order to guard the rear and flank of the army as it moved north. Meade kept Halleck informed of all his actions, and the latter concurred in every instance, limiting his comments to general observations and an expression of concern that military stores not be left for the Rebels under any circumstances. Benefitting from some remarkably accurate intelligence, provided principally by loyal citizens in the occupied regions of Pennsylvania and Maryland, Meade was able to prepare meticulously detailed plans for the advance of each corps. The movement began on 29 June and was almost a textbook study in how an army ought to move.

Hancock (seated) with his divisional commanders Barlow, Birney and Gibbon.

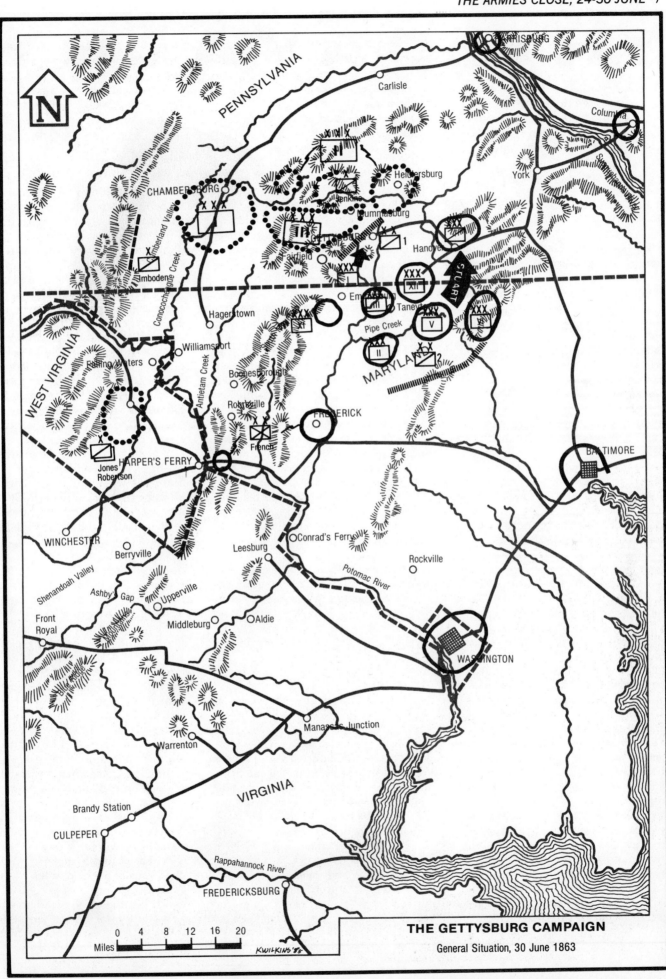

THE GETTYSBURG CAMPAIGN

General Situation, 30 June 1863

THE CAVALRY

The cavalry entered the Civil War looking to play a glorious role as the arm of shock on the battlefield, in the grand tradition of the eighteenth century and the Napoleonic Age. But even in Napoleonic times the boot-to-boot charge with lance and saber was beginning to become a risky venture, notably so against seasoned troops. By the time of the Civil War the rifled musket had made the cavalry charge not merely risky, but frankly obsolete against any but the greenest troops. As a result, the cavalry spent much of the war looking for a role.

As it developed during the war, the role of the cavalry came to encompass a considerable variety of activities. The missions of the mounted arm included conducting reconnaissances, establishing and maintaining contact with enemy forces, screening the movements of friendly forces, and raiding against enemy lines of communication. Any serious fighting was best done dismounted, using carbines and serving as light infantry, though the saber and the pistol, and even the shotgun, were useful in mounted skirmishes. The cavalryman's favorite role was raiding, for it gave him a chance to run free, causing as much destruction as possible, and avoiding the monotonous burdens of patrol duty. Moreover, raids tended to catch the attention of the public, already inclined to be overly fond of the troopers. Nevertheless, while raids sometimes could have a useful effect on the course of a campaign, they were distinctly less important than reconnoitering and screening before the army. These were missions which never ended, for the need to seek out information on the enemy, and to deny it to him, never ceased. Thus, unlike the infantry and the artillery, which relatively speaking had plenty of time to spare between campaigns, the cavalry worked most of the time. Patrolling, scouting, and serving on picket were boring, grueling tasks which placed a heavy burden on the troopers, and an even greater strain on their mounts. Casualties among the horses were always higher than those among their riders and a regiment could easily run through two or three issues of horses in a year.

The organization of the cavalry was very similar on both sides. A Union regiment consisted of a headquarters and twelve companies, which could be organized into battalions as the situation dictated. At regimental headquarters the officers included a colonel, a lieutenant colonel, three majors, three lieutenants serving respectively as regimental adjutant, quartermaster, and commissary, and a surgeon with his assistant. The headquarters staff included a sergeant-major, three sergeants serving respectively as quartermaster, commissary, and saddler, a farrier (blacksmith), and two hospital stewards. Each company had a captain, a first and second lieutenant, a first sergeant, a quartermaster sergeant, a commissary sergeant, five other sergeants, eight corporals, two teamsters, a waggoner, two farriers, a saddler, two musicians, and about 70 troopers.

A Confederate cavalry regiment normally consisted of a headquarters and ten companies. On paper, at least, the headquarters staff was virtually identical to that of the Federal regiment, though with only two majors. Each company was supposed to have a captain, three lieutenants, five sergeants, four corporals, plus a farrier and his assistant, and about 85 troopers. On paper then, the Union cavalry regiment had about 1200 men, while the Confederate one ran to only about 900. In practice, however, the numbers were far less due to casualties and a lack of replacements. At Gettysburg Union regiments averaged a little more than 360 men and Confederate ones about 280.

In both armies several regiments formed a brigade, with Federal ones having between three and six regiments and Confederate ones normally about five, but occasionally as few as two. In rare instances a battery of horse artillery was sometimes attached to a brigade, but this was more normally attached at a higher level. In both armies the usual cavalry division was of two or three brigades. However, in the Army of Northern Virginia, J. E. B. Stuart's cavalry division had six brigades plus a large contingent of horse artillery. This proved rather clumsy and the division was shortly organized into

a corps. The cavalry of the *Army of the Potomac* had been formed into a corps of three divisions and a sizeable contingent of horse artillery by Maj. Gen. Joseph Hooker in February of 1863. This marked the beginning of the maturation of the Federal cavalry, which until then had been significantly inferior to that of the Army of Northern Virginia.

Since the regular army had six regiments of cavalry at the start of the Civil War (the *1st* and *2nd Dragoons*, the *Regiment of Mounted Rifles*, and the *1st*, *2nd*, and *3rd Cavalry*, which were redesignated respectively the 1st through *6th Cavalry* in 1861) it might have been expected that the Union cavalry would have been more effective, at least at the onset of the war, than was that of the Confederacy. However, this was not the case, for the regular regiments had important duties to perform on the frontier. There was also a relative shortage of good riding stock and a relative lack of riding skills in the increasingly urban North. In addition, the Union army was tardy in forming brigades and divisions of cavalry, which left the mounted forces without centralized direction. As a result, it was the Southern cavalry which first developed as an efficient combat arm. This was partially due to the fact that riding was a common skill in the overwhelmingly rural South. In addition, at least at the onset of the war, many Confederate cavalry regiments were recruited from the hard-riding, fox hunting planter aristocracy. And the South benefitted from the fact that some of her sons were among the finest cavalrymen ever known, such as Turner Ashby, who died early, Nathan Bedford Forrest, who served in the West, and J. E. B. Stuart, who served with the Army of Northern Virginia. With such leadership, the Confederate cavalry developed an early and significant edge over that of the Union. It was only during the Gettysburg Campaign that the Federal cavalry began to be able to stand up and trade blows successfully with that of the Confederacy. This was due partially to the creation of the *Cavalry Corps* of the *Army of the Potomac*, which put the cavalry under central direction for operational purposes, and partially due to the introduction of the Sharps carbine, which gave the Union troopers a considerable advantage in firepower.

The first indication of this was Brandy Station and all the little cavalry skirmishes along the Blue Ridge and South Mountain chains in the early phases of the campaign. It became particularly evident when J. E. B. Stuart, in order to restore the luster to his bruised reputation, took half of his cavalry off on a raid into Maryland and Pennsylvania, disappearing from Lee's sight for over a week. To be sure, Lee still had three of Stuart's brigades plus one other, but there was no one in command of them, and thus no one coordinating their activities. Maj. Gen. Alfred Pleasonton, commanding the Union *Cavalry Corps*, was neither as brilliant nor as spectacular a cavalryman as was Stuart. Unlike Stuart, however, he wasn't looking for glory, he just did his job. Pleasonton kept his three divisions close in hand, screening before the advance of the *Army of the Potomac* and seeking out the enemy. As a result, Lee was taken totally by surprise when Henry Heth ran into Union cavalrymen on the Chambersburg Pike northwest of Gettysburg on the morning of 1 July. Stuart tried to set things aright with his attack against Union communications along the Hanover road on the afternoon of 3 July, but his troopers were outfought and outridden in a crazy melee fought on foot and horse. The old edge was gone, and gone forever.

Stuart's Raid —

As Lee moved northwards, he was legitimately concerned about the movements of Hooker and the *Army of the Potomac*. Although his cavalry had done an effective job of denying to the enemy information as to his own movements, it had been less successful in ascertaining the enemy's own movements. By 22 June, when the Army of Northern Virginia had already begun to debouche from the Shenandoah Valley into Central Pennsylvania, the *Army of the Potomac* had yet to cross to the north side of the river whose name it bore. Lee was generally uncertain as to the location and direction of Hooker's movements and decided to do something about it. He instructed his chief of cavalry, Maj. Gen. James Ewell Brown Stuart, one of the finest troopers of the age, to observe the enemy closely. Should he detect any movement northwards on the part of the *Army of the Potomac*, he was himself to advance northwards, placing his troops on the right of Ewell's II Corps as it advanced, to cover his flank and keep him informed as to the enemy's movements. Lee apparently intended that he should advance between the Army of Northern Virginia and the *Army of the Potomac*, so as to provide cover for the entire army during the advance, and to maintain contact with the enemy. Nevertheless, his orders did not specify the route which Stuart was to take. This permitted the latter to decide the matter for himself.

Now Stuart was rather sensitive about his reputation as a cavalryman. The unfortunate affair at Brandy Station seemed to him to cast a pall over that reputation. It—and the many skirmishes which had occurred since—also seemed to demonstrate that the edge which his troopers had held over the Yankee cavalry was gone. He decided that something spectacular was needed to restore luster to his image. He had ridden completely around the *Army of the Potomac* before. Another such raid would serve both to restore his reputation and to provide useful information on the enemy's movements. Reasoning thusly, he decided to take three of his brigades and some horse artillery on a ride around the *Army of the Potomac*. He was confident

that the move would be neither difficult nor dangerous. It would take perhaps four or five days to move the hundred miles or so through Virginia, across Maryland, and into Pennsylvania to reach Ewell in the Cumberland Valley. Moreover, Lee would still have available the services of three of Stuart's own brigades, those of Brig. Gens. Beverly H. Robertson, William E. Jones, and Albert G. Jenkins, plus the independent mounted brigade of Brig. Gen. John Imboden, which could be used for security and reconnaissance missions.

Stuart set out on 24 June, the very day when the lead elements of the *Army of the Potomac* began crossing the river. He had with him the brigades of Brig. Gens. Wade Hampton, Fitzhugh Lee, and W. H. F. Lee (the latter under the command of Col. John Chambliss) plus one battery of horse artillery. Almost immediately things began to go awry. Though a master at reconnaissance, operating over familiar terrain, Stuart managed to choose the worst possible route around the *Army of the Potomac*. Failing to realize just how slowly the Yankees were moving, Stuart put his column on the very same roads which the *Army of the Potomac* was using. He became enmeshed in the Federal rear guards, fighting a series of small, though occasionally sharp skirmishes. By 28 June he was finally clear of the Union rear guards. But at a time when he ought to have been well into Pennsylvania, he had advanced no more than 35 miles, and was actually only at Rockville, barely a dozen miles from Washington. There, while one brigade began tearing up railroad tracks, another overran a heavily laden Federal supply train, taking 400 prisoners and 125 wagons. Though he paroled the prisoners the next day, he decided to take the wagons along rather than burn them. This further slowed his march. Nevertheless, by great efforts, he managed to advance 45 miles in the next two days, skirmishing with elements of the *1st Delaware Cavalry* on 29 June. Late on the morning of 30 June he arrived at Hanover, where, unbeknownst to him, Brig. Gen. Judson Kilpatrick's Union *3rd Cavalry Division* had just arrived.

Shortly before 1000 hours, the 13th

Virginia Cavalry, Stuart's advance guard, ran into the rear of Kilpatrick's division. The surprised Union rear guards broke and fled. Chambliss' troopers drove right into the town, overrunning some Union ambulances, but Kilpatrick's *1st Brigade*, under the youthful Brig. Gen. Elon J. Farnsworth, rallied and drove the rebels off. Encumbered by the wagon train, and with Fitzhugh Lee's brigade and Hampton's both at some remove from the main column, Stuart was unable to respond. He fell back, detouring around the town, and advancing towards Carlisle, where he believed he would find Ewell, was, of course, by this time in the vicinity of Gettysburg.

Stuart reached Carlisle early on the morning of 1 July. There he found Union Brig. Gen. William F. Smith, with a division of militia. He demanded that Smith surrender. When the latter refused, Stuart leisurely shelled his positions and put several buildings to the torch. A more serious engagement might have resulted, but during the action a messenger from Lee reached Stuart, instruct-

The van of Stuart's advance

Where Was He?

ing him to return at once to the army, now concentrating in the vicinity of Gettysburg. Stuart immediately broke off the action and marched off. About noon the next day he brought his exhausted troopers back to Lee, who had sorely missed them. There was little to show for Stuart's week away from the army. To be sure, he had spread some disorder in the Federal rear, and captured some useful booty, but his absence had hindered Lee's efforts to locate the enemy, with the result that Lee was now engaged in a great battle in unfavorable circumstances. All that, of course, was in the past. With Stuart present, Lee intended to make use of him. On 3 July, Stuart would strike at the Union rear from behind their right flank, even as Lonsgstreet launched his great infantry attack against their center. Thus, if the *Army of the Potomac* should break and be forced to retreat, Stuart would be ideally placed to exploit the victory.

By noon on 3 July Stuart was in position with four brigades several miles east of the Confederate left flank. There,

on the Rummel Farm his division went into action at about 1500 hours against Brig. Gen. David Gregg's Union *2nd Cavalry Division,* reinforced by three brigades by the addition of George A. Custer's brigade of Michiganders from Kilpatrick's division. Gregg and his brigadiers were fully as tough and aggressive as were Stuart and his subordinates. A very confused engagement resulted. It began with an exchange of cannon fire and some skirmishing between dismounted troopers. In this, the outnumbered Union troopers seem to have gotten the better of their Rebel opponents, if only because many of them carried the Sharps and Spencer carbines but the difference was slight. A more serious mounted action followed. Several charges and counter charges followed, in one of which Custer is reported to have cried, "Come on, you Wolverines!" as he gleefully plunged once more into the fray. There was much hand-to-hand fighting, and at one time Gregg appears to have had actually surrounded most of Stuart's men, only to have them cut their

way out again. Tactically, it ended in a draw, and each side claimed to have forced the other to give up the fight. However, it should probably be labelled a Union victory in as much as Gregg did frustrate Stuart's efforts to disrupt the Federal rear. Losses were remarkably light, perhaps 250 for the Union and 200 for the Confederacy. The action had no effect whatsoever on the outcome of the great drama which unfolded simultaneously four miles to the southwest along Cemetery Ridge.

After Rummel Farm, Stuart and his cavalry returned to doing what they did best, serving as the eyes and shield of the Army of Northern Virginia as it retreated painfully back to its native soil. A good cavalryman, one of the greatest in history, Stuart had let his pride take him off on an unnecessary mission at a time when Lee's need for him had been greatest. In doing that, he had injured his reputation far more than had been done by Brandy Station.

Far left: *Brig. Gen. James J. Pettigrew*

Maj. Gen. Henry Heth

The army moved behind a thick screen of cavalry. Buford's *1st Cavalry Division* covered its left and front, while Brig. Gen. Hugh Kilpatrick's *3rd Cavalry Division* covered the right flank and Gregg's *2nd Cavalry Division* covered the right rear and chased Stuart, who had reached a position some 25 miles west of Baltimore. The advanced guard comprised *I Corps* and *XI Corps,* under the general direction of the very able Reynolds of *I Corps.* Behind these moved the main body of the army, with *II Corps, III Corps, V Corps, XII Corps,* and the *Artillery Reserve,* and with *VI Corps* in the rear acting as a general reserve. Despite considerable straggling, and some crossing of columns, it was probably the most well organized and most carefully conducted movement that the *Army of the Potomac* had ever undertaken. Though the average advance on 29 June was about 21 miles, some units exceeded this. Buford's cavalry advanced over 35 miles, a feat which could be matched by some of the infantry, notably Maj. Gen. Winfield Scott Hancock's *II Corps,* which covered 32 miles, mostly at night and with minimal straggling. Morale was good, and the troops were very determined, notably so among the Pennsylvanians, who constituted over a third of the army: 68 infantry and nine cavalry regiments, plus five batteries of artillery. On 30 June, Meade began to push the right of the army forward somewhat, so that by nightfall his front ran roughly southwest to northeast, just a few miles north of Pipe Creek, while the rear was just behind the creek. It was an excellent position in which to meet any possible Confederate advance. The bulk of the army concentrated

within a dozen miles of Taneytown, just below the Pennsylvania-Maryland border, so that no corps was more than a few hours march from any other. His cavalry was 'way ahead, with Kirkpatrick at Hanover, where he had a hot skirmish with Stuart's cavalry, and with Buford's pickets about four miles beyond Gettysburg, a small town of 2,400 souls. There Meade rested his army. He instructed his corps commanders to issue extra ammunition and rations, and to prepare their men for battle. He was careful to inform them of his plans. He believed that a great battle was imminent. For 1 July he prepared two sets of plans, one proposed a withdrawal to the Pipe Creek position should the enemy fall on the *Army of the Potomac,* while the other assumed a less aggressive foe, and envisioned a cautious advance in the direction of Gettysburg. If it came to a fight over the next few days, Meade was ready and so was the *Army of the Potomac.*

The Army of Northern Virginia was also on the move in the last days of June. Lee had bungled badly. By allowing Stuart a free hand, he had deprived himself of one of the finest reconnaissance forces in the world. Moreover, he had also failed to use the cavalry brigades which Stuart had left behind. The result was that as late as 28 June he remained ignorant of the movements of the *Army of the Potomac,* yet he continued to leave his army spread out over some 2000 square miles of Pennsylvania. Then, on the night of 28 June, he received some disturbing information. A spy dispatched to Washington by Longstreet on 24 June, had returned to the army with the news that the *Army of the Potomac* was in

Maryland in force. In haste, and somewhat carelessly, Lee began to issue orders to pull in the more dispersed elements of the army. Ewell, commanding the most exposed part of the Army of Northern Virginia, II Corps, was disappointed when orders to pull back were received. He had just fought a modest skirmish before the defenses of Harrisburg and believed that he could take the Pennsylvania capital at his leisure, bringing much glory and loot to Confederate arms. Nevertheless, he obeyed orders, or at least tried to, for he received two different sets of instructions. The first set, issued on the night of 28 June, directed him to march on Chambersburg, while the other, issued the following morning, ordered him to concentrate at Heidlersburg. Other commanders had similar experiences. As a result, when the Army of Northern Virginia began to move on 29 June, there was considerable confusion. Units already on the road, were forced to reverse their direction. Some formations found that the roads assigned to them had been assigned to other units as well. Johnson's Divison of II Corps ran into part of Longstreet's I Corps, resulting in a massive traffic jam which was resolved with difficulty. Most units did not have such serious problems, but there was considerable confusion. Fortunately morale was very high and the troops performed splendidly, despite their grumblings. When the movements were completed on 30 June, the army was concentrated in an area 30 miles long by ten wide, between Heidlersburg and Chambersburg. The army was still somewhat dispersed, and there was a good deal of intermingling of units, but it was the best that could be done in the circumstances, and Lee planned additional movements over the next day or so to concentrate the army in the vicinity of Cashtown and Gettysburg. Scouts were sent out and began to bring back some useful information, including the news that Meade had assumed command of the *Army of the Potomac*, but nothing substantial, such as the location of the enemy. Nevertheless, Lee appears to have felt confident that he could deal with any eventuality. Meanwhile, some of the troops were still on the march. The evening of

Cavalry on the skirmish line

Tuesday, 30 June was warm but not uncomfortably so, and the troops of Brig. Gen. James J. Pettigrew's brigade of Maj. Gen. Henry Heth's Division were still on the road, advancing on Gettysburg behind a thin line of skirmishers. At Gettysburg Pettigrew, whose men needed shoes, intended to levy yet another contribution on the already well-picked over town. In the gathering darkness, Pettigrew's skirmishers ran into some Federal cavalrymen along the Chambersburg Pike about four miles northwest of Gettysburg. They were from Buford's *1st Cavalry Brigade*, placed on outpost duty earlier that evening. Pettigrew halted his men about a mile from the Union vedettes. Both Buford and Pettigrew dispatched messengers to the rear. The two armies had made contact. The great battle which everyone had been anticipating and dreading for days was imminent.

George Armstrong Custer in an uncharacteristic pose. When the North was groping for heroes, Gettysburg made his reputation.

CHAPTER V

GETTYSBURG, 1 JULY:
Meeting Engagement

The first shots of the Battle of Gettysburg were fired not long after daylight—at 0430 hours—on the morning of 1 July by some Union cavalrymen on picket duty along the Chambersburg Pike just west of a small stream named Willoughby Run. Henry Heth had started his division on the road towards Gettysburg at about 0500, when elements of Pettigrew's Brigade formed a 2500 yard-wide skirmish line and began to advance slowly. Beyond the rebel skirmishers, the Union cavalrymen could discern considerable activity as the balance of Heth's Division formed up to move out. The pickets formed a slender skirmish line under cover, with no more than one man for every ten yards of front. As he became aware of how thin the Federal forces were to his front, Heth began pressing them harder. The Union troopers began to fall back slowly. At about 0800 their brigade commander, Col. William Gamble, was informed that his outpost line was under considerable pressure. Conferring with Buford, the latter immediately ordered him to put 1,200 of his men and a battery of artillery into battle line along Herr Ridge, a modest rise about two miles west of Gettysburg, which offered some

natural advantages. As a precautionary measure, Buford's other brigade, under Col. Thomas E. Devin, was posted to cover the approaches further to the north. Gamble's troopers went into action rapidly. Though greatly outnumbered, their position was a strong one. Moreover they carried Sharps carbines, with an effective rate-of-fire three times that of an ordinary rifled musket. Faced with more substantial opposition, Heth advanced cautiously, putting his men into six columns, three of which advanced on either side of the Chambersburg Pike. The Union cavalrymen maintained their line for nearly an hour before being forced to fall back about a mile, to the partially wooded McPherson's Ridge, an even better defensive position. Here the men held tenaciously, awaiting reinforcement.

Maj. Gen. John Reynolds, commanding both *I Corps* and the advanced guard, was the first reinforcement Buford received, arriving with his staff a bit after 1000 hours. Conferring with Buford, Reynolds commended him on the excellence of his deployment and his choice of ground, which was naturally quite strong and dominated any possible Confederate advance

Hall's battery delaying the Rebel advance on the Chambersburg Road

Assault on the stone barn of McPherson's Farm

Ready for battle. . .

on Gettysburg from the west. It looked to him like the ideal place to begin a major action with the enemy, with plenty of room to fall back later to even better positions. Reynolds ordered Buford to hold at all costs. He dispatched a message to Meade, informing him of the situation and concluding, "I will fight them inch by inch, and if driven into the town I will barricade the streets and hold them as long as possible." Then, after sending messages to Howard of *XI Corps,* Slocum of *XII Corps,* and Sickles of *III Corps* requesting their immediate assistance, he rode back to hurry on his veteran 3,700-man strong *1st Division,* under Brig. Gen. James S.

Wadsworth, about 30 minutes march away. Meanwhile action on Buford's line grew heated, as Heth attacked on a two brigade front. Buford's men began to fall back. Then, shortly after 1030 hours, Reynolds brought up his leading elements. Barely in time, Reynolds got the *2nd Maine Battery* into position, and then the *56th Pennsylvania,* of Wadsworth's *2nd Brigade,* which was followed by two other regiments north of the Chambersburg Pike while two more deployed to its south. Buford's tired troopers took up positions on the flanks. By 1045 hours the Federal line had been strengthened and lengthened somewhat, with about 2,000 infantrymen and six 3" field guns stretching from McPherson's Farm northwards for about 2000 yards across an unfinished railroad line, while some 1,600 tired cavalrymen covered the flanks. But the situation remained critical, as some 3,500 Confederate troops pressed the attack, supported by about a dozen pieces of artillery. Confederate forces began to lap at the flanks the Federal position, with Brig. Gen. Joseph R. Davis' Brigade working around his right, even as Brig. Gen James J. Archer's Brigade pressed the attack on his front and worked around his left. Reynolds ordered up the newly arrived Wisconsinites, Michiganders, and Indianans of the famed *Iron Brigade (1st Brigade, 1st Division, I Corps),* instructing them to ". . . drive those fellows out of those woods. . . ." The veterans of the *2nd Wisconsin* came up in their distinctive big black hats, loading their muskets at the run.

Shrugging off Confederate volleys, they plunged into the woods. Hitherto, many of the Confederate troops believed they were engaged against militia, they were soon disabused of this illusion. As the *2nd Wisconsin* attacked, some of Archer's men yelled "Thar come the black hats! 'Taint no militia! Its the *Army of the Potomac!*" as they fell back from the Federal left under their attack. Reynolds, who was observing the attack from horseback, was at that triumphant moment struck behind the right ear by a rifle ball, dying almost instantly. Even as he fell, the balance of the *Iron Brigade* came up, delivering a series of three echeloned hammer blows to Archer's front and right. Archer's Brigade fell back to Herr Ridge, battered and exhausted, even as its commander and hundreds of men were led to the rear as prisoners. The Federal left was saved. But the situation on the right grew worse.

Davis' Brigade had succeeded in flanking the Union position. Two of the regiments there were ordered back to Seminary Ridge. This exposed the remaining regiments of the *2nd Brigade*, and they shifted front, unmasking the Union center. Maj. Gen. Abner Doubleday, who assumed command of *I Corps* at about 1100 hours, after Reynolds fell, threw in everything available, the brigade guard and the *6th Wisconsin*, 450 men in all. Posted on the left flank of the *Iron Brigade*, the reinforced regiment turned to the right and rushed northwards behind McPherson's Ridge. Just below the Chambersburg Pike the regiment came upon the exposed flank of the Confederate forces who were in pursuit of the two Union regiments falling back to Seminary Ridge. The Wisconsinites halted along a rail fence and opened a voluminous fire into the Rebel flank. The Confederates took refuge in the unfinished railroad cut and opened fire in turn. A hot fire fight developed. Then the *95th* and *84th New York*, the regiments which the Confederates had been pursuing, formed up on the right flank of the *6th Wisconsin*. Lt. Col. Rufus Dawes of the *6th Wisconsin* ordered an attack. In a rough line the Union troops valuted the rail fence and drove straight at the enemy. Some of the troops managed to get across the railroad cut and a murderous fire began pouring in on the trapped rebels. It was over in a few minutes, with many of the men of the 42nd Mississippi and 55th North Carolina becoming prisoners and all of the 2nd Mississippi, the first full regiment ever to surrender in the history of the Army of Northern Virginia. Davis' Brigade had been virtually destroyed, only the 11th Mississippi and a

Above: *From the rooftop of this building Reynolds observed the opening battle.*

Two eyewitness sketches of Reynolds' death

Above: *Maj. Gen. Oliver O. Howard*

Above right: *Maj. Gen. Carl Schurz*

Below: *The railroad cut and the surrender of the 2nd Mississippi*

Below right: *Maj. Gen. Abner Doubleday*

few hundred other men escaping back across McPherson's Ridge. The Union right was saved.

By noon the situation on McPherson's Ridge had stabilized. The Union position was secure, at least for the moment, and Henry Heth had been given a serious drubbing. Firing died down and there was relative calm for two hours. Meanwhile, troops were on the march. One-armed Maj. Gen. Oliver O. Howard arrived on the field at about 1130 hours with the advanced elements of his *XI Corps* and assumed command of the battle from Doubleday. He designated his *2nd Division* and part of the corps artillery as a reserve, positioning them on Cemetery Hill, and began hurrying his forces forward as they arrived. At about noon he turned his corps over to Maj. Gen. Carl Schurz. The balance of *I Corps* came up and was rushed forward to McPherson's Ridge, where Doubleday put his *3rd Division* in on the left and held his *2nd* in reserve. By 1400 hours two full corps were at hand plus

Buford's cavalry, some 23,000 men and 60 pieces of artillery. Further back, other Union forces were beginning to move up.

Confederate troops were on the march too. Lt. Gen. A. P. Hill, commanding Lee's III Corps, decided to continue the action, apparently without clearing the matter with Lee. Heth brought up the balance of his division, putting some 7,000 men in front of McPherson's Ridge, while Maj. Gen. William D. Pender's Division was fast approaching with some 6,700 and Maj. Gen. R. H. Anderson's 7,100 men not far behind that. Other Confederate forces were on the move as well. On the morning of 1 July Lee had ordered Ewell's II Corps to march on Gettysburg, though carefully instructing him to avoid bringing about a general action. By 1400 hours Ewell was some four miles north of Gettysburg with the divisions of Maj. Gen. Jubal Early and Maj. Gen. R. E. Rodes, nearly 14,000 men, and with the 6,400 of Maj. Gen. Edward Johnson's following behind. But Longstreet's I Corps, some 21,000 of the finest troops in the Army of Northern Virginia, was a long way off, and some elements had not yet taken to the roads, nor even been informed that a general action seemed imminent.

Col. Thomas Devin, commanding Buford's cavalrymen to the north of Gettysburg, became aware of Ewell's approach at about 1230 hours. Informed, Howard began moving his forces into position almost immediately. He positioned the 1st and *3rd Divisions* of *XI Corps* along a 2,500 yard front in the broad valley north of the town. At the same time, Doubleday extended his front about 1000 yards northwards to the foot of Oak Hill by putting Maj. Gen. John C. Robinson's *2nd Division* into the line. These dispositions were unwise. The two Union corps now lay at

right angles to each other. Moreover, Doubleday's *I Corps* was now overstretched on a front of more than 3,000 yards, and his left flank was still engaged with Heth's men. However, neither Howard nor Doubleday seem to have been concerned about this. Howard dispatched several messages to Maj. Gen. Daniel Sickles of *III Corps* and Maj. Gen. Henry W. Slocum of *XII Corps*, informing them of the situation and calling for their help. He also reported to Meade. By this time Meade, who was a dozen miles southeast of the fighting at Taneytown, had become aware that a general action had begun. He also had been informed of the excellent work Reynolds had done in making a stand, and of the death of the latter, one of his closest friends. He ordered another trusted friend, Maj. Gen. Winfield Scott Hancock of *II Corps*, to turn his command over to Brig. Gen. John Gibbon and take over at the front. Still somewhat uncertain as to what the situation was, Meade instructed Hancock to report on whether the terrain and tactical situation at the Gettysburg position warranted a general battle, or whether the action should be broken off. But even as Hancock rode towards the fight, the action grew more general.

Left: *Brig. Gen. John Gibbon*

Below: *Gettysburg viewed from Cemetery Hill looking westward towards Seminary Ridge. The Lutheran Seminary is just visible to left of center.*

INFANTRY WEAPONS AND TACTICS

The infantry caused the overwhelming majority of the combat-related casualties of the Civil War. For a generation after the Napoleonic Wars the infantry had continued to be armed with a muzzle loading, smooth bore musket. This was essentially a somewhat improved version of the muskets which had been introduced in the late seventeenth century. It had served well, and organization and tactics were tailored to its use. Since it was highly inaccurate, slow firing, and of very short range, normal tactics dictated lining the troops up shoulder-to-shoulder, marching them within very close range of the enemy, and firing in coordinated volleys. This could be devastatingly effective, and was perfectly satisfactory for well over a century. Technologically, of course, the smooth bore musket was decidedly inferior to the rifle, a weapon which had shallow grooves cut into the barrel which helped stabilize the ball in flight, thereby greatly enhancing range and accuracy. But the rifled musket was even clumsier than the smooth bore and had an even lower rate of fire, for it required very careful loading. As a result its use by armies was rare. Then, in 1848 a French officer, Capt. Claude Etienne Minié, invented a practical rifled musket. What Minié actually invented was a more practical bullet for the rifled musket. The so-called "minie-ball" was a cylindro-conoidal (i.e., "bullet-shaped") lead projectile with a hollow base. The bullet was machined to a somewhat smaller diameter than the musket barrel. When the piece was fired the rapid generation of gas expanded the soft, hollow base of the round, forcing it to conform to the rifling grooves on the inner side of the barrel. The rounds were made up into paper wrapped cartridges of about two inches in length. Loading was thus no more difficult than it was for the old smooth bore weapons, while accuracy and range were greatly enhanced. The new weapon was soon adopted by most armies, to devastating effect. One reason for the devastation was a failure of tactical doctrine.

Tactics ought to be a reflection of weaponry. By the mid-nineteenth century the optimal tactics for the smooth bore musket were well understood, having been evolved over a period of more than a century. Unfortunately, when the rifled musket was introduced no one seems to have considered its possible effect on tactics. As a result, armies continued to use their existing tactics. Casualties were horrendous as lines of troops arrayed shoulder-to-shoulder marched up to short ranges and exchanged fire in formal Napoleonic style, or attempted heroic bayonet charges against rifle-armed foes. Tactics began to change, out of a combination of the instinct for self-preservation and an understanding of the futility of the traditional methods. Defensive tactics changed first and best.

In defense, presupposing that his flanks and rear were secure, a commander would put some of his troops out as skirmishers a couple of hundred yards before his main line. Firing from cover, their function was to entertain an advancing enemy, sniping at officers and generally attempting to disrupt the attack. As the enemy closed, the skirmishers could either filter out by the flanks, to regroup, or drift back to join the main line of resistance. Most of the troops, of course, would be on the main line. By 1863 both armies resorted to all available cover, and given time, attempted to improve their positions with rifle pits and other entrenchments. Firing from cover, the defenders could deliver an annoying shower of bullets at ranges out to a thousand yards, with increasing effectiveness as the foe came closer: since a 350-man regiment could theoretically pour out over 10,000 rounds in the time attacking infantry required to cover 1,500 yards, the defense had a distinct advantage. Should the enemy actually reach the main line of defense hand to hand combat was common, though far more frequently with clubbed rifles than with the standard 18 inch spike bayonets. A wise defender usually retained a portion of his troops behind the line as a reserve, and these could be thrown in should the enemy begin forcing the line. In addition, if his skirmishers regrouped on the flanks, they could be thrown in against the attackers' flanks at the critical moment. The Union stand on Cemetery Ridge on 3 July is a very fine example of what a properly conducted defense was supposed to look like. Now the principal impact of the rifled musket was to greatly improve the effectiveness of the defense. As a result, it made the offensive far more difficult.

Ultimately, no one managed to evolve proper offensive tactics during the Civil War. Initial efforts at Napoleonic style storming columns proved disastrously expensive, but the cult of the bayonet persisted. Attacks in waves, with skirmishers to the fore were also tried, to better effect, but these were by no means widely successful. Attempts were also made to attack with troops advancing by rushes in open order, again with mixed results. The best way

to conduct any attack was to avoid attacking the enemy's strength, but rather to use maneuver and surprise to strike where he was weakest, on an exposed flank or at a thinly held position or against a poorly deployed formation, or one already badly battered by infantry and artillery fire. In these circumstances, going in with the bayonet was possible, but most of the fighting was still by firepower, the principal effect of the bayonet being psychological: though few men were injured by it, most feared it. It was precisely this sort of attack which Lee effected at Chancellorsville. However, such an attack required considerable tactical skill. Even if successful, one had to pay the price.

Anyone undertaking an offensive, even against poorly organized opposition, had to be willing to take losses. Thus, on 2 July, the Confederate losses in their successful attack on Sickles' badly deployed *III Corps* were almost as great as those suffered by the defenders. The tactical defensive was just that strong. This was one reason for the repeated defeats suffered by the Union during the earlier years of the war, for Union forces were invariably on the offensive. It also helps explain why Confederate losses were often enormous, for Rebel generals had a predeliction for the tactical offensive even when on the strategic defensive. So fine a commander as Lee himself fought only one purely de-

fensive battle, when, at Fredericksburg on 13 December 1862, he held Marye's Heights in strength and accepted the repeated frontal attacks of the *Army of the Potomac*. Union casualties were almost double his own, whereas when he won by a tactical offensive his casualties were almost invariably greater than the enemy's. All of this makes Lee's grand assault on 3 July rather difficult to understand. None of the reasons which he subsequently offered to explain the attempt are convincing, particularly in view of Longstreet's reservations about the effort. In the end, not even Lee could shake the Napoleonic mold. Perhaps he had been winning too much.

SMALL ARMS

Small arms fire accounted for 91.3% of the combat casualties in the Civil War, artillery being responsible for but 7.5%; less than 0.1% were due to edged weapons, and the rest to land mines, hand grenades, and other causes. A great variety of small arms were used during the Civil War, particularly in the early period. This was due to a lack of adequate stocks and a shortage of industrial plants. As a result all sorts of weapons were procured abroad. As late as mid-1863 Union small arms were still not standardized, with many regiments at Gettysburg carrying odd weapons and some even being equipped with two or three different types. Confederate units were in even worse shape, often carrying a great variety of different weapons, many of them captured from the Union. The weapons included in this table made up over 90% of the long arms carried by the Union and Confederate infantry and cavalry during the Gettysburg Campaign.

Weapon is the official designation of the piece in question. *Load*, refers to whether the piece is muzzle-loading (ML) or breechloading (BL). *Cal* is the caliber, or diameter, of the bullet, expressed in inches; most of these rounds ran a half-ounce or better. *Range* is the normal effective range of the piece, in yards: most of these weapons could inflict lethal damage at up to four times that range, though accuracy was greatly reduced. *Weight* is the weight of the weapon, with its bayonet (except for the Sharps and the Spencer, which had none) in pounds. *R/F* is the number of rounds per minute which could be sustained in combat, given a trained soldier and a clean weapon. *Note* refers to the lettered comments which appear below.

A. This was the cavalry version of the British Enfield 1855 Rifle, which was immensely popular with Confederate cavalrymen, when they weren't exercising their penchant for carrying shotguns.

B. The standard British infantry rifle between 1855 and 1867, nearly 500,000 were procured for the Union and over 100,000 for the Confederacy in the early years of the war. Both the rifle and the carbine were subsequently manufactured in the South, along with a special "officer's" model of particularly fine quality. The Enfield was a good serviceable weapon, very popular with the troops, particularly in the South.

C. The first breech loading shoulder arm to be issued to U.S. troops, the Sharps was a cavalryman's weapon. Over 80,000 were procured during the war, and the Confederacy even began manufacturing them. The Sharps was loaded by a lever which doubled as the trigger guard. Pushing this forward dropped the breech block. The soldier would insert into the breech a linen-wrapped cartridge, and raise the block once more. Doing this would cut open the cartridge. The hammer had to be manually cocked. Firing was initially by means of percussion tape—similar to that used in child's cap pistol—but this was later replaced by percussion caps on a rotating disk. Very popular with the troops, at Gettysburg this was the most common weapon of Union cavalrymen.

D. The infantry version of the Sharps Carbine, only small numbers of these were issued during the war, mostly to units designated as "sharpshooters", which term does not, in fact, derive from the name of the rifle. At Gettysburg virtually all sharpshooter units, plus the *2nd New Hampshire* and the *1st Minnesota*, and several companies of the *14th Connecticut* and the *13th Pennsylvania Reserves* used the Sharps rifle to deadly effect.

E. The Spencer Repeating Carbine was the first regularly issued repeating firearm in the world. In mid-1863 Union cavalry regiments began receiving it and by the end of the war it was the principal long arm borne by Union cavalrymen, and had begun to appear in substantial numbers among the infantry. The Spencer had a tubular magazine with seven self-contained copper cased, rim fire cartridges. The magazine passed through the butt. As in the Sharps, pushing forward on the trigger guard lowered the breech block, ejecting the spent shell upwards. By pulling back on the level, the block closed and a spring in the magazine inserted a fresh round. The weapon was manually cocked, and a good man could easily get off twenty shots in a minute, changing the magazine as he went. Each man was issued ten spare magazines, which he carried in a special case, giving him a total of 77 rounds. During the Gettysburg Campaign it appears the Spencer was carried by some of the troopers in the *5th* and *6th Michigan Cavalry Regiments* of Custer's brigade.

Altogether Union forces at Gettysburg carried, in addition to the Sharps, and the Spencer, small numbers of nine other types of breechloading rifles and carbines.

Weapon	Load	Cal	Range	Weight	R/F	Note.
Enfield 1855 Carbine	ML	.577"	350 yds	8.0 pds	3	A
Enfield 1855 Rifle	ML	.577	450	9.2	3	B
Sharps 1848 Carbine	BL	.52	350	7.0	9	C
Sharps 1848 Rifle	BL	.52	450	8.0	9	D
Spencer 1860 Carbine	BL	.52	450	8.3	20	E
U.S. 1835 Musket	ML	.69	150	11.0	3	F
U.S. 1842 Musket	ML	.69	150	11.0	3	G
U.S. 1855 Rifle	ML	.58	400	10.12	3	H
U.S. 1861 Rifle	ML	.58	450	9.75	3	I

OF THE GETTYSBURG CAMPAIGN

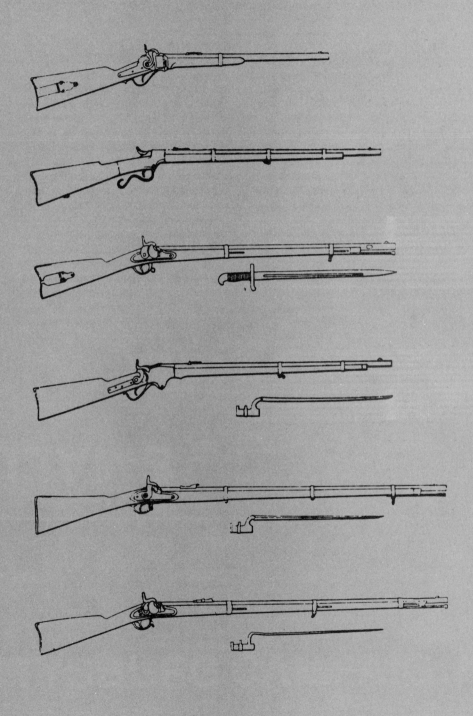

F. An obsolete weapon by the Civil War, this was the last flintlock adopted by the U.S. Army. In many respects it was virtually unchanged from the weapons which Washington's men had carried into battle. Numbers of these were used in the early days of the war and some remained in service with Confederate militia units well into the struggle. None appear to have been at Gettysburg—save that probably borne by John Burns—but they may have been used by second line and militia forces on both sides in some of the skirmishes which took place during the campaign.

G. This was essentially the U.S. 1835 flintlock musket, converted to percussion cap, or manufactured to the new specifications. Many units on both sides carried this with them in the early part of the war and some Confederate regiments still bore it at Gettysburg, along with a handful of Union ones, most notably the *12th New Jersey* on Cemetery Ridge. It was also carried by many of the emergency regiments raised in Pennsylvania during the campaign. It could be loaded with simple ball ammunition, or with "buck-and-ball", special cartridges which included some buckshot in addition to the musket ball. Troops would sometimes make up cartridges consisting entirely of buckshot, which could be particularly devastating at close range.

H. The first U.S. minié rifle, about 100,000 of these were produced in two slightly different versions before the war, and some remained in Confederate service at the time of Gettysburg and seems to have been used by some Federal militia regiments.

I. The famed "Springfield Rifle", over 900,000 of these were produced in three slightly differing versions during the war, some 150,000 of which found their way into the Confederate army. It was essentially an improved version of the 1855 rifle and was very popular with the troops of both armies. It was the last muzzle-loading weapon produced for the U.S.

All of these weapons were made of high grade iron, with hardwood stocks. The barrel was cast as a solid piece and then bored out to the desired caliber. Lock mechanisms, triggers, and other fittings were produced individually. While technically mass produced with interchangeable parts, following the technology introduced by Eli Whitney—whose invention of the cotton gin had done much to strengthen slavery, thereby helping to bring about the war—in practice there was wide variation even among pieces produced in the same plant. As a result, the final assembly of the piece was always done by hand, with much filing sometimes required. This was one reason why breechloaders were unusually expensive, for it was difficult to secure a tight seal on the breech mechanism with contemporary production methods.

Who Fired the First Shot?

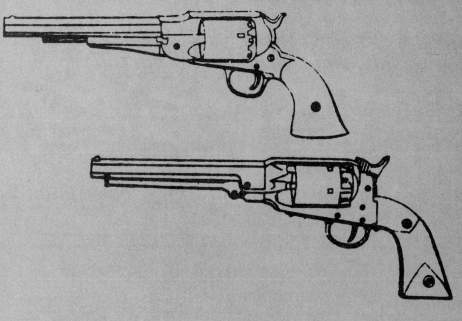

Who Fired the First Shot? The first shot of the Battle of Gettysburg was fired by Union cavalrymen on picket duty along the Chambersburg Pike at about 0530 hours—roughly an hour after sunrise—on the morning of 1 July against advancing Confederate skirmishers from Brig. Gen. James J. Pettigrew's brigade of Maj. Gen. Henry Heth's division. But who actually fired the first shot is a matter of some dispute. By some accounts the honors belong to Corp. Alponse Hodges of *Company F, 9th New York Cavalry,* an element of Col. Thomas C. Devin's brigade of Brig. Gen. John Buford's 1st Cavalry Division. According to his account, Hodges was in charge of a picket of three privates on the Chambersburg Pike just east of Willoughby Run. Some time after dawn Hodges spotted some men about a mile to the west. He dispatched the privates to notify the pickets on either flank and the brigade officer of the day, Col. William Sackett, of his own regiment. Shortly afterwards, Hodges advanced across the run by himself in order to better ascertain the situation. He appears to have gone forward about 600 yards, at which point he was sufficiently close in the early morning light to be able to determine that the troops in front of him were in fact Confederates. He

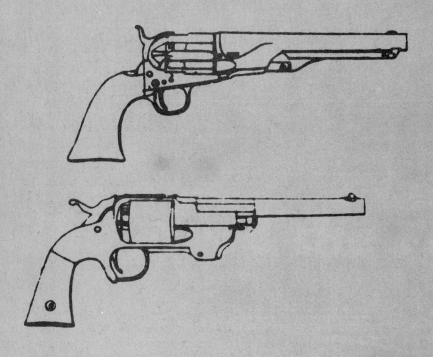

turned back, and at that point was spotted by the Rebels, who opened fire on him. Hodges got off a few shots from the bridge and then fell back to report to Col. Sackett, who was already getting his men into a skirmish line.

The alternative version has it that the first shots were fired by Lt. Marcellus E. Jones of the *8th Illinois Cavalry.* Jones was in command of some picket posted in roughly the same vicinity, but just south of the Chambersburg Pike. Shortly after dawn, he reported to his company commander that he observed activity in the distance along the Chambersburg Pike. Capt. H. E. Dana dismounted the company to form a thin skirmish line. As the Rebels approached cautiously, Lt. Jones became engaged in a fire fight. The *8th Illinois Cavalry,* formerly Col. William Gamble's regiment, and at the time in his brigade, was a politically important regiment. A great deal of regimental and state pride may be wrapped up in the latter's claim. Although the matter is not of great importance, and indeed, it is possible that both versions are correct, Hodges' account would seem to be the more reliable, particularly as, Cyrus W. James, a private of *Company G, 9th New York Cavalry,* is generally cited as the first Union soldier killed in the battle.

Loading the Musket

Holding his musket with his left hand, the soldier removed the ramrod from its slot beneath the barrel and swabbed out the tube to cleanse it of sparks, lest it flare while he was loading it. Then, placing the ramrod also in his left hand, he reached into his cartridge pouch for one of the paper-wrapped cartridges which it contained. Biting off the bottom end, he carefully poured the powder down the barrel, tapping the butt lightly on the ground as he did so. He then dropped the bullet into the barrel, shoved the paper in after it as a wadding, and tamped everything down with the ramrod, which he then replaced in its slot. Resuming the piece, he cocked the hammer. He then took a percussion cap from a second pouch which he placed on a little nipple which connected with the chamber by a tiny touch hole. [With the 1835 flintlock he actually had to put powder in the touch hole.] He was now ready to fire.

There was much that could go wrong. To begin with, it was extremely difficult to load any of these weapons in any but a standing position. In addition, in the heat of battle a man might spill some of the powder or drop the ball or the percussion cap. In such cases he might not even be aware of what had happened, and might reload, thinking he had fired properly. Double or triple loaded muskets were not uncommon. Of about 24,000 rifles and muskets salvaged from the field after the Battle of Gettysburg, about 6,000 were either empty or contained one round, about 12,000 had double charges, and about 6,000 more contained at least three rounds, with the record being ten. These, of course, where the ones which had not exploded in some soldier's face. A man might even forget to remove the ramrod from the barrel, with the result that he fired it off, and was then unable to reload. Not for nothing did the troops universally prefer breech loaders, when they could get them. Curiously, at the onset of the war the United States War Department had turned down a proposal to equip the entire army with breech loaders, citing the expense—about $30.00 to $50.00 apiece as against $20.00—and claiming that breech loaders would only encourage the waste of am-

munition. Whether anyone thought to consult the troops is unlikely.

Generally, the troops on both sides carried 40 rounds, in packets of 20. The standard ammunition pouch had two tin trays, each of twenty rounds, one above the other, so if he had more than 40 rounds, a soldier had to carry the extra ones in his knapsack or haversack. When the upper tray of his ammunition pouch was empty, he had to remove it and place it under the lower tray, this made carrying one's ammunition loose in a sack popular. Percussion caps were carried in a smaller pouch. It was not uncommon for extra ammunition to be distributed on the eve of battle, and, of course, one could always take it from the dead. Since both sides had mostly the same weapons, using captured ammunition was common.

Butler's battery moving into position

Ewell's II Corps struck in mid-afternoon. Rodes had concentrated most of his 18,000 strong division on Oak Hill, with one brigade in front of *XI Corps*, linking it to his main body by a line of infantry pickets, and held one brigade back as a reserve. Of his remaining three brigades, that of Brig. Gen. Alfred Iverson would hit the Union front obliquely, while to its left that of Col. E. A. O'Neal was to strike against Doubleday's right flank, and that of Brig.Gen. Junius Daniels was to cover the right of the two attacking brigades. At 1430 hours Rodes opened fire. Two batteries at the heavily wooded north end of Oak Hill took Doubleday's center, the *1st Division*, under enfilading fire. Brig. Gen. James Wadsworth, commanding, pulled his already battered right-hand brigade back diagonally across Seminary Ridge in an effort to link up with Robinson's *2nd Division*, on the corps' right. This movement split the corps, and Wadsworth's division as well, opening a 600 yard gap along the Chambersburg Pike. The left wing of the corps had 4,800 men in three brigades on McPherson's Ridge, while the right comprised Robinson's two brigades, plus Wadsworth's battered *2nd Brigade* and the *6th Wisconsin*, no more than 5,000 men. About 450 yards further to the right of *I Corps*, and roughly at right angles to it, was *XI Corps*. When Rodes' assault brigades moved out, *I Corps* seemed ripe for disaster. But even as the veteran Confederate regiments moved out smartly to the assault, the attack began to falter. Rodes failed to use his best brigade commanders, and neither Iverson nor O'Neal accompanied their men into action. Moreover, the latter attacked with only three regiments, rather than his full four, and did so on too narrow a front. Rapidly shifting his troops, Robinson took the attack of O'Neal's Alabamians frontally and threw the Rebel brigade back in disorder. This exposed Iverson's flank, but the latter kept coming anyway, with some 1,400 North Carolinians in near perfect alignment. They came under heavy artillery fire and they began to falter, drifting off to the left. Suddenly they came under direct rifle fire, suffering perhaps 30% casualties in a few seconds. Then several Union regiments went over to the attack, storming forward to capture many prisoners. The *Pennsylvania Bucktail Brigade (2nd of the 3rd Division of I Corps)* under Col. Roy Stone covered the left end of the gap in Wadsworth's front, facing northwards and began pouring a heavy fire into Daniel's Brigade and the remnant's of Iverson's. Elements of *I Corps'* left wing contributed long range fire into the flank of the retreating Rebels. Within minutes it was over, as the bulk of Iverson's brigade surrendered, to the distress of their commander, and as O'Neal's shattered commands drifted to the rear covered by Daniel's North Carolinians. Rodes' attack had failed, but he still had some fight left in him. Rapidly reorganizing the survivor's of his unfortunate attack, Rodes grouped them with his reserve, Brig. Gen. S. D. Ramseur's 1,000 strong brigade of North Carolinians, added 350 more of the 3rd Alabama, and held them ready for another attack. Meanwhile, Rodes' screen before *XI Corps* was having a busy afternoon.

Brig. Gen. George Doles' Brigade of Georgians had done well during the initial stages of the fighting on the ridge to his right. Assisted by the 300 men of the 5th Alabama, Doles' 1,300 men had gradually forced Union Col. Thomas Devin's cavalry pickets back. Infantry from the *3rd Division* of *XI Corps* came up, pushing Doles back. Counterattacking, he had run full into *XI Corps*, which promptly attacked on his right, intending to separate him from the balance of Rodes' Division. Doles' shifted two of his regiments to meet the attack, but by about 1530 hours his situation was becoming critical and his left was collapsing. At that moment Ewell dropped the other shoe.

Jubal Early's Division, about 5,500 veterans, had been getting into position north of Gettysburg while Rodes' troops were heavily engaged against both *I Corps* and *XI Corps*. Con-

Below: *The fighting around the Lutheran Seminary*

cealed by some thick woods, he had positioned a dozen guns just east of the Heidlersburg Road, and deployed Brig. Gen. J. B. Gordon's Brigade of 1,800 Georgians to the right of the road, Brig. Gen. Harry T. Hays' 1,300 Louisianans in the center, and Brig. Gen. Isaac Avery's somewhat weaker North Carolinians to its left, with Brig. Gen. William Smith's 800-strong Virginia Brigade behind Avery. By 1530 hours Early was ready.

Early's artillery opened up, enfilading the front of *XI Corps*. Gordon's Brigade stepped off, moving to Doles' support at an easy pace so as not to tire the troops. Gordon soon located the right-flank brigade of *XI Corps*, some 1,100 men under Col. Leopold von Gilsa, positioned with a stream to its front, on the crest of a wooded hill just west of the road. Though strong in front, von Gilsa's position could easily be turned on its right, unhinging not merely the brigade, but all of Brig. Gen. Francis C. Barlow's *1st Division*. Demonstrating little tactical finesse, Gordon quickly threw his men against von Gilsa's front, while Doles' Brigade and the remnants of

O'Neal's kept Barlow's other brigade, under Brig. Gen. Adalbert Ames, pinned down with rifle fire. Gordon's men were splendid, ignoring heavy rifle fire to race some 900 yards across all obstacles, fording the stream, and storming the hill. Despite the heroic efforts of the aptly named nineteen-year old Lt. Bayard Wilkeson, who kept the six Napoleons of *Battery G, 4th Artillery* in the front lines until mortally wounded, von Gilsa's brigade faltered. Barlow fell wounded trying to rally it. Ames took command, halted the rout, and began forming a new line. He had barely begun when Early threw in the rest of his division. The brigades of Hays and Avery struck Ames full in the right, shattering his improvised line, and unhinging the entire front of the division. This endangered the entire corps. By 1600 hours the corps had begun to fall back in considerable confusion. Schurz ordered it to rally on its reserve, Brig. Gen. Adolph von Steinwehr's *2nd Division* on Cemetery Hill. Meanwhile Confederate arms were enjoying success all across the field.

With Doles' and O'Neal's Brigades already

Laying a 12-lb. Napoleon

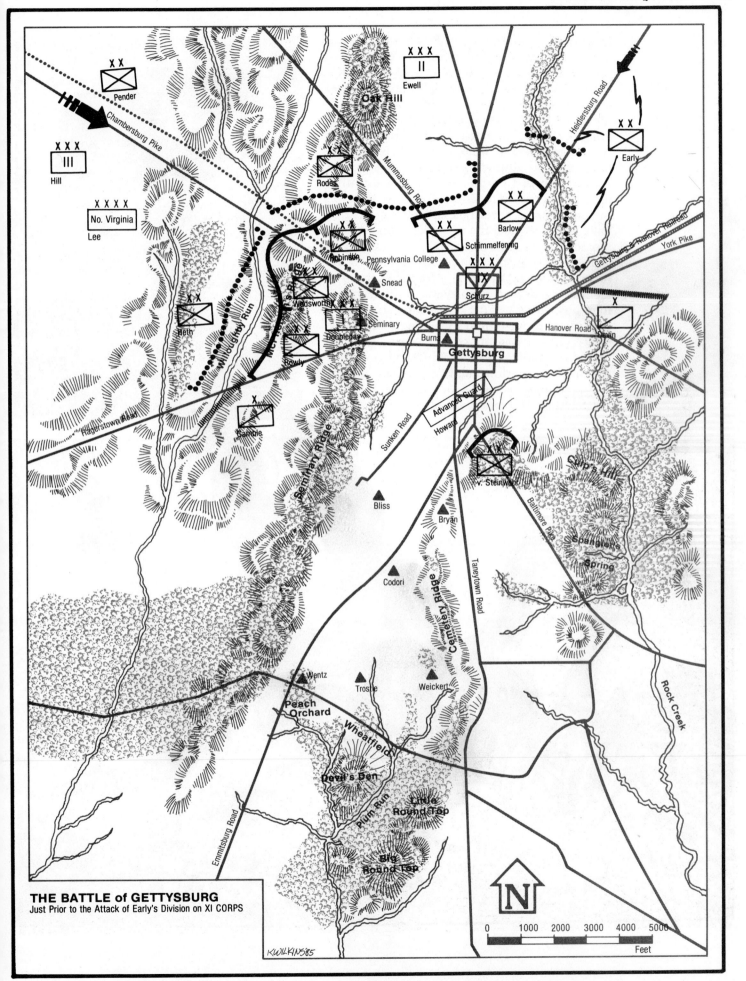

THE BATTLE of GETTYSBURG
Just Prior to the Attack of Early's Division on XI CORPS

KWILKINS85

Right: *Brig. Gen. Francis C. Barlow*

Below: *Lieutenant Bayard Wilkeson holds the 4th U.S. Artillery to its work in an exposed position.*

in action in support of Early, Rodes went over to the attack once more, pressing Daniel's Brigade against the weak southern end of the split *I Corps*'s right wing. Heavy fighting developed and the issue remained in doubt for some minutes until Rodes' threw in Ramseur's reinforced brigade against the northern end of the corps. At almost the same time, Heth's division reentered the lists, throwing four brigades against the left half of *I Corps*. The Yankees put up a terrific defense, inflicting heavy casualties on their assailants. Nevertheless, Heth's men gradually began to push the defenders back. At that moment, Lt. Gen. Richard Hill, commanding III Corps, threw in four completely fresh brigades from Pender's Division. Attacking through Heth's brigades on a milewide front, Pender's men pushed *I Corps* back. Resisting stubbornly, the Union troops retired to Seminary Ridge. As they did, a heroic Bucktail colorbearer turned briefly to defiantly wave "Old Glory" at the Rebels. He was cut down almost immediately. The Union troops reformed on Seminary Ridge, bolstered by 16 pieces of artillery firing almost

The Seminary grounds

hub-to-hub on a narrow front, and with Gamble's cavalrymen once more dismounting to cover their left flank. The Confederates still came on, though some regiments wavered. It was Brig. Gen. Abner Perrin's South Carolina Brigade, nearly 1,900 strong, which proved decisive. Never faltering, it advanced with the bayonet, smashing into the center of the newly formed Union line just south of the Lutheran Seminary which gave the ridge its name. Fierce fighting erupted around the buildings of the seminary, but the Rebels broke through and spread out, to roll up the tattered ends of the Union line. The retreat was ordered. Regiments began streaming to the rear through Gettysburg, to meet those streaming back from *XI Corps* to the north, each taking a different road to safety. The Union attempt to defend before Gettysburg had failed. But the defense had gained time. Moreover, though badly battered, with many missing—including both Barlow and

Schimmelfenning—neither corps had actually broken. Both had fallen back somewhat disorganized, but generally in relative good order. During the withdrawal they offered up stiff resistance in the town itself, notably on the grounds of Pennsylvania College, the tall cupola of which provided an ideal observation post. The fighting in the town was particularly difficult for both sides, with wild melees occuring as regiments blundered into each other merely by taking a wrong turn. Union rear guards were generally effective. Capt. Hubert Dilger positioned the six Napoleons of his *Battery I, 1st Ohio Light Artillery* right in the "Diamond", the main square of the town, sending round after round down the streets at the advancing Rebels. Nevertheless, by 1630 hours the position became untenable. As Dilger's battery pulled back, the 1st South Carolina charged up, securing the square and pressing on. The Confederates took many prisoners, perhaps 2,500 in the town itself

John Burns sitting on his porch, his flintlock propped by the door

and 5,000 altogether. But they came away with few other trophies, securing only two or three battle flags, and but two pieces of artillery, one from each corps. Slender pickings indeed had the Union forces been genuinely smashed.

The Union retirement ended on Cemetery Hill. There, amid the tombstones and the monuments, von Steinwehr had established a substantial defensive position. Von Steinwehr's troops provided covering fire for the retreating regiments, thereby checking the inadequate Confederate attempts to pursue. As additional troops came up they were put into the line, further bolstering the position. Meanwhile, Hancock had reached the field around 1615 hours. After a brief conference with Howard—who objected that *he* was senior and ought to be in command—Hancock assumed command. From atop Cemetery Hill, he discussed the situation with Howard, complimenting him on his choice of ground, finally saying, "Very well, sir, I select this as the battlefield", and began issuing orders to shift troops around. Characteristically, he met Doubleday's objections to the emplace-

The fighting for the Seminary

ment of Wadsworth's division on Culp's Hill with a burst of profanity that would have made a mule-skinner proud. The decisiveness of his actions, his bearing, and his determination, were themselves heartening and thus his very presence helped restore Federal morale. By 1800 hours Maj. Gen. Henry W. Slocum's *XII Corps* began to arrive, taking up positions on the right, and bringing manpower up to about 20,000 with over 75 pieces of artillery. Maj. Gen. Don Sickles' *III Corps* was near. The Federal position was solidifying. Slocum, who assumed command, concurred with Hancock's opinion that this new position could be held until Meade came up and decided whether to commit the balance of the *Army of the Potomac.* Hancock had already informed him that this was the place.

The day's fighting had not gone well for the Union, but neither had it resulted in a disgraceful rout. The Army of Northern Virginia had come off the victor in a hard fight against an inferior foe. But it was almost a pyrrhic victory. Confederate losses, while lower than the 12,000 killed, wounded, and missing suffered by the *Army of the Potomac,* had been substantial, perhaps 8,000 men. The results had not been worth the cost. To be sure, the advanced guard of the *Army of the Potomac* had been pushed back some miles, but it now occupied a position superior to that from which it had been ejected, and it was hourly receiving substantial reinforcements. Great tenacity and courage had been demonstrated, by the Confederate troops but little tactical finesse had been displayed by their commanders, resulting in too many frontal assaults when flank attacks would have served. The men

John Burns, the "Old Hero" of Gettysburg

Top left: *Brig. Gen. Adolph von Steinwehr*

Top Center: *Maj. Gen. Winfield Scott Hancock*

Top: *Maj. Gen. Henry W. Slocum*

THE FIRST DAY
Who Won?

★ ──────────────────── ★

The First Day. The Confederacy won the first day's battle. But Confederate leadership had been somewhat wanting. Lee made a number of serious errors. He insisted on holding Anderson's Division in reserve throughout the fighting, when it might have turned a Union reverse into a disaster. More importantly he had not directed the battle. As was his style, he had suggested when he ought to have commanded. On the defensive this was not a problem, on the offensive it could be. It was most evident late in the afternoon, when he gave Ewell the option of taking Cemetery Hill before dark, certainly one of the most unusual attack orders an army commander ever gave to one of his corps commanders. Lee also failed to coordinate the actions of his units, so that each division commander had pretty much fought independently. Such coordination as did occur was largely fortuitous, as a result of individual commanders seizing the initiative. His subordinates had not done well either. To be sure, Hill had performed excellently against McPherson's Ridge in the afternoon, effectively coordinating the actions of two divisions. But Heth had completely bungled the opening action with Buford's cavalry, and gone on to do likewise in his initial efforts against *I Corps* on McPherson's Ridge. Rodes' and his brigade commanders had badly mishandled their attack on *I Corps*, and Early had been slow in getting his division into action. Stuart's "raid" severely hampered a more skillful conduct of the battle, for the Confederate generals had to operate without information which only his cavalry could have provided. Great tenacity and courage had been demonstrated, but little tactical finesse, resulting in too many frontal assaults when flank attacks would have served. Had the action been better handled, the Union would have suffered a far greater

defeat at far less cost.

Although seriously defeated, the Union forces had done fairly well. But they could have done better. There was no question that the troops were skilled and determined, but some of their leaders were wanting. Buford's decision to dismount his troopers and fight north and west of Gettysburg was a good one, as was Reynolds' decision to support him. But it is doubtful that Reynolds intended to undertake anything but a delaying action, rather than seek a grand battle on two fronts, north and west of Gettysburg. For this Doubleday and Howard bear responsibility, particularly the latter, who put *XI Corps* into the broad valley north of the town. Howard's selection of Cemetery Hill as a reserve position was noteworthy, however. Hancock arrived on the field too late to influence the course of the action. However, once there, he had done very well, by not taking counsel of his fears, by rapidly putting together a viable defense on Cemetery Ridge and Culp's Hill so soon after a serious reverse, and by urging that a stand be made in the new position. On the other hand, Slocum had not done well, for, in failing to march to the sound of gunfire which his men heard shortly after noon whilst eating lunch at Two Taverns, not six miles from the battle, he had missed an opportunity to turn the action into a draw. Lower level leadership, however, seems to have done well, in the circumstances, despite Wadsworth's movements which split the front of *I Corps*. Had Union forces been better led, they might have inflicted a modest defeat on the advancing Confederates before falling back to the positions which they eventually ended up in anyway. They could, of course, have been worse handled, and an even greater reverse might have resulted.

The

"Old Hero of Gettysburg"

Around about noon on 1 July, as the men of *I Corps* were holding the line on McPherson's Ridge, Maj. Edward P. Halstead, of the corps staff, saw an elderly gentleman walking towards the ridge with a musket on his shoulder and a powder horn in his pocket. "Which way are the Rebels?" the old man asked, "Where are our troops?" Halstead told him that they were just ahead and that he would soon find them. The old man was John Burns, a resident of Gettysburg. His blood was up. About a week earlier Rebel foraging parties had taken away his cows. He had sat in his rocking chair all morning listening to the fighting and decided to get into it. Burns, who was about 70, was no stranger to war, for he had served in the War of 1812, against Mexico, and as an Indian fighter. He soon took his place in the line alongside men young enough to be his grandsons. Over the next three days Burns fought with the *150th Pennsylvania*, the *7th Wisconsin*, and other regiments.

The troops were at first amused by the little man who wore a swallow-tail coat with smooth brass buttons. They joked with him a bit. Seeing the ancient flintlock musket he carried they offered him a rifle. He waved it away, as he did also when given a cartridge box, saying "I'm not used to them new-fangled things." He fought well, like the veteran he was, and he accompanied the troops as they fell back to Seminary Ridge, in the retreat through Gettysburg, in the defense of Cemetery Hill, and in the defense of Cemetery Ridge on 3 July. He had high praise for the boys, telling Lt. Frank Haskell, "They fit terribly. The Rebs couldn't make anything of them fellers." The old man, who was wounded three times during the battle and at one point almost captured, soon became a popular figure, Lincoln himself asked to see him when he came to Gettysburg on the occasion of his famous address, and the two attended church together. Later a special Act of Congress granted him a pension of $8.00 a month. He died in 1872, full of years and honor.

had performed magnificently, repeatedly recovering the errors of their commanders by their courage and blood. But courage and blood can only do so much. Had the action been better handled, the Union would have suffered a far greater defeat at far less cost.

Union forces had done well, but could have done better. There was no question that the troops were skilled and determined, but some of their leaders were wanting. Had Union forces been better led, they might have inflicted a modest defeat on the advancing Confederates before falling back to the positions they ended up in anyway. They could, of course, have been handled worse, and an even greater reverse might have resulted.

The day's fighting had set the stage for a more decisive clash on the morrow. And during the hot, humid, and cloudy night of 1 July, as generals laid their plans, tens of thousands of men slept in fields and barns and houses, while still more tens of thousands marched through the darkness.

Field surgery during the Civil War

CHAPTER VI

GETTYSBURG, 2 JULY: The Battle for the Flanks

Meade arrived on the field long before dawn on 2 July and immediately conferred with Howard, Sickles, and Slocum at the cemetry caretaker's house. Reviewing the situation he decided to accept a general battle in the existing position, a decision which he had probably reached on the previous afternoon, for he had issued orders at that time directing the entire *Army of the Potomac* to march on Gettysburg. Then he took a quick look at the Union position on Cemetery Ridge, followed just before dawn by an extensive ride along the entire Federal line in the company of Howard and Brig. Gen. Henry Hunt, his chief of artillery. With the help of an engineer officer he produced a sketch map of the terrain, indicating on it the positions which he desired each corps to occupy. Copies of this were sent to each corps commander, who adjusted their lines accordingly. At about 0800 hours he sent Hunt to survey the lines once more for the purpose of selecting artillery emplacements.

The Union line was on ground averaging some 20 to 30 feet higher than that in front of it. Greatly resembling a fish hook, it was anchored on the right on heavily wooded, rocky Culp's Hill, 140 feet above the valley floor, facing northwards and eastwards, fronting on some very broken ground and partially covered by Rock Creek. Culp's Hill was itself covered on the right by an extension of the line southward along Rock Creek for about 1400 yards. Slocum's *XII Corps* with some 9,800 men held the eastern side of the line here, with Wadsworth's 2,500 strong division of *I Corps* on the northern face of the hill. About 450 yards northwest of Culp's Hill across some lower ground lay Cemetery Hill, some 600 yards south of the main squire of Gettysburg. The northern end of Cemetery Ridge,

Confederate skirmishers at the foot of Culp's Hill.

this hill rises some 60 to 80 feet above its surroundings, with a panoramic view of everything to its northeast, north, and west, and has a fine, broad top suitable for several batteries of artillery. Here lay the 7,000 survivors of Howard's *XI Corps*. Cemetery Ridge stretches roughly south-southwestwards from there for about 1500 yards, before turning roughly southeastwards for a similar distance. The ridge is not much more than 30 feet above the valley floor, and grows gradually shallower as it trails off southwards. From its crest, the western slope of the ridge is deceptively easy, but the slope is considerably more formidable than it appears, rising in places at more than 30°, with patches of broken ground and tangled vegetation. Here, facing roughly westwards, were to be found the balance of *I Corps*, perhaps 4,000 men now under Maj. John Newton (Meade having sent Doubleday back to his division) and, to its right, Han-

Little Round Top seen from the west a short time after the battle. Note the rough nature of the ground and Big Round Top to the right.

cock's newly arrived *II Corps*, 11,300 strong. To Hancock's left Maj. Gen. Dan Sickles brought the 10,700 men of his *III Corps* into the line shortly after 0900 hours, after a reprimand for dawdling by Meade. Sickles' left was at the end of Cemetery Ridge, just short of Little Round Top, a prominent, wooded, very rocky hill rising 170 feet above its surroundings. About 500 yards further south was Big Round Top, an extremely rugged, wooded, rocky hill rising over 300 feet above the valley floor. To the north and west of the Union lines the ground was relatively flat open farmland with a scattering of buildings and occasional orchards and stands of timber. The countryside in the vicinity of the Round Tops and to their south became increasingly rugged, with many trees, rocky outcroppings, and stray boulders. The entire Union front covered perhaps 6000 yards. It was an old position, with broad fields of fire, many natural

Above: *Maj. Gen. Dan Sickles.*

Above right: *Maj. Gen. John Newton*

Right: *Maj. Gen. Gouverneur K. Warren*

defenses, and short lines of communication. A thin line of skirmishers had been advanced from Cemetery Ridge, and these covered the entire left of the Union line, giving additional security. With Meade's concurrence, Brig. Gen. Robert Tyler, commanding the *Artillery Reserve,* placed his guns in a central location in the rear, from which they were no more than 2,200 yards from any point in the line. When Maj. Gen. George Sykes' *V Corps* began to reach the field at about 0800 hours, after having marched some 50 miles in three days, Meade placed it next to the artillery. Meade had approximately 45,000 men and about 200 cannon holding the line behind breastworks and stone fences, plus 12,000 men and 124 pieces of artillery in reserve. When Maj. Gen. John Sedgwick's strong *VI Corps,* with 13,600 and 30 guns, marched up Meade would have on hand some 70,000 men and over 350 guns.

Meade had several options. He briefly considered reinforcing his right and attacking Ewell's II Corps, but gave up that notion when both Maj. Gen. Gouverneur K. Warren, his Chief of Engineers, and Slocum reported that the ground in front of Culp's Hill was unsuitable. As a result, he had second thoughts about attempting an offensive move. He had to expect that the enemy would not remain inactive. Lee was a resourceful, wily foe, and it would be best to see what he was about before committing the army. The natural strength of his position gave further encouragement to the adoption of a defensive stance. Thus, even as Union and Confederate troops exchanged rifle and artillery fire

Heavy skirmishing on Cemetery Hill

at a distance, Meade spent his time getting his troops into order, issuing instructions, and surveying his lines. He left the details of the deployment of each corps to its commander, merely indicating in a general way the positions he wished covered. This generally worked well, for both officers and men were well trained and experienced. Most of the corps commanders understood that their corps were but individual parts of the whole and made their dispositions accordingly, being careful to establish contact with the neighboring corps on each flank. Un-

fortunately Sickles of *III Corps* was an amateur soldier. Though commendably aggressive and a good leader of men, he had a tendency to be careless. Initially he had positioned his troops properly to the left of Hancock's *II Corps*. But in the afternoon, he pushed forward. Sickles' deployed his two divisions at roughly a 45° angle to each other, forming a triangular salient with its apex nearly 1,500 yards in advance of the Cemetery Ridge position, and its base over 2,000 yards wide. When fully deployed, Sickles' right would consist of Brig. Gen. A. A.

Maj. Gen. John Sedgwick and the staff of the VI Corps. He was graduated from West Point, 1837, a class which included Braxton Bragg, Jubal Early, Joseph Hooker and John C. Pemberton. The VI Corps was kept in reserve throughout the battle and only lightly engaged. He was later killed by a sharpshooter at Spotsylvania.

The Leister house. During the battle this served Meade as a headquarters.

Humphrey's *2nd Division*, with 4,900 men in three brigades along the Emmitsburg Road for some 650 yards, and his right hanging in air about the same distance in front of Hancock's left hand brigade, which he partially masked. On Humphrey's right would be Brig. Gen. Charles Graham's 1,500-strong brigade of Maj. Gen. David B. Birney's *1st Division*. Graham's men would form the knuckle of the salient, with half the troops holding a front of about 450 yards along the road, and the other half at an immediate right angle, holding a similar front along a country lane running just around a peach orchard measuring about twelve acres. About 400 yards to Graham's left the balance of Birney's division, 3,600 men in two brigades, were already occupying a very strong position stretching about 1000 yards in front of some wheat fields and an almost lunar landscape of rocky outcrops and boulders called the Devil's Den, with its left at Plum Run, a small freshet running through a broad, boggy valley just west of the Round Tops. As Henry Hunt observed, the deployment of Sickles' units was not too bad, taken individually. The brigades were generally in good positions, well covered to their front, with excellent fields of fire. Unfortunately,

taken as a whole, the situation of the corps was not good. The front was too long for the manpower available, with only 1.6 rifles per yard of front. Then too, there was the awkward angle in the middle of Graham's brigade. What was worse, the entire corps merely hung in the air, with no flank protection, and no liaison with the rest of the army. Moreover, Sickles had neglected to inform Hancock, to his right and rear, of his deployment. In short, the left flank of the *Army of the Potomac* was exposed. A determined attack could easily crush *III Corps* and then proceed to roll up the entire Union line.

Lee was determined to attack on 2 July. Generally satisfied with the outcome of Wednesday's fighting, he believed he would again do well on Thursday. It was a belief generally shared by all of the officers and men of the Army of Northern Virginia. The problem was how to go about it. Longstreet, Lee's closest and most able subordinate, disliked the looks of the Union positions. Conferring with Lee on the evening of 1 July, he pointed out the significant natural advantages of the lines held by the *Army of the Potomac*, and the fact that, in the absence of adequate reconnaissance, they could not be certain as to the strength of the Union forces. He

The *"Council of War"* at the Leister house (see photo facing page). *During the night of July 2–3 over twelve generals were crowded into this small front room.*

then suggested a broad sweeping movement on the Confederate right. A strategic maneuver rather than a tactical one, such a move would put the Army of Northern Virginia between the *Army of the Potomac* and Washington, thereby forcing Meade to abandon the excellent position which he now held. More importantly, the maneuver would permit the Army of Northern Virginia to stand on the defensive, for Meade would be forced to attack it in order to restore his communications with Washington. And the Army of Northern Virginia had never yet done badly in a defensive fight. Lee seems to have considered Longstreet's proposal, but demurred. This decision has at times been attributed to exhaustion, illness, or even blood lust, but it was by no means irrational. Though Longstreet's proposal was attractive, it had several drawbacks. The absence of Stuart made dangerous any spectacular movements in the face of the enemy, particularly as Lee had no knowledge of the locations of Meade's corps beyond the two he had already encountered. Nor could the movement be made immediately, for only about 70% of the Army of Northern Virginia would be on hand on the morning of 2 July; delaying the maneuver to await the arrival of the balance of

the army might give the day to Meade. Then too, the morale of the army might suffer if it appeared to be abandoning its hard-won gains and be moving south once more. When Longstreet urged that they at least stand on the defensive in their present position, Lee also disagreed. The army could not long remain inactive in such close proximity to the *Army of the Potomac* in the heart of Pennsylvania. Meade might choose not to attack, but rather to essay a strategic maneuver of his own. Or he might remain in position, thereby pinning the Army of Northern Virginia, while additional Union forces poured into central Pennsylvania from all directions to reinforce him, or, worse, to develop a strategic trap by moving into the Shenandoah Valley and blocking his line of retreat. The Army of Northern Virginia would have about 50,000 mostly fresh troops and some 200 pieces of artillery at hand on 2 July, to face a somewhat superior, but already battered foe. Lee had Meade pinned, and he intended to hit him.

Lee proposed to attack on the Union flanks. Over on the Confederate left, Ewell's II Corps would hit the Federal right in the morning, followed soon after by Longstreet's I Corps, which would assault Cemetery Ridge. Ewell's attack

Above right: *Brig. Gen. A.A. Humphrey*

Above: *Brig. Gen. Charles Graham*

Below: *Col. D.H. Lee Martz (on left) and the battle flag of the 10th Va. Cavalry*

would be primarily a diversion, designed to pin Union forces. Longstreet's would be the main blow. It took Lee a while to come up with this plan, and he changed it several times in the face of objections from his generals. In the end he had to insist on it, despite the fact that Ewell believed his corps should stand on the defensive and leave the attacking to Longstreet, while the latter was in favor of a defensive posture for the entire army. Lee's authority as a commander overruled their objections, and they set about preparing for the day's action.

Lee ought to have tidied up his lines a bit. The Army of Northern Virginia held a concave front stretching nearly six miles. Ewell's II Corps, on the Confederate left, had one division covering its left flank and holding a line running

about 1,200 yards on a roughly northwest-southeast axis, and two others holding about 1,800 yards on an east-west axis, running right through the heart of Gettysburg. Most of Ewell's units were between 500 and 1,200 yards from the Union forces holding Culp's Hill and Cemetery Hill. With a bend in his front, a few low hills to the left, Gettysburg in his center, and open fields on his right, Ewell's lines were not particularly suited to the defense, but Lee appears to have ignored the matter. To the right of II Corps, and at almost right angles to it, was Hill's III Corps, with one division in reserve and two holding about 3,000 yards of front along Seminary Ridge, a useful defensive line, running slightly west of parallel to the Union forces along Cemetery Ridge, some 1,200 yards to the east. To Hill's right was Longstreet's I Corps, which on the early morning of 2 July had yet to arrive on the field. When deployed, Longstreet would hold a front of about 2,500 yards. Unknowingly, his lines would be right before the ground into which Sickles would intrude his *III Corps* later that morning. With perhaps 40,000 troops in line, Lee would have about four men per yard of front, which was not bad, particularly as he had 10,000 more in reserve. But the curvature of his front left much to be desired. Ewell's II Corps was badly situated, too far from the rest of the army to be able to shift forces rapidly to its support, and at the same time too far to easily support the right and center. Ideally, it ought to have been pulled back towards the left, thereby greatly shortening Lee's front and improving his communications. As it was, Lee had suggested doing this during the heated staff conferences on the night of 1–2 July. However, he had allowed himself to be talked out of it by Ewell and his very persuasive subordinate, Jubal Early, merely making a general few suggestions, including one that Ewell occupy Culp's Hill, which had been reported to be free of enemy troops. Then he left his commanders to prepare the details of the coming day's action.

During the night the Army of Northern Virginia made ready for battle. For Longstreet it meant more than merely siting his batteries and seeing that his troops got adequate rest. Longstreet's corps was not on the field yet. Maj. Gen. Lafayette McLaws' division camped nearby at about 0100 hours, after eight hours on the march. The corps' reserve artillery and Maj. Gen. John B. Hood's division marched up through the night to reach the vicinity of the battlefield during the pre-dawn hours. Before he

d have to be
the artillery
roops would
of these diffi-
ewhat. Long-
preparations
ed to defer his
of Longstreet's

ctions. During
g complication
. Gen. Edward
Advancing on
d it swarming
a captured dis-
XII Corps was
two divisions of
es to his left and
Johnson held his
s still rethinking
ell learned of the
he received new
virtually complete
instructed him to
st the Yankee right
g rounds of Long-
r a general assault
unity right. Ewell
cover his left, and

id morning of 2 July,
ederate attack were
ngstreet's troops, his
0800 hours, and im-
mediately took to their blankets for a couple of hours rest. Lee was everywhere, visiting in turn

each corps. The delay was fortuitous. There was some uncertainty as to the nature of the ground over which Longstreet would have to attack and as to the location of the Union lines. Several officers had brought back useful but inconclusive information. Shortly after dawn, Lee decided to dispatch Capt. S. R. Johnston, an engineer from his staff, on a proper reconnaissance. With a small group of companions, Johnston explored the ground between Seminary Ridge and Cemetery Ridge, quietly penetrating the Union picket lines, and scouting out the entire area up to the woods at the southern end of Cemetery Ridge. He even climbed the steep slope of Little Round Top, to observe that there were no concentrations of Union troops anywhere to be seen south of Cemetery Ridge. By coincidence, Johnston's party missed the movement of the leading elements of Sickles' *III Corps* into the line south of Cemetery Ridge by no more than a few minutes, their location being

Above: *Maj. Gen. "Buddy" Smith steadies his militiamen while Stuart sends a few rounds into Carlisle, Pa.*

Below left: *The rugged terrain of Devil's Den*

Below: *Maj. Gen. John Bell Hood*

Maj. Gen. Lafayette McLaws

concealed by Cemetery Ridge and the woods themselves. At about 0900 hours Johnston returned to Lee. Lee was pleased, for Johnston's report suggested that there were no Union troops directly in front of Longstreet's corps. He began to discuss the tactical details of the attack with Longstreet and McLaws, whose division was to be part of the attack, while Hill looked on.

Lee wished the attack to be delivered along the Emmitsburg Road, to drive northeastwards into the Union lines on Cemetery Ridge. Longstreet disagreed, wanting the attack to be made directly eastwards, across ground that Johnston said was bare of Union forces. Lee overruled him, but the latter persisted and an unpleasant scene developed between the two old friends. In the end, of course, Lee had his way. Longstreet's corps would attack in two stages: there would be an initial attack by his right into the area west of the Round Tops to secure artillery positions, followed by an advance along the Emmitsburg Road designed to drive in the Union left flank at the southern end of Cemetery Ridge. By about 1000 hours, Longstreet was issuing orders for his artillery to get into position to support the attack. Lee then rode off to see Ewell. At this point Longstreet was still awaiting the arrival of Maj. Gen. George E. Pickett's division and a stray brigade of Hood's division. He was also still concerned about the wisdom of the proposed attack and did not believe he had

enough strength to bring it off. Lee discovered this delay at about 1100 hours, when he returned to Longstreet's headquarters. He demanded that the attack be made as soon as all of Hood's division was at hand.

Longstreet's corps finally began to deploy about noon, moving somewhat to the right in order to get into the best position from which to launch the attack. The movement was badly conducted, despite the fact that Capt. Johnston was assigned to guide McLaws' division along a route concealed from Yankee observers. Unfortunately, the ground over which the division moved was not that which Johnston had spent much of the morning exploring. The result was that the movement became confused, with lengthy counter-marches and tiring cross-country marches being required. Some of Hood's men became entangled with some of McLaws'. Federal signalmen on Little Round Top observed at least part of the movement at about 1330 hours, which was precisely what Lee had hoped to avoid. The troops only began to occupy their assigned positions at about 1500 hours. And at about that time, McLaws' advanced guard, of Brig. Gen. Joseph B. Kershaw's brigade, encountered strong Union forces in the vicinity of the Peach Orchard. Longstreet had run into Graham's brigade of Sickles' *III Corps*. McLaws halted his division and prepared for an attack. Longstreet suggested that the troops to his front were insignificant, to which McLaws countered, stating that he was faced by a superior foe. Convinced, Longstreet called up Hood's division and ordered a full-scale attack.

The attack would be made as soon as the troops were in position. McLaws' division was to attack on the left, with two brigades up and two following behind, on a front of roughly 1,000 yards, not 500 yards from the apex of Sickles' salient at the Peach Orchard. To McLaws' right, and at roughly right angles to it, was Hood's division. Hood's right rested just short of Big Round Top, and he had four brigades in line on a front of about 1,400 yards, between 500 and 800 yards from Sickles' line. Longstreet committed 54 pieces of artillery under the able Col. Edward P. Alexander, who sited them on a 1,000 yard front some 1,800 yards west and southwest of the Peach Orchard. By 1600 hours all was in readiness for Longstreet to fall on Sickles' *III Corps*.

The deployment of Sickles' corps began to disturb Meade in the mid-afternoon. He ordered *V Corps* to move to the left, replacing it in the reserve with the newly arriving *VI Corps*.

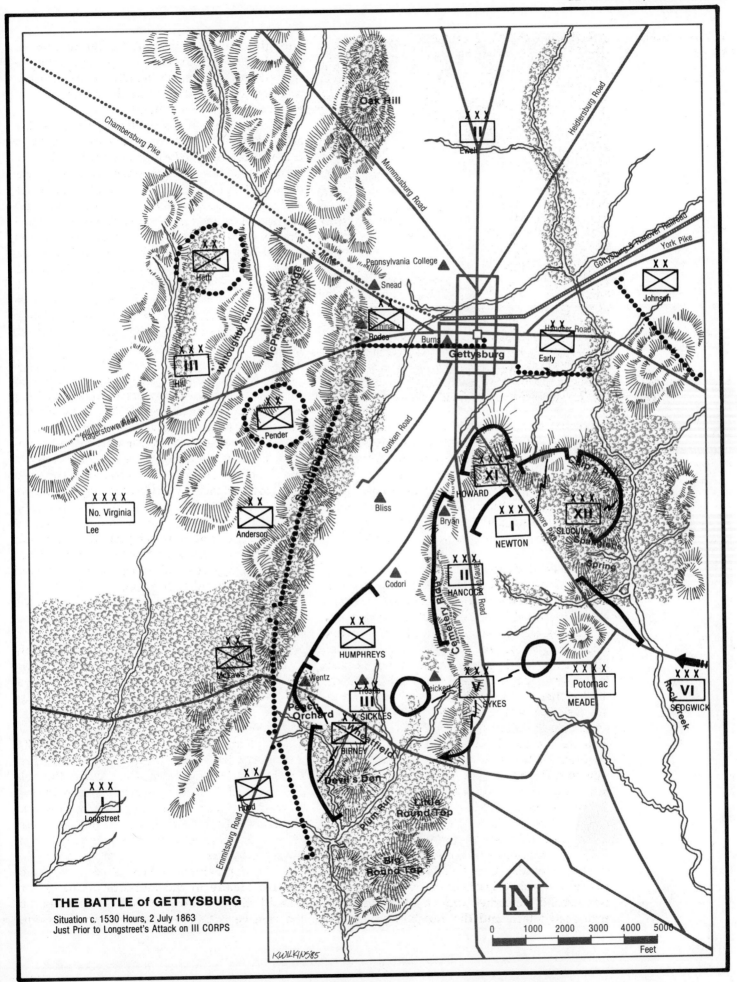

THE BATTLE of GETTYSBURG

Situation c. 1530 Hours, 2 July 1863
Just Prior to Longstreet's Attack on III CORPS

KWILKINS85

ARTILLERY WEAPONS

During the Civil War artillery was eclipsed by the rifle-armed infantry. While the first half of the nineteenth century had seen significant improvements in artillery technology, they were not as spectacular as the advances in small arms. Most artillery pieces during the Civil War were direct fire weapons, that is, they had to see their targets in order to hit them. In Napoleonic times it had been possible to site batteries within a thousand yards or less of enemy formations. The rifled musket made this a highly dangerous undertaking, for the infantry could now deliver reasonably accurate fire at such ranges, cutting down gunners and horses alike. Nevertheless, artillery did play a useful, and often vital role on the battlefield.

In an attack artillery was used to soften up the defenses, showering them with explosive shells and solid shot, inflicting casualties and destroying the cohesion of the defenders. This was most effectively done at relatively short ranges, to insure accuracy. Unfortunately, this put the gunners within range of enemy riflemen. As a result, unless the guns could be put under cover of woods, fire had to be delivered at rather long range. The Confederate guns which fired the preparatory bombardment on 3 July were mostly sited in the woods atop Seminary Ridge. None of the guns were less than 1,200 yards from the Union lines along Cemetery Ridge, with most at about 1,500 yards, and, aside from two very long range pieces, some guns were as much as 2,200 yards away. This was one reason why the two-hour bombardment, involving perhaps 15,000 rounds, was relatively ineffective. It was difficult for the gunners to observe the fall of shot, and they tended to overestimate the range. As a result, a substantial proportion of their fire fell behind Cemetery Ridge, rather than atop

it. When it was possible to deliver a preparatory bombardment from closer range, as Longstreet's batteries did on the afternoon of 2 July against *III Corps* or as Williams' did on the morning of 3 July against the Confederate forces on Culp's Hill, the results could be particularly effective. In both cases, of course, the guns were firing from cover at fairly close ranges.

Artillery could be used to bring enemy artillery under fire. However, although opposing artillerymen often engaged each other in gun battles, counter-battery fire was relatively ineffective. The guns all used black powder, which generated considerable volumes of white smoke. As a result, after a few rounds, the guns were literally shrouded in great clouds, making it difficult to observe one's targets. Continuing to fire in such circumstances was merely a waste of ammunition. It was for this reason that Meade's chief of artillery, Brig. Gen. Henry Hunt, preferred not to return fire during the Confederate bombardment of Cemetery Ridge. There was no point in consuming ammunition which could be more usefully reserved to meet the expected infantry attack.

As with the infantry rifle, it was in defense that artillery was particularly useful. A single well-handled battery could often hold up the advance of thousands of troops, especially if the attackers had to cross wide stretches of relatively open ground. An attacking formation could be brought under fire at ranges upwards of 2,000 yards, albeit with relatively low effectiveness. As the troops got closer, effectiveness increased. Solid shot could bowl swathes through the attacking ranks, and explosive shell could burst in the midst of the troops with greater slaughter. When the enemy came to within 300 yards the gunners would switch to canister, which were effectively giant shotgun shells literally capable of tearing a man to pieces. At the very last, the guns could be double-loaded with canister, which could be discharged right into the faces of the enemy as they reached the muzzles of the guns.

Consider a charge from 1,500 yards against a battery of six 12-pounder Napoleons:

VOLUME OF FIRE DELIVERED

Attacker	Time*	Type of Projectile Fired			
		Shell	Ball	Canister	Total
Cavalry	4.9 min	42	12	12 +	66 +
Infantry	16.9	120	42	66 +	228 +

[*Time required for the attackers to reach the battery at normal attack rates.]

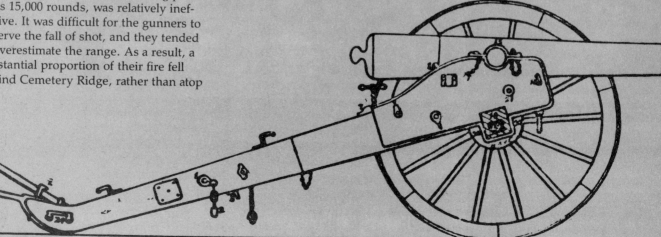

AND TACTICS

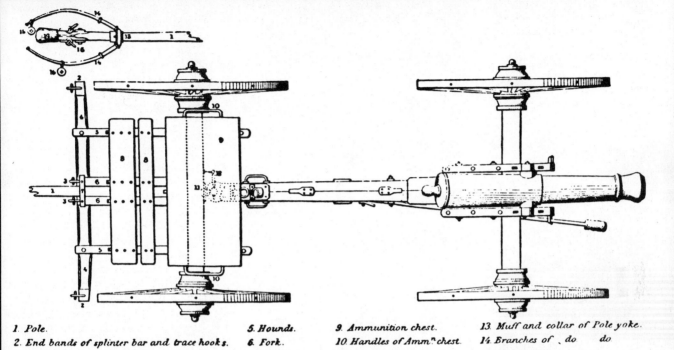

1. Pole.
2. End bands of splinter bar and trace hooks.
3. Middle bands of splinter bar and trace hooks.
4. Splinter bar.
5. Hounds.
6. Fork.
7. Fork strap.
8. Foot boards.
9. Ammunition chest.
10. Handles of Amm.ⁿ chest.
11. Pintle hook.
12. Pintle hook Key.
13. Muff and collar of Pole yoke.
14. Branches of   do   do
15. Sliding rings.
16. Pole strap iron. 17. Pole pad.

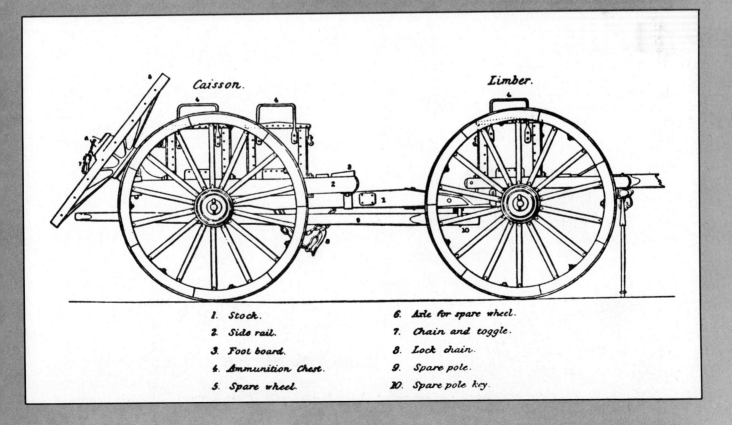

Caisson.   Limber.

1. Stock.
2. Side rail.
3. Foot board.
4. Ammunition Chest.
5. Spare wheel.
6. Axle for spare wheel.
7. Chain and toggle.
8. Lock chain.
9. Spare pole.
10. Spare pole key.

FIELD ARTILLERY OF THE

As can be seen, even cavalry, which can charge at a considerably faster rate than can the infantry, would receive an enormous volume of fire. Given that the attackers would also be receiving increasingly accurate rifle fire as they closed with the defenses, it is not difficult to see why frontal attacks were so costly.

This table includes the specifications for virtually all field artillery pieces used during the Gettysburg Campaign. *Type* indicates whether the piece was a *Howitzer*, able to use high angle fire to drop explosive shells behind obstacles, or a *Gun*, designed for a relatively flat trajectory, and able to fire shells or solid shot to relatively long ranges, or a *Gun-Howitzer*, theoretically capable of being fired in either mode. The designation given a piece is the official one, within the year normally that of introduction, though sometimes that of design. *Ri* indicates a rifled piece, all others being smooth bores. *BL* indicates a breech loading piece, all others being muzzle loaders. *Bore* is the diameter of the tube,

in inches. *Weight* is the total weight, in pounds, of the piece, with carriage, but exclusive of limber, caisson, and ammunition. *Round* is the weight, again in pounds, of the *Projectile* and the propellant *Charge*; for howitzers the projectile weight given is for shells, for other pieces it is for solid shot. Note that official pounder designations were not always a reliable indication of actual projectile weight. *Range*, in yards, is the maximum range of the piece, that at which it would project rounds, though not necessarily with any accuracy; for guns the range given is for solid shot, for explosive shell it was about 25% less. Effective range, that at which most of the rounds fired reached the vicinity of the target, was usually about 60% of maximum range. *Notes* refers to the lettered paragraphs below.

A. The standard U.S. howitzers of the pre-war period, both models, plus a lighter mountain version of the 12-pounder had been widely used early in the war, but by the time of Gettysburg were rapidly being phased out by both sides, due primarily to their short range and the difficulty of observing their accuracy. A less serious

problem, that of properly setting fuzes, was shared with all artillery pieces able to fire shell. Howitzers could also fire canister. They were made of gun metal, normally called "brass", but actually a bronze of about 10% tin plus some other minor alloying ingredients. Cast solid, they were then bored out on a lathe.

B. The famed "Napoleon", this was actually an American version of the field piece designed by Napoleon III in 1853. Though heavy and relatively short ranged, it was the most commonly used artillery piece of the war, and accounted for about 40% of the guns in each of the armies at Gettysburg. It could fire all types of ammunition, but was particularly effective firing canister in support of defending infantry. At least theoretically it could fire both as a gun and a howitzer, though rarely employed in the latter role. As with the howitzers, Napoleons were cast in gun metal, and bored out, though some Confederate versions were made of weaker cast iron, with a reinforcing jacket at the breech, and consequently were considerably heavier.

C. Variously referred to as the "Ordnance Rifle" or "Gun", or as the "Rodman Gun" or "Rifle", or as the "Griffen Gun" this was, after the Napoleon, the most commonly used piece at Gettysburg, equipping the entire Union horse artillery and many field batteries as well. The piece was so good that many 10-Pounder Parrott guns were converted to take the same ammunition. Like all rifles the 3" gun was not really good at firing canister, since the latter scoured the inside of the barrel, damaging the rifling. The piece was made by welding together wrought iron strips which had been wound in a spiral around a solid core,

Type	Bore	Weight	Round	(pds)	Range	Notes
HOWITZER	(in)	(pds)	Proj	Chg	(yds)	
12-Pdr U.S. 1841	4.62	788	8.9	.75	1072	A
24-Pdr U.S. 1841	5.82	1318	18.4	2.00	1322	A
GUN-HOWITZER						
12-Pdr U.S. 1857	4.62	1227	12.3	2.50	1680	B
GUNS						
3" U.S. Ri 1861	3.00	820	9.5	1.00	2788	C
6-Pdr U.S. 1857	3.67	884	6.1	1.25	1523	D
10-Pdr Parrott Ri 1863	3.00	890	9.5	1.00	2970	E
12-Pdr Blakely Ri BL 1859	3.10	700	12.0	1.50	1760	F
12-Pdr James Ri 1857	3.67	875	12.0	0.75	1700	G
12-Pdr Whitworth Ri BL 1860	2.75	1100	12.0	1.75	8800	H
20-Pdr Parrott Ri 1861	3.67	1750	20.0	2.00	4400	I

GETTYSBURG CAMPAIGN

which was then drilled out and seven rifling grooves cut into the tube.

D. This was the light field gun version of the Napoleon, but little used in the Eastern Theater by the middle of the war.

E. Designed by Robert P. Parrott, Superintendent of the West Point Iron and Cannon foundry, both armies made considerable use of this piece, which had originally been designed with a 2.9" bore but had been rebored to take the same ammunition as the 3" Ordnance Rifle in 1863. It was made of cast iron, poured solid and then bored out, and was reinforced at the breech by a wrought iron band which was shrunk on. Since Confederate attempts to duplicate the gun were not successful—the end products weighing nearly 70% more than the originals—the Rebels relied on captured stocks.

F. A small number of these highly unusual guns were obtained in England by the Confederacy. Although impressive enough in performance, and highly suitable for horse artillery due to

their lightness—indeed, Wade Hampton actually imported a battery at his own expense—they had a terrific recoil, making relaying them difficult. The guns were made of cast iron poured solid and drilled out. The shells had flanges which fit the rifling grooves in the barrel.

G. The James rifle was the invention of Charles James, a Rhode Islander. It proved unsatisfactory in service, due to unstable projectiles. Indeed, James himself was mortally wounded by the accidental detonation of one of his shells in 1862. Most James guns were cast in gun metal, but a few seem to have been made of high grade cast iron. Very few James rifles were actually produced, however, though numbers of existing cannon were experimentally converted to the James system and referred to as "James" guns.

I. This was a heavier version of the standard Parrott field gun, and the heaviest normally carried into the field. It was substantially similar to the 10-Pounder version.

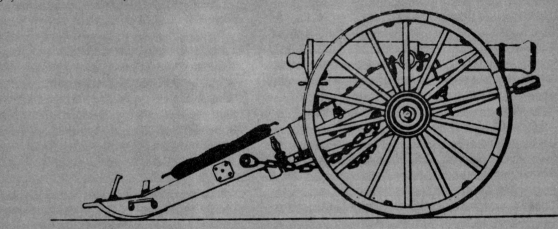

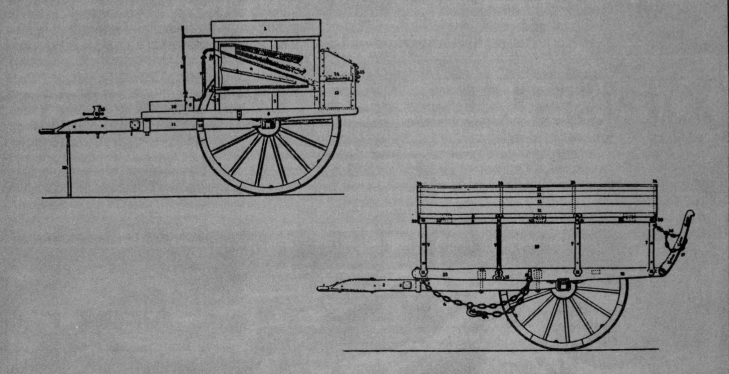

SERVING THE GUNS

The artillerymen were the most professionally expert soldiers in either army, due partially to the technical demands of their trade, and also the care which both armies took with their training. What follows applies to a Union battery, which normally had six guns, while Confederate ones often made due with four. Allowing for this difference, however, the description is applicable to the Confederates as well, as arrangements and procedures were essentially the same in both armies.

The battery was divided into three sections, each under a lieutenant. Each section had two complete artillery equipments, including gun, two limbers, and a caisson. There was, in addition, a spare limber and caisson with extra ammunition. The battery itself had six more ammunition caissons with limbers, plus a traveling forge, and a battery wagon with tentage and supplies. Altogether, including officers, staff non-commissioned officers, gunners, teamsters, buglers, and blacksmiths, the battery officially had 155 men, though at Gettysburg Union batteries averaged about 105, Confederate ones about 90. The number of horses depended upon the type of guns. Heavier pieces, Napoleons or 20-Pounder Parrotts, required six horses, so a battery of such had about 115 horse, while a lighter battery ran a half dozen less. The difference between horse artillery and foot batteries was that in the former the gunners were mounted on the teams, while in the latter they mostly rode the limbers. All pieces in Union batteries were usually of the same type, but many Confederate batteries had two or even three different types, a matter which ought to have been resolved by a proper redistribution of the available pieces from time to time. Union batteries were organized on paper into regiments, though never deployed as such. Some Southern states followed a similar procedure, often organizing batteries into permanent battalions which actually served together. Operationally, both armies formed groups of four or five batteries for tactical control, called brigades in the Federal service and battalions in the Confederacy.

Normally guns were deployed 14 yards apart, which, with each piece occupying two yards, gave the battery an 82 yard front, with a depth of almost 50 years for limbers and caissons. Given time, the gunners, and available infantry supports, would often strengthen their position by building log and earth breastworks. But batteries frequently went into action without advanced preparation, moving directly from the march. A trained crew could unlimber and fire their first round in 30 seconds. A full battery could do so in about a minute. The working of the guns was actually in the hands of the senior non-commissioned officers, the lieutenants and the battery commander being responsible for tactical control. Most pieces could be fired two or three times a minute. This, however, depended upon the skill of the crew and the tactical situation, and when hotly pressed it was not unheard of for a gun to fire four canisters in a minute. Since virtually all the guns used in the Gettysburg campaign were muzzle loaders, the basic procedure for loading and firing was fairly standard.

The gun crew moved into action even as the piece recoiled from its previous shot. As the ventman covered the touch hole with his padded thumb, the tube was damp swabbed out, to insure that there were no live embers left over from the last shot. Meanwhile, the loader selected the indicated type of round. Ammunition came fixed, that is, it was made up into bundles in which a projectile, a wooden wad, and a cloth-wrapped powder charge were all loosely bound together. This was placed in the tube and rammed home. Directed by a gunnery sergeant the crew then relaid the piece, pushing it into position to fire. The sergeant adjusted the aim, using a screw mechanism and main force. The ventman then shoved a priming wire down the touchhole, piercing the powder bag. As everyone stepped clear of the rear of the piece, the trigger mechanism, a friction primer, was set and the gunnery sergeant awaited the command to fire. When it came, he gave the lanyard a sharp pull, which set off the friction primer and discharged the piece. Lacking any recoil mechanism, the gun would leap back several feet as the projectile roared on its way in great burst of fire, smoke, and noise. The crew began to move into action for the next round.

Generally a battery carried about 100 rounds of ammunition per gun. About three-quarters of the supply was usually evenly divided between solid shot and shrapnel, while the balance was divided between canister and shell. Army supply columns usually carried about as many more additional rounds, but during the Gettysburg Campaign Union artillery chief Henry Hunt brought along even more, so that there was well over 220 rounds available per gun, about 10% to 15% more than Lee's pieces had. In action a battery could run through its basic supply of ammunition in less than an hour, though it could stretch that limit by deliberately firing slowly, which tended to increase accuracy considerably. This was, of course, a luxury of which a hotly engaged battery might not be able to avail itself.

If they had to, gunners could get out of a fight quickly. A single gun could be limbered up and begin moving in about a minute, and an entire battery required but three minutes. This, of course, assumed that casualties—among both men and horses—were minimal. The guns themselves were virtually indestructible, though their carriages were highly vulnerable to enemy artillery fire. If a battery lost too many men and horses, it began to have problems. A gun could sustain fire for some time

The Guns At Gettysburg

Type	U.S.	C.S.
HOWITZERS		
12-Pdr U.S. 1841	2	26
24-Pdr U.S. 1841	4	
GUN-HOWITZER		
12-Pdr U.S. 1857	146	111
GUNS		
3" U.S. Ri 1861	142	76
3" U.S. Navy Ri	4	
6-Pdr U.S. 1857	1	
10-Pdr Parrott Ri 1863	64	44
12-Pdr Blakely Ri BL 1859	4	
12-Pdr James Ri 1857	4	
12-Pdr Whitworth Ri BL 1860	2	
20-Pdr Parrott Ri 1861	6	10
TOTAL	366	282

with as few as three men, though nine was the norm. Now horses were invariably killed or wounded in greater numbers than men. With two horses a light gun could still be moved, though with difficulty. A heavier piece, a Napoleon or 20-Pounder, required at least four. And in either case, it meant abandoning the spare caisson. The biggest cause of lost artillery pieces was casualties among the horses and smashed carriages. At Gettysburg less than a dozen pieces changed hands undamaged, a remarkable tribute to the dedication and courage of the artillerymen.

Footnote: *Artillery Ammunition.* There were four types of artillery ammunition commonly used during the Civil War, each designed for a particular task. Smooth bore pieces fired mostly spherical ammunition, while rifled guns fired cylindro-conoidal bolts looking like nothing less than a modern artillery shell.

Canister. Canister, one of several types of "case shot", consisted of a light tin can filled with musket balls or slugs packed in dry sawdust. For a 12-Pounder Napoleon, the can was a bit larger than a standard 46 ounce juice can, contained between 26 and 76 balls depending upon size and weighed a bit more than 12 pounds. When fired, the can disintegrated, scattering the bullets like a great shotgun blast. Ineffective at more than 400 yards, canister could be devastating to assaulting infantry at close ranges. Canister was best used with smooth bore artillery, for the great number of balls could damage the lands and grooves of a rifled gun. Canister was sometimes mistakenly referred to as "Grape Shot"

Grape Shot. Grape was another form of case shot. It consisted of a number of large iron or lead balls packed between two light metal plates or into lightly reinforced canvas bag. For a Napoleon, the number of balls was only about nine. When fired the package would disintegrate, and the balls would smash anything before them. Since the balls were larger than those used in canister, grape shot was effective at longer ranges, up to about a thousand yards. However, it was going out of fashion by the

Civil War, since it was unsuited to rifled guns, and was anyway being replaced by Shrapnel. Grape was rarely used on the battlefield after 1861.

Shell. Sometimes called "Explosive Shell", this was a light, hollow cast iron sphere of "shell" filled with explosives. For a Napoleon, the standard shell weighed aobut 9.75 pounds, seven ounces of which was explosive charge. When set off by a fuze, fragments of the casing, and, if detonated against the ground, pieces of wood and rock, would be scattered in all directions. A variety of fuzes were available. Spherical shell could be set off by concussion fuzes, which worked mechanically upon impact. Explosive shell for rifled cannon had a fulminate detonator in their tips which would go off on impact. Both of these had to impact against something in order to go off. Since detonation of a shell above the heads of massed troops would give the maximum results, time fuzes were also used. The typical time fuze was a wooden or paper tube filled with punk or other relatively slow-burning combustible. When a shell was loaded the gunner would cut the fuze to the length desired. If he cut it right, and if it burned at the prescribed rate, and if the gun was properly trained, the fuze would set the shell off above, and just in front of the target, so that the shell fragments would be thrown downwards in the direction in which the shell was going, scattering shell fragments right into the assembled troops. This did not always happen. In their bombardment of Cemetery Ridge on 3 July, the Confederate gunners not only misjudged the range, but also tended to cut their fuzes too long. In addition, it appears that about half their

shells failed to go off, due either to faulty fuzes or faulty shells. Nevertheless, at anything but extreme ranges, shell was more effective than solid shot against troops, though its effectiveness was reduced at under 800 yards.

Shot. Often called "Solid Shot" or "Round Shot," this was a ball or cylindro-conoidal rifle shell of cast iron used to smash things, such as walls, buildings, and masses of troops. Round shot would upon hitting the ground, often bounce several times, and could cut great swathes through large formations. Shot was the ammunition of preference when firing at long ranges.

Shrapnel. Invented by Henry Shrapnel, a British general, this was more correctly, but less clearly, called "Case Shot"—both canister and grape shot are also forms of case shot—or "Spherical Case Shot," though it was provided for both rifled and smooth bore guns. Shrapnel was essentially a combination of canister and explosive shell. A hollow, cast iron projectile was filled with lead bullets packed in hardened sulphur and provided with a bursting charge which could be set off by a percussion or time fuze, which would scatter the balls. Since it could be used at the same ranges as grape shot, and had the advantage of having an explosive charge as well, it rapidly replaced the latter. Since it was essentially a variant of explosive shell, shrapnel suffered from the same drawbacks as did shell.

Maj. Gen. Warren at the signal station on Little Round Top

Then, prompted by Henry Hunt's report, he rode over to examine Sickles' lines, reaching *III Corps* a little before 1600 hours. He was appalled by what he found. Sickles' advanced position threatened to unhinge the entire *Army of the Potomac*. Sickles apologetically offered to withdraw his corps to Cemetery Ridge, but Meade pointed out that it was too late for that. He was right, for within minutes Rebel artillery began to open up on Sickles' front. Meade directed Hunt to bring about 50 guns from the *Artillery Reserve* to the support of Sickles, and ordered *V Corps* to come up as quickly as possible. Throughout the day there had been little skirmishes and brief artillery exchanges all along the front. Now it was time for more serious fighting.

Alexander's artillery opened up at 1600 hours, taking the Peach Orchard under heavy fire. Within minutes Confederate infantry had begun to advance. As planned, Hood's men would go in first, followed within the hour, by those of McLaws. Hood's troops advanced at a fast pace, with their front well covered by skirmishers. The right hand brigades, under Brig. Gen. Evander Law with 1,900 men and Brig. Gen. Jerome Bonaparte Robertson with 1,700, drove somewhat westwards, towards Big Round Top. Union artillery opened up. Skirmishers

from two regiments of Yankee sharpshooters were active, but the bulk of the Federal infantry held their fire. Despite the artillery and musket fire, and the broken ground, the Confederate ranks maintained their cohesion, and swept aside the thin line of skirmishers. Reaching the gorge of Plum Run, on the western foot of the Round Tops, Law's Alabamians swung to their left, some of the men advancing over rugged Big Round Top to drive on Little Round Top, while the balance moved up the creek and on to the slopes of Little Round Top, to get around Sickles' flank at Devil's Den. Over on Law's left, Robertson's men, mostly Texans with a regiment of Arkansans, stormed right into the left flank of Brig. Gen. John Ward's brigade with 2,200 men of Sickles' *1st Division*, holding the ground in front of Devil's Den. Seeing the battle beginning to develop nicely on his right, Hood ordered his other two brigades, Brig. Gen. Henry Benning's with 1,400 and Brig. Gen. George T. Anderson's with 1,900, to support Law and Robertson. Ward's men held their fire until the Rebels were but 300 yards away, and then delivered a brigade-sized volley fully into the charging Confederates. The attackers faltered momentarily. Hastening to reload, Ward's men got off yet another volley, further confusing the enemy.

Then Ward counterattacked, driving the Confederates back and securing a stone wall forward of his original position. The Confederates came on once more, driving Ward back. Once more he counterattacked. Some of the fiercest fighting of the war developed along the entire front of Birney's *1st Division*, as Hood's brigades came into action one after another. Sickles' veterans fought hard and well, and held their ground, but the position was inherently flawed, and the flaws began to take their toll.

Over on Sickles' left was Little Round Top, rising high above the surrounding countryside. Earlier, before the crisis erupted in front of *III Corps*, Meade had instructed his chief engineer, and good friend, Maj. Gen. Gouverneur K. Warren, to investigate the situation on Little Round Top. Riding swiftly there with a few aides, he arrived shortly after Longstreet's attack on Sickles got underway. Warren was stunned to discover that, save for a few signalmen who were packing up to leave, the hill was bare of Union troops. He ordered the signalmen to get back to work as conspicuously as possible, and then, knowing that Maj. Gen. George Sykes' *V Corps* was approaching, he dispatched two messages. The first went to Meade, recommending that a division be brought up immediately. The second was an effort to pry some troops out of the hard-pressed Sickles. The latter refused. Meade overruled him, ordering A. A. Humphreys' division, already under enemy fire, but not yet deployed on the Emmitsburg Road, to reverse its march. Within minutes, Meade learned that *V Corps* already had one division in Sickles' rear. He cancelled the order. Humphreys' countermarched once more. Warren, meanwhile, was impatiently watching the progress of the battle in front of Ward's brigade. He rode out to locate *V Corps*, and within a few minutes found Sykes, who was examining the ground in the rear of *III Corps*. Warren apprised Sykes of the situation on Little Round Top. The latter immediately dispatched an order to Brig. Gen. James Barnes, of his *1st Division* instructing him to place a brigade on the hill. The courier could not locate Barnes. He did, however, run into 26-year old Col. Strong Vincent, commanding Barnes' *3rd Brigade*, of 1,300 men. Vincent pried the message from him. Recognizing its importance, on his own initiative and in complete disregard for his orders, Vincent immediately got his brigade on the march to Little Round Top. The brigade swiftly covered the half-mile to Little Round Top, racing over fields and pastures at the "double quick," crossing

Plum Run, and, under fire, sweeping up the west side of the hill and on to its wooded, rugged crest. Col. Joshua L. Chamberlain's *20th Maine* was in the lead, and as it streamed down the southern face, Vincent placed it on the extreme left. Then he directed the deployment of his other regiments to its right as they came up. Before he left, his instructions to Chamberlain were clear, "hold at all hazard." Chamberlain had the high and dangerous honor of anchoring the left flank of the entire *Army of the Potomac*. Within minutes his men were hotly engaged.

With the 47th Alabama, Col. William C. Oates' 44th Alabama had been assigned the task of covering the right of Law's Brigade as it

Above left: *Brig. Gen. Evander McIvorlaw*

Above: *Col. Strong Vincent*

Below: *The view from Little Round Top*

Above: The struggle for Devil's Den

The charge of the 20th Maine under the command of Col. Joshua L. Chamberlain

swarmed up Plum Run in an attempt to flank Ward's brigade in the Devil's Den. Advancing to Law's right, the regiment had swept aside some Union skirmishers and begun to scale Big Round Top, in the face of light opposition from elements of the *2nd United States Sharpshooters*. As Oates' men reached the crest of the craggy hill, the Union troops fell back, disappearing. Thinking this portended an attack by a superior Union force, Oates halted his men. Just then one of Law's staff officers rode up, demanding to know why the regiment had halted. Oates explained his misgivings, the staffer ignored them, however, insisting that he continue the advance. Oates therefore got his weary men to their feet and led them forward once more. Minutes later, at about 1630 hours, the 15th Alabama reached the foot of Big Round Top, coming out into the lightly wooded valley which separated it from Little Round Top. From there, Oates was surprised to spot what appeared to be a major Union wagon park, standing completely unguarded not 600 yards away to the right. As he began to advance on this, he came under heavy fire from the base of Little Round Top. Thinking the Federal skirmishers had retired thence, he ordered his regiment, perhaps 400 men, to sweep them away. The Alabamians advanced and ran into Joshua Chamberlain and some 385 determined men of his *20th Maine*.

While the 350 men of the 47th Alabama, to his left, engaged the *83rd Pennsylvania*, which had some 300 men, and Chamberlain's right, Oates threw his regiment up the steep—45°— rocky, scrub and tree covered slopes, against

Chamberlain's left, hoping to crush it in and roll up the entire Union position. His men drove off Chamberlain's *B Company*, which was trying to form a skirmish line covering the regiment's left. As the company rallied to the left behind a stone wall, where it found a dozen of the sharpshooters who had been entertaining Oates earlier, the Confederates attacked Chamberlain's main line. The fight grew hotter as Oates made repeated uphill assaults against the *20th Maine*, each time being beaten off in the thick woods. Despite this, Confederate pressure did not let up. Hand-to-hand fighting developed, but the Maine Staters held firm. Great heroism and dedication were displayed on both sides. Chamberlain kept his men well in hand, prepared to meet each new attack, and Oates was repeatedly able to rally his men and lead them forward again. But finally, the limits of endurance were reached. Battered by both the *83rd Pennsylvania* and the *20th Maine*, the 47th Alabama fell back. Oates' men wavered, thirsty and exhausted. But the *20th Maine* was nearly out of ammunition, having fired over 20,000 rounds. Realizing that another Confederate attack might succeed, Chamberlain ordered his men to charge with the bayonet. Beginning from the left, the men rose from their places and stormed forward. Covering the 30 yards or so which separated them from the 15th Alabama in less than a minute, they threw the enemy into confusion. The Rebels fell back, hotly pursued by the determined Yankees. *B Company* and the sharpshooters returned to the fray, rising from behind their protective stone wall to deliver a shattering volley into the flank of the retreating Confederates. The 15th Alabama broke and, as Oates himself put it, "we ran like a herd of wild cattle." They were closely pursued by Chamberlain's victorious men, who bagged over 400 prisoners. From start to finish, the fight for Little Round Top had taken little more than an hour. In one of the hottest fights in American history, the *20th Marine* had suffered about 30% casualties, but the 15th and the 47th Alabama had been shattered, losing over 40% of their men. But even as Chamberlain's men swept the enemy from the southern face of Little Round Top, the defenses on the western side of the hill began to crumble.

To the right of Little Round Top, Brig. Gen. John Ward's brigade was putting up a stiff resistance to Law's and Robertson's Confederate troops in the Devil's Den. As Col. William F. Perry of the 44th Alabama noted, this was an area in which "Large rocks, six to fifteen feet high, are thrown together in confusion over a considerable area, and yet so disposed as to leave everywhere among them winding passages. . . ." There were hundreds of places

Another view of Devil's Den

Above: *Dueling with the Union Batteries on Little Round Top*

Below: *The return fire*

which could shelter a soldier, scores of routes among the boulders, and lots of timber and rock with which to erect breastworks, all of which favored the defense. In an effort to get past Ward, Law's men had been slipping around his left, up Plum Run. Some of them had begun climbing the western face of Little Round Top. This had entangled them in the fighting there. Gradually the rest of the brigade was drawn into the struggle, which grew even more intense.

Observing from the Devil's Den Col. Perry remarked that Little Round Top "resembled a volcano in eruption"; Capt. Praxiteles Shaw, a preacher turned soldier with the 5th Texas, put it differently, but with equal poetry when he said that Yankee "fire came down the hill in blizzards." Holding the western side of the hill was the *16th Michigan*. A seasoned, veteran regiment, with good officers, it was the weakest outfit in Vincent's brigade, and it was in the

wrong place. With perhaps 250 rifles in the line, it could not cover Vincent's flank, which hung some 450 yards to the left of Ward's brigade, above Plum Run and the wooded ground at the foot of Little Round Top. Struck by elements of both Law's and Robertson's Brigades, which advanced up the steep bare western slopes with considerable courage and determination, the *16th Michigan* recoiled, some say broke and ran, with its commanding officer, Col. Norval E. Welch, in the lead. The *44th New York,* to the left of the Michiganders, tried to refuse its flank, bending it back and fighting on two fronts. With his right in imminent danger of collapse, Vincent came up exhorting and rallying his men, only to fall mortally wounded. Little Round Top hung ripe for the plucking, as Confederate forces advanced up its western face. But Gouverneur Warren was on the scene once more, having returned to the hill sometime after Vincent's men had occupied it. Even as Vincent fell, Warren had been supervising the emplacement on the craggy summit of the 10-pounder Parrott guns from Lt. Charles E. Hazlett's regular army *Battery D, 5th Artillery.* As Hazlett's guns began to open up on the Confederate troops beneath Little Round Top and assailing Devil's Den, word came that Vincent had fallen and that the entire position was crumbling. From the crest of Little Round Top, Warren spotted a brigade to the northwest, on the march towards the Peach Orchard. He rode down to it with his aides and was pleased to discover that it was his old brigade from the *2nd Division* of *V Corps,* now under Brig. Gen. Stephen H. Weed. Sykes had ordered Weed to reinforce Little Round Top, but whilst on the march the latter had been intercepted by Sickles, who had preemptorally instructed him to march on the Peach Orchard, where he was under considerable pressure. Weed had ridden ahead, and the brigade was temporarily under Col. Patrick H. O'Rorke of the *140th New York.* Warren countermanded Sickles' orders and within minutes the brigade began streaming up the north side of Little Round Top. At that moment Warren's brother Edgar, one of Weed's aides, came up demanding to know what was going on, as the brigade was needed elsewhere.

Warren explained the situation and the brothers agreed that O'Rorke's regiment should remain with Warren, while the balance of the

The Rebel advance on Little Round Top

brigade resumed its march for the Peach Orchard. O'Rorke, who had recently graduated from West Point at the head of his class, quickly ran his 450 men up the steep slope to the summit of Little Round Top, where Hazlett now had six guns in position. Without pausing—and with empty rifles—the regiment plunged down the other side with fixed bayonetts. Within minutes Weed came up with the balance of his brigade, Sykes having overruled Sickles. The attack by nearly 1,500 men threw the Rebels back in bloody disorder. O'Rorke fell at the head of his troops, Hazlett as he commanded his battery, Weed as he rushed forward. There were a few minutes more of heavy fighting and then it was over, as the Rebels gave up their efforts to take the hill. Soon after, the balance of Sykes' *2nd Division* came up, firmly anchoring the Union left. But the situation to the right, along Sickles' front was still fluid, and the Union could still lose the day.

During the fighting for Little Round Top, the left wing of Sickles' *III Corps* front had been repeatedly battered back in a bloody, confused series of actions characterized by an erratically

A 20-pounder Parrott

drawn front, a continuing commitment of reinforcements, a constant juggling of regiments from place to place in the line, and a near total lack of higher direction. Sickles stripped Col. George C. Burling's brigade from Maj. Gen. A. A. Humphreys' *2nd Division*, on his right, to reinforce Maj. Gen. David B. Birney's *1st Division*, on his more exposed left, bringing the latter up to nearly 6,500 men. Birney, in turn, did much the same thing, stripping regiments from Col. Philip de Trobriand's brigade and Burling's, to reinforce Brig. Gen. Charles K. Graham's 1,500 men covering the Peach Orchard on his right, and Brig. Gen. John Ward's 2,200 on his left. Sickles even secured Meade's permission to draw troops from elements of *II Corps* and *V Corps*. This practice did little for the morale or the cohesion of the affected troops. Forced to participate in ill-coordinated actions, under unknown officers, with strange regiments on their flanks, often on broken, wooded ground, the men could not perform to the best of their ability. Able officers, but with few troops, both Burling and de Trobriand were unemployed for much of the fight, when they might have

THE GETTYSBURG CAMPAIGN

A Color Portfolio

ROAD TO GETTYSBURG

Lt. Gen. James Longstreet pauses to gaze as he and his beloved First Corps march to Gettysburg.

COUNCIL OF WAR

Robert E. Lee and his generals determine tactics before Gettysburg.

© by Don Stivers. Reproduced by special arrangement with the American Print Gallery.

FOLLOWING PAGE:

REILLY'S BATTERY

Reilly's Battery of the famed Hood's Division are shown here engaged in counterbattery action against Hazlett's Union Battery on Little Round Top.

© by Dale Gallon. Reproduced by special arrangement with the American Print Gallery.

"I Select This as the Battlefield"

Maj. Gen. W.S. Hancock (shown in upper right, conferring with his staff) *gives the order to charge. Union infantry and artillery hurry toward the fighting. Little Round Top rises in the background.*

Courtesy of Eastern National Park and Monument Association

PRECEEDING PAGE:

HAZLETT'S BATTERY

The magnificent view from Little Round Top at Gettysburg stretches out before the men of Hazlett's Battery as they fight to hold the position, 2 July 1863.

High Watermark of the Confederacy

Pickett's famous charge is shown here as Confederates, dressed in brown (right) follow their red battleflags into the center of the Union line at the "copse of trees." General Armistead falls mortally wounded to the right of the flags.

Courtesy of Eastern National Park and Monument Association.

THE ANGLE

Pickett's charge reaches its climax at "the Angle," as a tangle of Confederate troops meet the Union line, and then fall back.

Courtesy of Eastern National Park and Monument Association

AFTER THE BATTLE

Scenes like this must have been common during and after the battle. At the lower right a surgeon amputates the leg of a wounded soldier in a ravaged shed which serves as a makeshift hospital.

Courtesy of Eastern National Park and Monument Association.

THE LAST CAVALIER

"Jeb" Stuart, who fought light cavalry like no one ever has; embodies the look and spirit of the Southern Army.

© by Michael Gnatek, Jr. Reproduced by special arrangement with the American Print Gallery.

usefully commanded sections of the front. The result of all this was that the defense suffered. Another result is that it is virtually impossible to elucidate the movements of the units involved as they struggled with each other, nor even to get a clear notion of the sequence of events which took place on the front of III Corps on the afternoon of 2 July.

Ward's brigade, to the west of Little Round Top, had been under heavy pressure from the moment the rebel guns opened up on the Peach Orchard, over in the center of III Corps. But this had begun to slacken during the heaviest part of the fighting on Little Round Top, for almost all of Law's and Robertson's Brigades had become involved there. As a result, Robertson soon found himself facing Ward with but two regiments. He requested reinforcements from Hood, only to discover that the latter was down with a shattered arm, and had not yet been replaced, for the next ranking officer in the division was Law, who was with his troops on Little Round Top. Robertson therefore requested generals Henry Benning and George T. Anderson, commanding Hood's other brigades, to reinforce him, while sending messages to Longstreet. Benning's brigade was immediately available, for he had become lost and followed Robertson rather than Law. Anderson brought his men up as well. With two full brigades and a portion of a third, Robertson renewed the attack on Ward's brigade, and took on de Trobriand's weakened outfit to Ward's right as well. Apprised of the renewed Confederate onslaught against Ward, Sickles committed three regiments from Burling's brigade. But even these could not stem the Rebel tide. Despite favorable terrain, Ward and de Trobriand finally began to fall back, giving up the Devil's Den and the southern end of the Wheat Field. To make the situation even worse, Sickles' fell wounded soon after ordering Burling's men forward, removing overall direction of fight. Even as this took place, reinforcements arrived to bolster the Federal line, in the form of two brigades from Caldwell's division of II Corps, and two more from Ayres' division of V Corps. These launched a counterattack, which halted, and then partially threw back the enemy. By about 1730 hours the line had temporarily stabilized. Then two brigades of Brig. Gen. James Barnes' 1st Division of V Corps began to come up, swinging around the Union right, and endangering the left flank of Anderson's attacking Confederates. Hood's division, perhaps 6,800 strong at this point, was facing over 10,000 men and imminent disaster.

The fierce fighting on his right had by now attracted the attention of Longstreet. He ordered up McLaws' Division, which had inexplicably delayed its attack much longer than planned. Brig. Gen. Joseph B. Kershaw's brigade of South Carolinians went in first with some 2,200, at just about 1800 hours, followed almost immediately by Brig. Gen. Paul J. Semmes' 1,300 Georgians. The two brigades drove towards the 400 yard gap between de Trobriand's right and the Peach Orchard, held by Graham's Pennsylvanians. It was into this area that Col. William S. Tilton and Col. Jacob B. Sweitzer, of Barnes' 1st Division, had intruded their brigades, thereby threatening to flank Anderson with 2,000 men. Finding himself now flanked in turned by Kershaw, Tilton pulled his small brigade back, twisting his right around until it faced westwards. This exposed Sweitzer's flank. Barnes ordered Sweitzer to break off his attack and fall back, which the latter did, despite an inclination to fight it out. Kershaw advanced under artillery fire into the ground vacated by Tilton and Sweitzer, only to have his right flank smashed by the brigades of Brig. Gen. Samuel Kosciuzkó Zook and Col. John R. Brooke, some 1,800 men from Caldwell's division. With his right crumbling, Kershaw called Semmes to his aid, and the latter's brigade came up quickly, though he fell mortally wounded as it did. Under Col. Goode Bryan, Semmes' men advanced under heavy fire, until halted. At this moment, at about 1800 hours, perhaps 20 minutes after Kershaw and Semmes had advanced, Brig. Gen. William Barksdale's Brigade of 1,600 Mississippians leaped forward, smashing into Brig. Gen. Charles K. Graham's brigade at the Peach Orchard. The 1,400 Georgians of Brig. Gen. William T. Wofford's Brigade followed within minutes, with Longstreet himself in the lead. As the troops cheered him, Longstreet plunged forward, waving his hat and crying, "Cheer less, men, and fight more!" Barksdale's men swung to their left and proceeded to take Humphrey's Division in the flank along the Emmitsburg Road, while Wofford's troops pressed eastwards and then to their right. Graham's men were driven from the Peach Orchard in considerable disorder, some 250 of them falling prisoner, including Graham himself, as Wofford's men linked up with Kershaw's, forming a single battle line. Maj. James Dearing, of Longstreet's corps artillery, quickly got eight cannon forward and into action and began to belabor the retreating Union troops. The situation on the Union front was now critical, for Hood's men had turned the right of III

Corps at the same time that McLaws' had broken its center. Seven brigades—the equivalent of a full army corps—were in danger of being enveloped on the left of *III Corps*, and Humphreys' division, already engaged frontally with Maj. Gen. Richard Anderson's Confederate division, now lay exposed to a flank attack from its left.

Union Brig. Gen. John C. Caldwell tried to secure the Union line running from the Wheatfield to Devil's Den. With Zook's, Brooke's and Sweitzer's brigades, Caldwell charged across the corpse-filled Wheatfield, supported on his left by two brigades of regulars from Brig. Gen. Romeyn B. Ayres' *2nd Division, V Corps*, who attacked the Devil's Den. The troops pressed hard, driving back the enemy in a bloody charge. Then, even as the victorious Federal troops pressed the attack, they were struck on their right flank by Wofford's Rebels, just emerging from the Peach Orchard. The attack faltered, as bloody hand-to-hand fighting developed. Pressed from both front and flank, the Union troops suffered heavy casualties and gave way. Some units broke, fleeing before the advancing enemy to the shelter of Cemetery Ridge and Little Round Top, hundreds of yards to the rear. The front line had dissolved. Three full divisions had been badly battered. The entire Union left was now at risk. Ordering elements of *VI Corps* and *XII Corps* to help fill the gap in the Union lines south of *II Corps*, Meade placed Hancock of *II Corps*, in command of the entire flank. Hancock thrust Brig. Gen. Samuel W. Crawford's *V Corps* division of the *Pennsylvania Reserves* into the gap to cover the Devil's Den area and Little Round Top from the west. Crawford soon had his veteran troops in position with one brigade on the hill itself, and the

The innocent victims

other massed to its north. As thousands of fugitives streamed past them, the Pennsylvanians stood patiently awaiting the enemy for twenty minutes. When the tight Rebel columns came into view out of some woods in the direction of Wheatfield, Crawford ordered the attack. Thousands of muskets spoke, as the Pennsylvanians discharged two volleys, then, with Crawford in the lead, charged, racing downhill and sweeping the advancing Confederates back once more to the edge of the Wheatfield, halting the threat to the Union left. If the center and right of the *III Corps* front could be held, disaster might yet be averted.

Over on the *III Corps*' right, Humphreys' had been doing well most of the afternoon, being only lightly engaged against elements of Confederate Maj. Gen. Richard Anderson's Division to his front. As the crisis began to develop on the Union left, he had been subject to

The advance of the horse batteries

conflicting orders. When Sickles' was wounded, Maj. Gen. David B. Birney, commanding the corps' *1st Division*, had assumed command. Rather than direct the fighting on the left flank of the corps, Birney had abandoned his division and gone off to meddle with Humphreys' dispositions. The aggressive Humphreys' had planned to attack into the face of the impending enemy attack, catching the Rebels off balance. Birney cancelled this, ordering him instead to fall somewhat, and draw back his left, in a maneuver which Birney fondly hoped would restore the Union line as soon as Birney's own division could similarly refuse its right. But even as Humphreys ably shifted his division to form this new line—despite the fact that there was no one on whom he could form up—Graham's brigade collapsed in the Peach Orchard. This put Barksdale's Mississippians on Humphrey's exposed left flank, even as Anderson threw two brigades against his front and right. Birney now intervened once more, ordering Humphreys to fall back all the way to Cemetery Ridge, over 850 yards in his rear. This was an unwise maneuver, for the division had to retire whilst receiving the full attentions of three Confederate infantry brigades and a considerable number of cannon. Humphreys' made the best of it. He pulled his men back slowly, repeatedly halting them so that they could get off a few volleys. Despite heavy casualties, the troops held together well, inspired by Humphreys' heroic example, as he rode from place to place, exhorting the men and issuing orders. Artillery from Cemetery Ridge began to support him, and several regiments came out to lend a hand. The entire maneuver took perhaps twenty minutes, and the division suffered 1,200 dead and wounded, over 35% casualties, but it came out intact, with morale sound and still full of fight. And even as

Humphreys' men reached the security of Cemetery Ridge, other elements of *III Corps* managed to escape from the disaster as well.

About 50 pieces of artillery had been concentrated in the area just east of the Peach Orchard and north of the Wheatfield. Having supported the fight all afternoon, these batteries were suddenly exposed to capture with the collapse of Graham's brigade at the Peach Orchard, and the disintegration of Birney's line. Coordinated by Lt. Col. Freeman McGilvery they held off the advancing Rebel tide as long as possible, offering an island of resistance in a sea of shattered divisions and regiments. At about 1800 hours they fell back some 250 yards to the vicinity of Trostle's farm. There they engaged in a number of desperate rear-guard actions against Kershaw's, Barksdale's and Wofford's Confederates. As pressure grew, McGilvery fell back once more. Under cover of the half-dozen

12-pounder Napoleons of Capt. John Bigelow's *9th Massachussetts Battery,* he formed a new gun line on Cemetery Ridge, about 400 yards to the rear. Bigelow's men fought on without infantry support until down to two guns. Then, with most of their horses dead and nearly all of their canister exhausted, and with Rebel infantry closing in on their flanks and front, they pulled back to McGilvery's new line. As the enemy closed on this new artillery line, elements of Kershaw's Brigade overran several batteries. The *141st Pennsylvania* came up and retook them in a bayonet attack. In the end, but four guns were taken by the enemy, though many more were disabled or destroyed. The balance were brought safely away and by about 1915 hours were lining up along Cemetery Ridge, just as Hancock came up to their support, personally leading a brigade from his *3rd Division*.

Hancock threw three regiments into a front

Trostles' Farm during the action

The 9th Massachusetts Battery under fire

The 9th Massachusetts Battery galloping into action

counterattack downhill against Barksdale's troops, while a fourth went in to recover a battery which the *21st Mississippi* had overrun on the left. In the bloody clash which followed Barksdale's Mississippians were thrown back, and he himself killed, by the desperate charge of the *111th, 125th,* and *126th New York Regiments,* while the *39th New York,* a polyglot outfit of Italians, Poles, and Hungarians, quickly recovered the captured guns. The Federal line began to solidify on Cemetery Ridge, as regiments and brigades fought their way back. Two brigades which Meade had ordered up from *XII Corps* began to arrive, led personally by acting corps commander Brig. Gen. Alpheus Williams. Williams threw his two leading regiments into the fighting, driving off still more Confederate troops and recovering several more guns. Then he pressed hard against the Rebels, pushing forward in the gathering dusk almost to the Peach Orchard, nearly 850 yards beyond Cemetery Ridge, while he deployed the rest of his troops along the ridge itself. With these troops, and those which retreated out of the disaster, the final gap in the Union left was plugged, and a continuous front established from Little Round Top to Cemetery Hill.

Meanwhile the fighting became more gen-

eral. As Humphreys withdrew his division under pressure to Cemetery Ridge, A. P. Hill launched his III Corps against it and against the northern end of the Cemetery Ridge line. Soon the entire front of I Corps and II Corps was hotly engaged. Small units performed prodigiously, making limited attacks at every opportunity. The fighting grew intense, as Hill fed brigade after brigade into the attack. Wilcox' 1,700 man brigade of Anderson's Division was halted by a desperate charge of 262 men of the 1st Minnesota, which sustained one of the highest regimental losses in a single action in American history, fully 215 men—82%—became casu-

Left: "Going into Action" by war artist Edwin Forbes showing the 9th Massachusetts Battery on 2 July 1863. [from L.W. Baker's, History of the Ninth Massachusetts Battery]

Top: Trostle's field: Bringing the guns away by prolongs

Above: Brig. Gen. William Barksdale

alties, including Col. William Colville, Jr., who had been released from arrest to participate. Meade pulled the *2nd* and *3rd Divisions* of *I Corps* out of reserve and plugged them into the lines, personally leading their skirmishers forward. A series of local counterattacks resulted, gradually merging into the semblence of a general counterattack. The Confederate attack faltered. As darkness began to fall, Hill's brigades retired, closely pressed by Hancock's regiments. And as the Union forces pushed the Confederates back to Seminary Ridge, heavy fighting began to develop on their right as well, in front of Cemetery Hill and Culp's Hill.

Save for some desultory shelling of Union positions on Cemetery Hill and Culp's Hill, Richard Ewell's II Corps had been virtually unengaged for most of 2 July. Although Lee had instructed him to attack if he thought conditions suitable, Ewell appears to have had no clear notion of what he was going to do. At about 1600 hours, 16 pieces of artillery had begun to lay down a more vigorous barrage against the eastern side of Cemetery Hill in response to the opening rounds of Longstreet's offensive over on the Confederate right. As Federal artillery began counter-battery fire against the Rebel guns, Yankee infantrymen posted in the vicinity prepared to meet a general assault. But none came. Instead, the artillery duel dragged on for hours and hours, with the more numerous and heavier Union guns gradually gaining the upper hand. At about 1800 hours, as his gunners began to slacken off their fire, Ewell briefly toyed with the idea of launching an attack. Having second thoughts, he soon gave it up. This permitted Meade and Slocum to strip most of *XII Corps* away to reinforce the shattered Union left. Some time later, Ewell once again decided to attack. He issued the appropriate instructions to his subordinates, but thereafter appears to have done little to supervise the operation. As a result, Maj. Gen. Robert E. Rodes' Division, on Ewell's right, completely failed to get into action. Maj. Gen. Edward Johnson's division, over on Ewell's left, did better, and Maj. Gen. Jubal Early's, in Ewell's center, did best of the three. The attack began at about 2000 hours, when 32 guns opened up on the Union positions. Johnson attacked Culp's Hill from the northeast and east. He went in with three brigades, being forced to use the famed Stonewall Brigade to cover his left, where Union cavalrymen under Brig. Gen. David Gregg were constantly probing his rear. The attack did not go well. The troops encountered great difficulties in getting across

Brig. Gen. George S. Greene

deeply cut Rock Creek under fire. By the time they finally cleared the creek, pushed back the Yankee skirmishers, and began to grapple with the main line of resistance, it was already dark, sunset having been at about 2030 hours. The Union troops, the battered veterans of Wadsworth's Division of *I Corps*, with a brigade from *XII Corps* to their right, were posted atop steep, wooded slopes and rocky cliffs which they had strengthened with breastworks of logs, rocks, and earth. Johnson's principal effort hit Brig. Gen. George S. Greene's brigade of the *3rd Division* of *XII Corps*, numbering little more than 1,400 all told, and with a long front to cover. Although already under attack himself, Wadsworth immediately reinforced Greene with two weak regiments, which were soon followed by several more from Carl Schurz' *XI Corps* division, over to the left of Culp's Hill, and one from *II Corps*, which returned almost as soon as it arrived. These were few in number, bringing Greene's total up to at best 2,200 men, but they were enough, given his excellent position. By careful supervision of his troops and by rotating regiments into reserve from time to time to rest and resupply their men, Greene managed to hold the attacks of Brig. Gen. John M. Jones' Virginia brigade and of Col. J. M. Williams' "Louisiana Tigers" brigade against his front. Over on Greene's right, however, Confederate Brig. Gen. George H. Steuart's Brigade achieved considerable success, for it attacked against an unoccupied section of the defenses which had been evacuated earlier in order to free troops to go to the support of Sickles' beleaguered corps. Green refused his right, and moved troops to cover it. But the real defense was provided by the lunar landscape of the southern end of Culp's Hill and the ground falling away from it, which was full of rocky outcroppings, woods, depressions, and hollows. The Confederates advanced cautiously in the moonlight, fearing a trap. And as they did, Brig. Gen. Thomas Ruger marched up with his division, which had been taken from *XII Corps* to bolster the left. Ruger's division deployed quickly, covering the Rebel positions from across Spangler's Spring, a small

brook running down from Culp's Hill into a broad boggy area up against Rock Creek. The lead elements of the other division of *XII Corps,* that of Brig. Gen. John W. Geary, began to come up at about 2300 hours, after having gotten lost and wandering aimlessly in the Federal rear for several hours. By midnight, Geary's men had deployed so as to cover Steuart's front. Neither Union commander thought it wise to attempt an attack against Steuart during the night, particularly in as much as his men were occupying earthworks which their own men had built, but had then abandon in order to march off to bolster the line on Cemetery Ridge.

In Ewell's center was his best division, under his best officer, Jubal Early. Early attacked Cemetery Hill at about 2000 hours, with about 3,500 men on a two-brigade front. As they emerged from cover the troops began to come under heavy artillery fire from four batteries. Veterans all, Early's men kept coming, crashing

Below: Early's charge on the evening of July 2, upon Cemetery Hill.

into a line of Union infantrymen in the hollow ground at the foot of the hill. The defenders, from *XI Corps*, poured in a deadly fire. But *XI Corps* had been heavily engaged on the previous day. It was weak and its men were tired. Col. Leopold von Gilsa's brigade of Ames' division, on the corps' right, was down to little more than 650 men, and Col. Andrew L. Harris' brigade, at right angles to its left, was even weaker. As Brig. Gen. Harry T. Hays' brigade of Lousianans and Col. Isaac Avery's North Carolinians slammed into them, the two brigades crumbled away, officers and men alike fleeing to the rear despite

efforts to rally them by some steadfast artillerymen. As his infantry got onto the top of the hill, Early began to move some artillery forward. The Confederate pieces opened up. A heated hand-to-hand fight developed in the cemetery as Union gunners tried to beat off Confederate infantrymen. Placing his hand on a piece, one triumphant Rebel yelled "This battery's ours!" only to receive the guttural reply, "*Nein*, dis battery is *unseres!*" A crisis was at hand. Maj. Gen. O. O. Howard, commanding the corps, was conferring with Maj. Gen. Carl Schurz, of his *3rd Division*, when the Rebels erupted onto

the top of Cemetery Hill. Schurz gathered up two regiments immediately at hand, threw them into the fighting with fixed bayonets under Col. Wladimir Krzyzanowski, and then personally followed them into the fray with his staff. Brig. Gen. Adolph von Steinwehr, his sector further to the left relatively secure, sent a brigade from his *2nd Division*. Col. Charles R. Coster's York Staters and Pennsylvanians came up swiftly, delivered a couple of volleys into the enemy, and then threw them back on their right. At almost the same time, in response to a message from Howard, Col. Samuel S. Carroll's brigade of *II Corps*, came up. Carroll's men, from Indiana, Ohio, and West Virginia, decided the issue, as they threw the last of the Confederate troops off Cemetery Hill. Then they launched themselves over the edge and attacked downhill, clearing the enemy away from the foot of the hill. Early's attack had failed. By 2230 hours it was all over, save for occasional rifle and artillery fire. Gradually the firing died down all along the line, and the second day of the Battle of Gettysburg was over.

It had been a good day for Confederate arms, but not the victory which Lee was seek-

The wreckage of a Federal caisson of a 12-pounder gun around the wheatfield.

THE SECOND DAY
Who Won?

The Second Day. The fighting on 2 July was once again a Confederate victory, but it was an incomplete one at best, casualties had been high and the *Army of the Potomac* had escaped a potential complete diaster to retire to a secure defensive position. Again Lee's leadership had been wanting, nor had that of his subordinates been better. Longstreet's original plan of battle was probably technically superior to that which was eventually adopted. However, his execution of the final plan had been somewhat careless, with the result that it was badly coordinated, and McLaws' men struck much later than they ought to have. Both Hill and Ewell should have been far more closely supervised than was the case. Hill had remained almost completely inactive for the entire day. Worse, by not getting Ewell to attack against the Union right at the same time that Longstreet struck their left, Lee permitted Meade to weaken himself on that side in order to restore the left flank after the collapse of *III Corps*. Ewell's inexplicable lack of activity permitted a likely victory to turn into something approaching a drawn fight. Moreover, his attack on Culp's Hill later in the day, was foolish, unnecessary, and hours too late to effect events in the center. Yet again the Confederate troops had fought splendidly, only to have little to show for all their courage and devotion.

Despite the reverse, Union leadership had done somewhat better. Meade had kept his head, appearing on all parts of the field, to inspire the men and gain an understanding of the situation. He had confided in his most able subordinates, and eased the burden of command by placing Hancock and Slocum over the left and right wings of the army, respectively. They had done well, particularly Hancock, who seemed to be everywhere on the field at critical moments. Slocum handled the potential disaster on the Union right with considerable skill, and Gouveneur Warren had been superbly effective, with his marvelous improvised defense of Little Round Top. Indeed, save for Sickles and Birney, the Union corps and division commanders had performed ably, and sometimes brilliantly. Sickles, of course, had been the cause of the disaster which involved his corps, and many other troops, and he ought never to have been permitted to do so. Indeed, had *III Corps* held its assigned position along Cemetery Ridge, it would have been ideally placed to take in the flank of Longstreet's attack along the Emmitsburg Road. Birney contributed to the disaster when he left his division to go off and assume command of the disintegrating *III Corps* after Sickles had been wounded. Perhaps the most magnificent performance by a division commander had been that of

Humphreys, who had kept his head and pulled his men out of the disaster in remarkably good order. Carl Schurz, commanding up on Cemetery Hill, had also handled his division well. The lower ranking Union officers had generally, almost universally done well, most notably in the fighting around Little Round Top and in the collapsing center. Their performance set the stage for the Union victory the next day.

One of the many dead in and around Devil's Den

Confederate prisoners

ing. Although great blows had been dealt the *Army of the Potomac*, it had not collapsed, but rather had taken the blows and gone on to establish a substantial line of defense along Cemetery Ridge. Yet again the Confederate troops had fought splendidly, with but little to show for all their courage and devotion. They had not attained a decisive success. For the Union it had been a hard day, due primarily to Sickles' careless disposition of his corps. Nevertheless, the situation had been stabilized. Moreover, save for the collapse of Ames' division, the troops, by and large, had performed ably, and in many instances splendidly. Of course, as in the case of the Army of Northern Virginia, the *Army of the Potomac* had taken some heavy losses. About 13 brigades had suffered casualties of 30% or more, some of them having been so badly battered that they were unfit for further service. But the army had held together. The troops were still determined. That hot, humid night, as the armies bedded down in the moonlight, their commanders contemplated the morrow.

Confederate infantry man killed around Devil's Den. A number of photographs were taken of this man from different angles; in one instance the body was moved for dramatic effect.

CHAPTER VII

GETTYSBURG, 3 JULY:
Day of Decision

The sun rose strong and hot on Friday, 3 July. Lee had spent much of the night planning an attack. Despite the poor results of the second day's fighting, the army was still determined and still full of fight. Unfortunately, rather than bring his principal subordinates together for a staff conference, so that they could express their views, Lee issued his instructions by courier. The plan was simple, he would simultaneously hit both ends of the Union line, collapse them, and force the *Army of the Potomac* to retreat. Ewell was ordered to reinforce his left, under Johnson, with three brigades drawn from his right, under Rodes. He was then to attack the Union forces remaining on Culp's Hill early in the morning, in an effort to exploit the gains Johnson had made after sunset the previous night. Meanwhile, Longstreet was to renew the attack against the Union left and center along Cemetery Ridge. And, J.E.B. Stuart's cavalry, having finally turned up the previous afternoon, was to undertake a diversion against the Union rear, threatening to cut Meade's line of communications. Unfortunately, Lee was neither clear nor forceful in detailing his desires. Longstreet, believing that the Cemetery Ridge line was much too strong for a frontal attack, began planning a flank march to the right, in order to get around the Federal left beyond Big Round Top, which he believed to be but lightly held. At about dawn, soon after Longstreet had issued orders designed to get his troops into position for such an attack, Lee rode up to his headquarters, curious as to why the attack had not yet begun. The resulting conversation between the two officers left Longstreet disappointed and depressed, and Lee stunned and frustrated. As it was too late to get an attack going in time to coincide with Ewell's, he had to improvise. Collecting up Longstreet and a few staff officers, he rode along Seminary Ridge, observing the Federal positions opposite. His eye soon fell upon a section of the Union front which looked particularly suitable, a 650 yard wide stretch of almost bare ridge crowned by a prominent copse of trees, just at the north end of Cemetery Ridge, before it rose to the higher ground of Cemetery Hill. There was about 1,300 yards between his skirmish line along the foot of Seminary Ridge and the Union front. Most of this was level, open fields, crossed by the Emmitsburg Road and uncluttered save for a few farm buildings and fences, and some stands of timber. Lee explained to Longstreet, Hill, and the others present that he would smother the defenses with an unprecedentedly large artillery bombardment and then storm it with 15,000 men. Longstreet vigorously expressed his opposition to the plan, but Lee would not be moved. As Henry Heth later put it, "The fact is, General Lee believed the Army of Northern Virginia, as it then existed, could accomplish anything."

Longstreet was to attack as soon as practical with eleven brigades. Aside from Maj. Gen. George E. Pickett's newly arrived division of Virginians of his own corps, most of the troops would come from Hill's III Corps. These included all of Maj. Gen. William D. Pender's relatively fresh division of Carolinians and Georgians, now under the command of Maj. Gen. Isaac Trimble, an elderly but game officer who had been serving as Lee's chief of engineers. In addition, there was Maj. Gen. Henry Heth's division, temporarily under Brig. Gen. James J. Pettigrew, which had been unengaged since its battering on the first day, plus a pair of brigades from Maj. Gen. Richard Anderson's division. Lee apparently also intended that the balance of Longstreet's corps, the divisions of Hood and

McLaws, were to support the blow in some fashion, probably in the form of a follow up attack further to the right, soon after the main assault. However, he was again unclear as to his intentions, and Longstreet appears to have believed these troops were to be held back until significant success had been gained in the center. Thus, as the troops began to deploy for the attack, their commanders were still not in complete agreement as to what was to take place, nor even as to its wisdom, for Longstreet still expressed reservations about the attack. These do not seem to have troubled Lee. Although aware that the Union position was a strong one, he had complete confidence in his troops, and no doubts that they could take Cemetery Ridge, thereby splitting the *Army of the Potomac* in two and winning the battle.

Unlike Lee, Meade had convened a meeting of his senior officers soon after the fighting ended on 2 July. They met at about 2100 hours, at the Leister house, conveniently located just behind Cemetery Ridge in the *II Corps* sector, at roughly the center of the Federal line. Into the tiny front room of the house crowded Meade, Slocum and Hancock, his wing commanders, seven regular or acting corps commanders (Newton, *I;* Gibbon, *II;* Birney, *III;* Sykes, *V;* Sedgwick, *VI;* Howard, *XI:* and Williams, *XII*), chief engineer Warren, and chief of staff Maj. Gen. Daniel Butterfield. Looking in through a window of the tiny room, Lt. Frank Haskell, aide to Brig. Gen. John Gibbon, observed that ". . . some sat, some kept walking or standing, two lounged upon the bed, some were constantly smoking cigars." As the wounded and exhausted Warren slept against the wall in a corner, the officers exchanged views of the day's action and on their prospects for the morrow. There was some discussion of the state of the army's supplies, for there was but one day's rations left at hand, but it was concluded that these could be eked out through local resources. Dispirited by the disastrous battering which his corps had received, Birney expressed doubts about the possibility of holding much longer. Newton, respected engineer, had reservations about the security of the army's flanks. Some officers debated the possibility of a general withdrawal to the Pipe Creek position, about a day's march to the southeast. However, Hancock, Howard, and Slocum were all in favor of fighting it out. Meade, who was somewhat concerned with the irregular character of the Union front, suggested that should a withdrawal become necessary a tactical one of about 2,000

W. L. Sheppard—

The 29th Pennsylvania forms a line of battle on Culp's Hill in the early morning of 3 July.

Steuart's brigade renews the Confederate attack on Culp's Hill in the early morning of 3 July.

yards would be best, to a line running just east of Rock Creek. Meanwhile, Butterfield calculated that the *Army of the Potomac* had perhaps 58,000 infantrymen available, which was probably a bit high. Then, with Meade's consent, he polled Hancock, Slocum, and the corps commanders, asking each three questions. The first, as to whether the army should remain in position, was unanimously answered in the affirmative. On the second question, as to whether the army should stand on the defensive or attack, the response was equally unanimous for the defensive. Finally, on the matter of how long the army should remain in position, the majority of the officers recommended that Meade consider alternative courses of action if the enemy delayed attacking by more than a day. Although he was not bound by this poll, Meade was pleased with it, for he had already decided to stay and fight it out, and had expressed as much in a

message dispatched to Henry Halleck shortly before the meeting. It then being about midnight, the meeting broke up. As it did, Meade turned to Gibbon of *II Corps*, saying, "If Lee attacks tomorrow, it will be on your front." When asked why he thought thusly, Meade replied, "Because he has made attacks on both our flanks and failed, and if he concludes to try again it will be on our center." Then the officers went out of the house and rode off into the dark.

Most of the Union corps commanders had little to do after the staff conference. They toured their lines, spoke quietly with some of their officers and men, and then turned in for a few hours sleep. Not so Maj. Gen. Alpheus Williams, the acting commander of *XII Corps*. He had much to do before he could rest. He was concerned about the Rebel brigade which had secured a lodgement at the southern end of Culp's Hill on the previous night. Strongly en-

sconced in trenches and earthworks, Brig. Gen. George H. Steuart's men posed a threat to Union tenure of the entire hill, and potentially could unhinge the Union right. With permission from Slocum and Meade, Williams planned to eject the Rebels in the morning, and spent three hours preparing his attack. The enemy position was strong, with a stone wall as well as the earthworks covering it in front, and its left flank secured by some 700 yards of boggy ground stretching southwestwards from the junction of Rock Creek and Spangler's Spring. But it was not impregnable, for Steuart's men did not hold the crest of Culp's Hill. And Brig. Gen. George S. Greene's heroic brigade of Geary's division still held the northern end of the hill, over on Steuart's right flank. So Steuart's brigade held a salient in the middle of *XII Corps*, subject to fire from two sides. Williams took advantage of this. Finding some excellent sites for his artillery, he

Maj. Gen. Daniel Butterfield

This is a view of Cemetery Ridge around the turn of the century. The "Angle" is roughly in the center, and the Round Top is in the left background.

proceeded to position 26 guns at ranges varying between 600 and 800 yards from the enemy, in such a way that they could pound every part of Steuart's position. These would open the attack, with a 15 minute bombardment. Then Brig. Gen. John Geary's *2nd Division* would go in against Steuart's right while Williams' own *1st Division*, now under Brig. Gen. Thomas Ruger, would pin the enemy's attention by applying steady pressure against Steuart's left, and one brigade would be held out as a reserve. At about 0300 hours on 3 July Williams was satisfied with his arrangements. Rolling himself up in a blanket, he lay down on a broad, flat rock beneath an apple tree to snatch a half-hour's sleep. By that time, men were already stirring in anticipation of the day's fighting to come.

Maj. Gen. Edward Johnson, commanding the Confederate forces in the vicinity of Culp's Hill, was also planning an attack for that morning. He had been reinforced by four brigades, Brig. Gen. James A. Walker's famed Stonewall Brigade from his own division, plus the brigades of Col. E. A. O'Neal and Brig. Gen. Junius Daniel from Rodes' Division over on the right of Ewell's II Corps' right, and Brig. Gen. William Smith's brigade from Early's Division, in the corps' center. With three brigades already in the line, this gave him seven brigades for an attack on Culp's Hill. He already had Col. J. M. Williams' brigade of Louisianans holding the ground beneath the northeastern side of the hill, on his right, and he had shifted Brig. Gen. John M. Jones' brigade of Virginians to cover his left. In his center was, of course, Steuart's mixed brigade of Virginians, North Carolinians, and some secessionist Marylanders, holding a portion of the hill itself. Johnson placed some of the reinforcements to cover his exposed left flank, but put most of them behind Steuart and Williams, intending that they attack directly up Culp's Hill. Johnson's dispositions were not sound. The terrain was highly unfavorable to an attack, being mostly wooded slopes, with rocky outcroppings, cliffs, and depressions. Nor was there any place suitable for artillery to be deployed in any numbers. Moreover, neither Johnson nor Ewell held out any forces as a reserve, available to exploit success should the Yankees be driven from the hill. It would almost seem as though the attack was being staged because an attack had to be staged. Johnson planned to hit the Union lines at about 0500 hours. Alpheus Williams hit first.

Williams' 26 guns opened up at about 0430 hours. For 15 minutes they subjected the Rebel positions to heavy fire. Then, as scheduled, they ceased firing. Geary's division was supposed to attack at this point. But the course of events becomes unclear. Both Geary and Ewell reported that a furious attack was made and repulsed with heavy losses. Yet neither Brig. Gen. George Greene's brigade nor Brig. Gen. Thomas L. Kane's incurred any serious losses in the course of the day's fighting. What actually appears to have happened is what Wiliams himself reported, that the cannonade had barely ceased when Johnson unleashed his own assault. It was a confused, ill-coordinated attack uphill against superior force. Walker's famed Stonewall Brigade appears to have carried it out unsupported save for a large volume of rifle fire delivered by the other brigades. Kane's Pennsylvanians and Greene's New Yorkers poured a deadly fire into the attacking troops. Walker's men came on repeatedly, in a series of attacks, renewing the assault each time with a fresh regiment. Walker was a seasoned veteran, and his men were superb soldiers, but the Union position was too strong and too stoutly defended. The attack faltered. As Walker's troops streamed back down the slopes, Johnson's other brigades pressed forward, so that the entire front along Culp's Hill was soon enveloped in a furious fire fight between the well-entrenched Yankees at its top and the Rebels at its foot, sheltering behind trees and boulders. The fire fight continued for some time. Then, at about 0800 hours, Johnson ordered in O'Neal's Alabamians. The entire brigade attacked in line, easily storming up the lower slopes in an attack of such furor that it frightened Geary. But then heavy artillery and rifle fire pinned O'Neal down, and his men sought such shelter as they could find. At about 0900 Johnson threw in Walker's men once more, to the right of O'Neal's pinned troops. Once again attacking with great skill and great elan, Walker's men were once again beaten off. At about this time Slocum interfered in William's conduct of the battle. Believing that the withdrawal of Walker's men presaged a general Confederate retirement, he ordered an attack across the boggy meadow along Spangler's Spring. The order bypassed Williams and went directly to Ruger. Ruger referred it back to Slocum for clarification, and the latter permitted skirmishers to first probe the enemy position. Unfortunately, a courier garbled Ruger's oral instructions to Col. Silas Colgrove, commanding his *3rd Brigade.* Against his better judgment, and without thinking to refer the matter back to Ruger, Colgrove immediately committed two regiments.

JENNIE WADE

Jennie Wade, the only "civilian" casualty of Gettysburg, and the house in which she died

Jennie Wade was a 20 year-old resident of Gettysburg, engaged to be married to Corp. Johnston H. Skelly of the 87th Pennsylvania. Her sister had given birth with great difficulty on 28 June and Jennie was caring for her at her home on Baltimore Street, less than 50 yards north of Cemetery Hill. On 1 July the Battle of Gettysburg engulfed them. Protected by the sturdy brick walls of the house, Jennie, her sister, and the infant lived for three days in the midst of the greatest battle ever seen in this hemisphere. On the morning of 3 July, while Jennie was making bread, a Confederate musket ball smashed through a door on the north side of the house, pierced another into the kitchen, and struck Jennie in the back killing her instantly, the only civilian casualty of the battle. Nor was the tragedy complete, for unbeknownst to Jennie, her fiancee, Corporal Skelly, had been wounded and taken prisoner at Winchester on 13 May. Transferred to Virginia, he died in a hospital on 12 July.

At about 1000 hours, 650 men of the *27th Indiana* and *2nd Massachusetts* charged right into the front of Jones' Brigade, which had been shifted there during the morning. The Rebels laid on very heavy fire. The Indianans advanced about 200 yards and then wavered, falling back with over 30% casualties. The *2nd Massachusetts*, was even more determined. Advancing nearly 400 yards, it seized a portion of the Confederate lines, holding it for perhaps five minutes before retiring reluctantly under heavy pressure both to front and flank. As it fell back, it made at least one counterattack to beat off pursuing Rebel troops. By the time the regiment reached the safety of Union lines once more it had lost nearly half its men. It was an unnecessary maneuver did nothing to bolster the defense.

Meanwhile, at 1000 hours Johnson ordered the brigades of Steuart and Daniel to storm Culp's Hill, despite the protests of both commanders that the attempt was clearly suicidal. Steuart formed two lines facing at right angles to his former lines, with Daniel to his right. The troops attacked "in a most gallant manner." Nevertheless, as soon as they emerged from the sheltering ridge they were subjected to a deadly cross fire. Rifle balls and canister raked the lines in what one officer observed was "the most fearful fire I ever encountered." Daniel's brigade had some modest success, getting to within 50 paces of the Union lines before going to ground. But Steuart's brigade fared badly. Its exposed left was unable to stand the fire and broke, fleeing to the rear. The right pressed on briefly, wavered and then fell back in turn, forcing Daniel's men to pull back as well. Johnson's attack had failed. Williams now went over to the attack himself, ordering a general advance to recover the positions lost on the previous night and to press the enemy back to Rock Creek. This was done skillfully and swiftly, with units all along the line helping to drive back the exhausted Rebels. It was shortly after 1100 hours. Though artillery fire would continue another hour, and skirmishers would trade shots for even longer, the fight for Culp's Hill was over.

Williams' defense had been masterful. He had skillfully rotated regiments into and out of action, drawing upon his reserves as needed, and thus bringing the brigades of Col. Charles Candy and Brig. Gen. Henry Lockwood to the relief of Greene and Kane. He had even drawn upon Brig. Gen. Alexander Shaler's brigade of *VI Corps* for assistance, after it had been thoughtfully sent to his assistance by Meade at about 0800 hours. He had generally retained good control over his units and during the fight had conducted limited counterattacks to brush Rebel skirmishers back from his front. It was a difficult defense, but well conducted. Of course, it had been marred by tragedy. There had been the foolish, unnecessary, and wasteful, if spectacular heroism of the *2nd Massachusetts* and the *27th Indiana*. And the very nature of the position had resulted in many casualties from "friendly fire," as Union artillerymen were forced to shoot over the heads of their infantry in several places. Despite the great courage and dedication of the Confederate troops, the Union right remained securely anchored.

While their comrades to the left drove the enemy off Culp's Hill, the Union troops on Cemetery Ridge spent the morning of 3 July putting their positions into a state of readiness. The Union front remained much as it had been at the end of the fighting on the previous night. On the extreme right there was some cavalry and a battery posted on Wolf's Hill. About 500 yards west of these was *XI Corps*, still relatively uninjured, facing eastwards on a front of about 2,200 yards along Culp's Hill and on the ground south and east of it across Rock Creek. Supported by a fairly fresh brigade from *VI Corps*, the corps amounted to perhaps 8,500 infantrymen. Wadsworth's battered division of *I Corps*, perhaps 2,500 riflemen in all, held some 500 yards along the northern face of Culp's Hill. To Wadsworth's left, holding about 2,000 yards of front on three sides of Cemetery Hill as it jutted northwards like a great prow was Howard's unfortunate *XI Corps*, which, with 6,000 infantry, had but little fight left in it. About 300 yards to Howard's left was the main Union line along Cemetery Ridge, facing westwards and running roughly southwards. There were about 5,500 infantrymen from two relatively unscathed divisions of *II Corps*, occupying some 700 yards of front. Doubleday's battered division of *I Corps* held the 200 yards to their left with about 3,000 men. To their left was Caldwell's depleted *1st Division* of *II Corps*, holding about 900 yards of front with the assistance of two fresh brigades from *VI Corps*, for a total of a little more than 4,000 rifles. The extreme left of the Union line was held by the *V Corps*, which had been heavily engaged on the previous day but could still put over 8,000 men into a line that stretched over 2000 yards, all the way down to, and around, Big Round Top. Beyond *V Corps*, there were two brigades of cavalry on picket. In reserve were over 7,500 fresh riflemen from *VI Corps*, with one division covering the army's left

Little Round Top

flank from a position behind *V Corps* and its other two divisions behind *III Corps*, which was behind Caldwell and amounted to little more than a division in strength, with perhaps 5,000 men. In addition, Robinson's battered division of *I Corps*, with about 2,500 men was at the southern end of Cemetery Hill, able to support either *XI Corps* or *II Corps*. The entire front was liberally seasoned with artillery. There were about 32 guns on Culp's Hill, 26 facing eastwards with *XII Corps* and six more facing northwards with Wadsworth. Howard's *XI Corps* had about 55 on Cemetery Hill, 20 of which faced northwards and the rest westwards. Facing westwards along Cemetery Ridge *II Corps* had 26 pieces of artillery and there were 33 from the *Artillery Reserve* supporting Caldwell. *V Corps* had 12 guns in the line, six of which were on Little Round Top, and about 18 in reserve. Also in reserve were 48 guns with *VI Corps*, 20 with *III Corps*, and about 50 more from the *Reserve Artillery*. Altogether the *Army of the Potomac* had available perhaps 54,000 infantry and about 280 pieces of artillery—with some 6,500 artillerymen—to cover a front of over 9,000 yards. Thus, including reserves there were about six rifles per yard of front and about one gun for every 200 men. This was a comfortable average, although the line was rather thin in some areas, notably in Caldwell's sector. Most of the Union troops were under cover, even if only behind the shelter of a fence or a hastily dug trench, with their positions selected so as to give maximum fields of fire. Where the contour of the ridge permitted, there were two lines of infantry, one able to deliver fire over the heads of the other. The Union position had some flaws, but it was fairly sound. By 1100 hours Meade's preparations were complete. He had toured the front, and been generally satisfied with the dispositions of the men and guns. In addition, he had issued orders to two important subordinates who were not present on the field.

Maj. Gen. William H. French commanded about 10,000 troops at Frederick and on Maryland Heights above Harper's Ferry, and Maj. Gen. Darius Couch commanded the 32,000 militia and home guards along the Susquehanna. In the event of a victory, they were to bring pressure on the retreating enemy, French by striking against Lee's line of retreat in the Shenandoah Valley, and Couch by advancing southwards and coordinating his movements with those of the *Army of the Potomac*. Should the battle turn out badly, both officers were to fall back, French through Frederick and thence on to Washington, and Couch back across the Susquehanna to cover central Pennsylvania. This done, Meade broke for lunch, accepting the invitation of John Gibbon to share some stewed chicken with Hancock, Newton, Pleasonton, and some staff officers.

Not far from where Meade and Gibbon and the others lunched, over on the right flank of *II Corps'* front, there stood a large stand of timber known as Zeigler's Grove. About 50 yards southwest of this was the start of a low stone fence in rather poor repair, with a rail fence built over it in places. This ran roughly southwards for about 200 yards, before turning 90° to the right to run west for nearly 100 yards more, whereupon it made yet another 90° turn, to the left, to run southwards once more to end about 125 yards further on. Sheltering right behind the angle formed by this wall, directly in the middle of the corps' line was 28-year old Brig. Gen. Alexander Webb's brigade of Philadelphians from Brig. Gen. John Gibbon's *1st Division*, supported by 22-year old Lt. Alonzo H. Cushing's *A Battery, 4th Artillery*, a regular army outfit with six 3" rifled cannon. Crowning the almost bare ridge at this point was a very prominent copse of trees. It was these which had attracted Lee's eye whilst on his reconnaissance that morning, and towards which he intended to direct his attack.

Lee's army spent the morning preparing for the attack. Col. Edward P. Alexander, ablest of the artillerymen in I Corps, directed the emplacement of the guns which would fire the preliminary bombardment, assisted by Col. R. Lindsey Walker and Col. J. Thompson Brown, who commanded the artillery in III Corps and II Corps. The guns, numbering around 150, were deployed on a 7,500 yard front stretching from Oak Hill—where two very long range Whitworth cannon were located—to the Peach Orchard. Most of them were placed in two grand batteries. About half, 75, were almost hub-to-hub on a 1,300 yard front stretching from the Peach Orchard roughly northwards along Seminary Ridge, and another 35 were similarly posted on an 800 yard front about 300 yards further north along the ridge, and then yet another 26 about 300 yards further along the ridge. The balance were scattered at odd sites all along the front. Many of the guns were, in fact, poorly placed, being much too far from the main objective for their fire to be really effective. Nevertheless, Brig. Gen. William N. Pendelton, Lee's chief of artillery—an ordained Episcopal minister—approved all of Alexander's dispositions. About two dozen howitzers were held in re-

Brig. Gen. Alexander Webb

Maj. Gen. George E. Pickett

Brig. Gen. James L. Kemper

serve, to be moved forward when the preliminary bombardment was over in order to lend close artillery support to the attacking infantry. Much to everyone's surprise, the Union artillery made no effort to disrupt the work, which was readily visible from Cemetery Ridge, for Brig. Gen. Henry Hunt had decided to conserve ammunition for use in the forthcoming attack.

As the guns moved into position, the infantry also began to get ready. Under the direction of Maj. Gen. George E. Pickett they deployed on a front about 1,350 yards wide, behind the western side of heavily forested Seminary Ridge. Their lines were drawn somewhat obliquely to the Union front, roughly northeast-southwest rather than north-south. When they advanced, the troops would have to correct this. Pickett's own fresh division of Virginians was on

Brig. Gen. Richard B. Garnett

Brig. Gen. Lewis A. Armistead

the right, deployed in two waves on a front of about 825 yards, each wave consisting of two ranks with a thin line of file closers behind. On the right were 1,600 men of Brig. Gen. James L. Kemper's brigade, resting in the Peach Orchard. To its left was Brig. Gen. Richard B. Garnett with 1,500 more men. About 100 yards behind one of these brigades—it is unclear as to which—was Pickett's second line, the large brigade of Brig. Gen. Lewis A. Armistead, over 2,000 men on a front of about 500 yards. About 325 yards to Armistead's left was Heth's division, under Brig. Gen. James J. Pettigrew, which had been badly battered on the first day, but had been unengaged since. Pettigrew's men were also deployed in two waves, but rather differently. He had four brigades in line on a front of about 700 yards. Each brigade had half of each regiment deployed in the first wave and the other half in the second wave, about 100 yards to the rear. On the right were the Tennesseeans and Alabamians of Brig. Gen. James J. Archer's Brigade, now under Col. B. D. Fry, perhaps 500 men. Then came the North Carolinians of Pettigrew's own brigade, some 1,200 men under Col. J. K. Marshall, with Brig. Gen. Joseph R. Davis' 1,200 Mississippians and North Carolinians to their left, and the 500 Virginians of Col. J. M. Brockenbrough's Brigade, under Col. Robert M. Mayo. About 100 yards behind Pettigrew's troops was a third wave, consisting of two small brigades of North Carolinians from Maj. Gen. William D. Pender's Division, under Maj. Gen. Isaac Trimble, with Brig. Gen. Alfred Moore Scales' 1,200 men on the right and Brig. Gen. James H. Lane's 1,700 on the left, on a front of about 550 yards. In addition, there were two brigades from Anderson's Division deployed on a 400 yard front some 250 yards to the front and right of Pickett's Division. Brig. Gen. Cadmus A. Wilcox' 1,200 Alabamians, on the right, and Col. David Lang's 700 Floridians were to slip rightwards to cover the exposed right of the attacking brigades. Quite surprisingly, no such arrangements were made to protect the equally exposed left flank of the attacking brigades. In addition to the nine brigades actually making the attack, plus the two covering its right flank, three other brigades of Anderson's Division, Brig. Gen. Ambrose Wright's Georgians, Brig. Gen. William Mahone's Virginians, and Brig. Gen. Carnot Posey's Mississippians, were available, and were to hold themselves ready to support the attack on orders.

In the attacking brigades, each front line regiment had about 10% of its men out as skirmishers. These had filtered into the area between the two armies, to get within rifle shot of the Union lines. During the morning they had helped pull down fences and other obstacles which might hamper the orderly advance of the attacking brigades. Now they lay quietly under cover, awaiting the attack. When it came, they would open a harassing fire on Cemetery Ridge and then advance in two lines, the first about 100 yards in front of the main line and the other 100 yards in front of that. Just before the attack struck the Union lines they would be reabsorbed into their brigades.

Preparations for the attack appear to have been largely completed by about 1100 hours. The troops rested as best they could as the temperature rose into the high 80's. Some men napped, others had lunch. Wilcox, who was commanding one of the flank guard brigades, invited Garnett, who was to lead one of the attacking brigades, to a bit of lunch with one of Pickett's staff officers. It was a simple meal of tepid mutton, eked out with some very hard and very cold well water liberally doused with some very good whiskey liberated from a local farm house.

All through that hot morning there had been firing along the Cemetery Ridge position. Some of it was just casual shooting by bored soldiers or sniping by skirmishers posted in advance of the front by both sides. But there were also some artillery rounds fired, mostly for ranging purposes, and there had been one or two small artillery exchanges. At one point the *1st Company, Massachusetts Sharpshooters* went into this no-man's-land for a while to clear away some Rebel snipers. At about 1000 hours a considerable skirmish occurred at Bliss' barn, some 400 yards from the Union lines, when elements of the *12th New Jersey* ejected some Confederate skirmishers who were sniping at Cemetery Ridge. The Jerseyites no sooner withdrew, however, than the snipers returned. The *14th Connecticut* went in, retook the place, and burned it to the ground, to the accompaniment of an exchange of artillery. By about 1100 hours this skirmishing had come to an end, and only the distant sounds of the firing around Culp's Hill disturbed the air. That ended at about noon. An odd silence descended over the battlefield. On both sides the troops were remarkably confident. Their officers largely shared this sentiment, save for Longstreet himself.

Longstreet grew nervous. He remained unhappy about the entire enterprise and at one point even attempted to delegate to Alexander

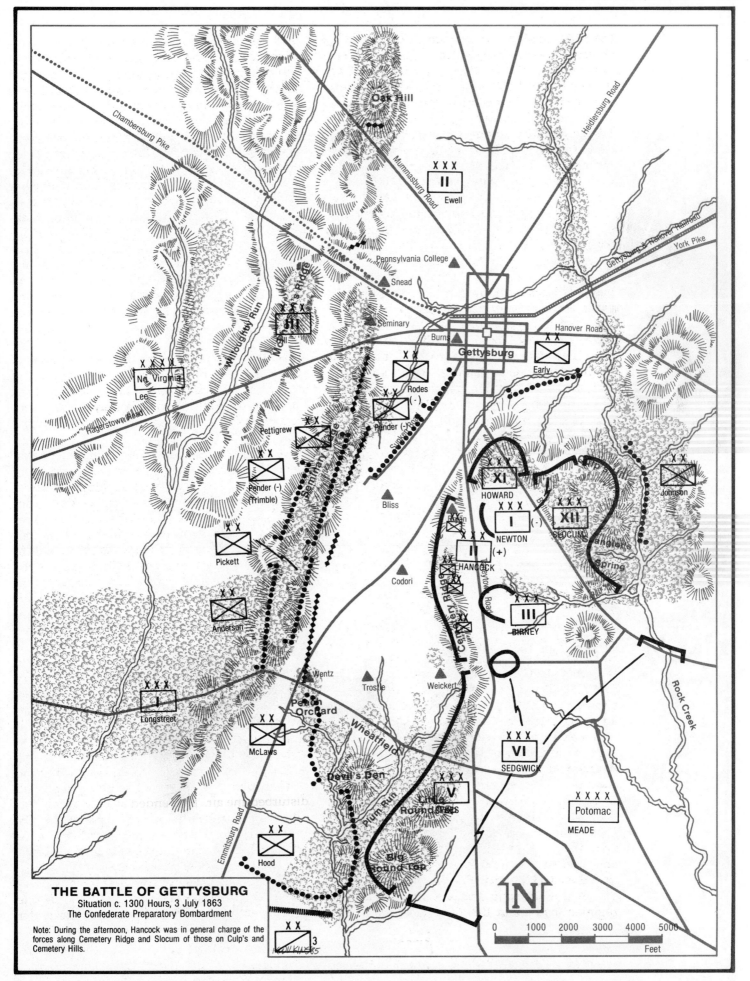

THE BATTLE OF GETTYSBURG
Situation c. 1300 Hours, 3 July 1863
The Confederate Preparatory Bombardment

Note: During the afternoon, Hancock was in general charge of the
forces along Cemetery Ridge and Slocum of those on Culp's and
Cemetery Hills.

On 3 July, Confederates wait for the end of the artillery bombardment before "Pickett's Charge."

the authority to call off the attack, writing "If the artillery does not have the effect to drive off the enemy or greatly demoralize him so as to make our effort pretty certain, I would prefer that you should not advise Gen. Pickett to make the charge," a remarkable order for a corps commander to give a colonel. Alexander penned a brief note pointing out that if there remained any doubt as to its wisdom, the attack should be called off before the bombardment began, for it would consume most of the remaining artillery ammunition. This seems to have brought Longstreet back to his senses, for his next message more reasonably instructed Alexander to notify Pickett when he thought the artillery had done its work, to which Alexander replied, "When our Arty. fire is at its best I will advise Gen. Pickett to advance." Soon after, reluctantly satisfied that all was in readiness, Longstreet passed a note to Col. J. B. Walton, his chief of artillery, "Let the batteries open." Walton passed the order to fire the agreed upon two signal rounds. At 1300 hours Capt. M. B. Miller's 3rd Company of Louisiana's Washington Artillery fired a single shot within seconds, giving the requisite second shot. Almost instantly a wave of flame and smoke leaped from the nearby batteries and spread rapidly along the line northwards, some 150 guns began the most intensive bombardment ever yet seen.

As shot and shell began to rain down, the Union front became alive with activity. Infantrymen sought cover, as artillerymen stood to their pieces. Henry Hunt, chief of artillery, on Little Round Top, tarried briefly to observe the scene, later recalling that it was "indescribably grand," and then rode off to see about bringing up more guns and more ammunition. Lingering over the remnants of lunch, Gibbon leaped up, grabbing his sword and shouting for his orderly to bring his horse. As the man led the mount up he was struck in the breast by a shell fragment, dying instantly. The horse fled. Gibbon headed for the front on foot. The imperturbable Hancock continued dictating an order concerning fresh beef for *II Corps*, the command of which he had just resumed from Gibbon. When he finished, he walked up to where Gibbon stood, to engage the latter—who had written the standard text on gunnery—in a professional discussion as to the effectiveness and purpose of the bombardment. Gibbon was of the opinion that it presaged a retreat, Hancock felt certain it was preparatory to an attack. Meanwhile, the rain of shot and shell continued. Chaplain Alanson A. Haines of the *15th New Jersey*, a *VI Corps* outfit posted in reserve, later wrote, ". . . a terrific rain of hundreds of tons of iron missiles were hurled through the air. The forests crashed and the rocks were rent under the terrible hail. . . . the smoke was impenetrable, and rolled over the scene of action, concealing all. . . ." Most Union batteries withheld their fire as ordered, though a few in *XI Corps* and those atop Little Round Top were permitted to open a selective reply, attempting to find targets through the smoke which shrouded the enemy's guns.

The barrage enveloped the entire Union front from Cemetery Hill down to the end of Cemetery Ridge. Men and horses were killed and wounded. Guns were disabled. Ammunition wagons were struck, disappearing in huge explosions, which elicited great cheers from the Rebel ranks. After the opening rounds Confederate fire tended to be a little high, so that many shots missed the ridge entirely, falling behind it. Several landed among the wagons of the *Reserve Artillery*, forcing its commander, Brig. Gen. Robert O. Tyler, to pull it back about a half mile. Other overs disrupted troop concentrations and supply wagons, and panicked rear-area personnel and sutlers. As Meade's headquarters at the Leister house was behind Cemetery Ridge, it took a number of rounds. Butterfield, the chief of staff, was wounded, other officers had close calls, and 16 of the staff's horses were killed. Meade stood fast through most of the bombardment, preferring to be at the post of danger than to change his headquarters and thereby possibly disrupt communications, though he later wandered over to Powell's Hill for a while to confer with Slocum, thereby missing most of the subsequent events. Hot as it was behind Cemetery Ridge, it was hotter still on the front itself.

Nowhere along the ridge was it hotter than on the lines of *II Corps*, where the fire of over 100 guns was concentrated. Cushing's battery alone lost half its guns, three ammunition chests went up and several men with them. The other batteries and the infantry along the stone wall suffered as well. At about 1315 hours Hancock ordered the batteries to reply, as much to bolster morale as to inflict damage upon the enemy.

Five batteries opened up with 25 guns, much to Hunt's annoyance, but with salutary effect on the troops. By then the Rebel gunners had slowed their rate of fire, coordinating it in battery volleys for better accuracy and in order to maintain a relatively high sustained fire. The Union batteries on Cemetery Hill deliberately fired intermittently, convincing the enemy that many guns had been put out of action. The bombardment continued relentlessly.

The infantrymen took the pounding well, clinging to the trembling earth in the broiling sun and shouting back and forth at each other over the thunderous roar, as their officers walked back and forth along the lines, shouting encouragement. Casualties among them were relatively light, due partially to the rudimentary shelter behind which most of them lay, and partially to the fact that many Rebel shells were duds, but mostly to the fact that overages tended to increase as time passed, a phenomenon of the necessity of relaying the guns after each shot. Indeed, the number of shells falling behind the lines was so great as to discourage the fainthearted from fleeing. It seemed safer at the front than behind it. Nevertheless, some units suffered greatly. The 25 guns in front of *II Corps* seem to have been reduced to no more than half that number by the shelling, and several had to be pulled back. Two regiments, the *108th* and *126th New York*, posted behind Lt. George A. Woodruff's *I Battery, 1st Artillery*, a regular army outfit with six 12-pounder Napoleons, discovered that Zeigler's Grove offered little protection. Shells bursting among the trees sent wood splinters in all directions, killing or wounding many. A brigade of *III Corps* had the misfortune to be the target of a number of explosive shells, with severe losses. Psychologically of course, the question as to whether the bombardment was or was not accurate was unimportant. The troops were being pounded, probably in preparation for a grand assault. No man knew when a shell might seek him out, and when the shelling did stop it would only mean that they would soon be locked in a titanic death struggle with the enemy's infantry.

The Rebel infantry was being pounded as

well, albeit more lightly, by such Union guns as were permitted to return fire. Though most of the troops were under cover, casualties were taken, in some cases in substantial numbers. The most exposed brigade, Kemper's, suffered a loss of about 15%, and Pickett's Division took perhaps 300 casualties overall. For the Confederate troops the shelling was doubly terrible, for it gave a foretaste of the pounding they would be subjected to as they advanced across the more than 1300 yards of open ground which separated them from their objective. But the men had confidence in their officers and almost literally worshiped Lee. They stood their ground, and steeled themselves for the attack, much as their foes opposite did in anticipation of it. To inspire and calm them, their commanders passed among them, ignoring shot and shell.

On Cemetery Ridge general officers also deliberately, often recklessly, exposed themselves to fire in order to steady the men. Brig. Gen. Alexander Hays, commanding the right hand division of *II Corps*, ran exuberantly from place to place behind the lines, shouting out boyish slogans, laughing, and cheering for the troops. Gibbon—who admitted to being frightened—spent part of the bombardment sitting quietly with his aide, Lt. Frank Haskell, just behind the crest of Cemetery Ridge. Later the two of them went for a stroll along the lines, pausing now and then to chat with the infantrymen crouching behind whatever shelter they could find. Then they descended part way down the west face of the slope, to sit in the shade of some elms, with a magnificent view of the enemy batteries blazing away over on Seminary Ridge. Brig. Gen. William Harrow, commanding Gibbon's left hand brigade, walked quietly up and down his lines with his arms folded, coolly ignoring the shower of fire. Brig. Gen. Alexander Webb, a New York aristocrat commanding a bunch of Irish roughs from Philadelphia, stood quietly in an exposed position, leaning on his sword, calmly puffing on a fine cigar. Doubleday sat on the ridge eating lunch and, when a shell threw some gravel on his sandwich, cracked "That sandwich will need no salt!" Howard sat down with his staff on the forward slope of Cemetery Hill, right beneath one of his batteries, watching the spectacle. And Hancock appeared everywhere, neatly uniformed and riding a magnificent black horse. At about 1400 hours he trotted down to McGilvery's silent batteries, on a rise just south of Cemetery Ridge, and ordered them into action,

despite McGilvery's reference to Hunt's orders that he withhold fire. The latter obeyed.

Over 80 guns were now replying in some fashion to the Confederate barrage. But Hunt, who was also all over the field that afternoon, was incensed. He had been busy arranging for the replacement of exhausted batteries and the movement of ammunition, and wanted no interference in his arrangements. He wished to conserve ammunition for the expected infantry assault. Moreover, having consulted with several other officers, including *XI Corps* chief of artillery, Maj. Thomas W. Osborn, he had concluded such counter-battery fire as the Union guns were already delivering had been relatively ineffective. He rode over to find Meade. Meanwhile, Gouverneur Warren had been back on Little Round Top carefully observing the fall of shot on the enemy's lines. He too concluded that the counter-battery fire was ineffective and informed Meade. Meade decided to conserve ammunition. Although Hunt failed to find Meade, he soon received orders to cease firing and issued the necessary instructions. As the batteries were widely dispersed, they received their orders at different times. Thus Union artillery fire did not cease abruptly, as if by design, but rather died down gradually, as if the gunners were running out of ammunition. By 1445 the Federal guns were silent.

In the Confederate lines, Col. Alexander, had been carefully observing the effects of the bombardment. He believed that the nearly two hours of shelling had done their work. He had noted the ragged way the Union counter-fire had slackened and then ceased and he had also noted that on the *II Corps* front some batteries seemed to have been pulled out of the line. He concluded that the Yankees were running out of ammunition, and had stopped firing to conserve what they had for the expected infantry attack. As his own batteries were themselves getting low on ammunition, he decided that the time was ripe. He hastily penned a short note to Pickett, beginning "For God's sake come quick," and followed it with two verbal messages. Then, as the Confederate guns fell silent, he waited impatiently. Alexander's written message found Pickett in conversation with Longstreet. Upon reading it, he passed it to the latter. Longstreet sat silently, message in hand. Pickett, who had twice asked Alexander if the time was ripe, spoke up, "General, shall I advance?" Unwilling to speak, Longstreet bowed his head. Pickett saluted, saying "I shall lead my division forward, sir," then he passed Longstreet a note for his fiancee, and rode off to his troops. Longstreet rode over to Alexander's post. There he discovered that the reserve guns were nowhere to be found—Pendelton had moved them to the rear and neglected to inform Alexander. This meant that the attacking infantry could not be accompanied by artillery, for the available batteries had participated in the bombardment, and had but little ammunition and tired gunners. Longstreet suggested halting the advance until the guns could be resupplied. Alexander informed him that it would take at least an hour to do so. But in an hour the effect of the bombardment would be lost. Though stunned, and now very dubious about the wisdom of the undertaking, Longstreet had no choice, the attack had to go forward immediately.

The ranks of the attacking brigades stirred.

Orders were issued. The troops prepared for battle each after his own fashion. In some units they joined their officers in prayer. In others they listened, attentively or not, as their commanders exhorted them with patriotic slogans or heartened them with folksy comments. A couple of generals conferred together briefly. Some officers assigned reliable men to keep an eye on those less so. It required but a few minutes to get the men ready, perhaps 13,000 of them. It was at most about 1505 hours. The smoke of the cannonade had drifted away and it was a bright, clear day with the temperature at 87° and the humidity high. In well-dressed ranks the troops stepped off smartly behind the shelter of Seminary Ridge, and began to advance at a steady 110 steps a minute. Brigade followed brigade and the great attack was underway.

Maj. Gen. Daniel Butterfield on his horse

TIME OF THE TIMES

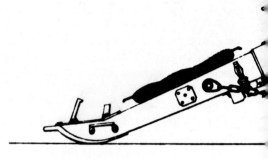

Time. Time presents a difficult problem when dealing with any pre-twentieth century event. Timepieces were not reliable, nor did standard time exist before 1884. As a result, all time was local solar time. In the case of the Gettysburg Campaign the times given for particular events by various participants frequently differ by as much as 30 minutes. A good case in point is the Confederate bombardment of Cemetery Ridge on 3 July. Col. J. B. Walton, chief of artillery of the Confederate II Corps, recorded receipt of Longstreet's order to fire at 1330 hours. Since he almost immediately ordered the signal shots to be fired, by his reckoning the bombardment could have been no later than 1335. On the other hand, Col. Edward P. Alexander, who was actually in charge of the bombardment, reported that fire commenced at almost exactly 1300 hours. And in Gettysburg, the Reverend Dr. M. Jacobs, Professor of Mathematics and Chemistry at Pennsylvania College, an inveterate note taker, recorded that it began at 1307 hours. Similar discrepancies exist in observations on the duration of the bombardment and the time of its end. Prof. Jacobs, who recorded that the bombardment ended just before 1550 hours, is probably to be most relied upon, at least for the bombardment since, he was, after all, a local resident. For other events, the matter is less easily settled. While most first hand reports agree that the attack on Cemetery Ridge on 3 July required about 20 minutes, there is little agreement on anything else. All times cited in this account have been based as much as possible on a consensus of available reports, modified by knowledge of the military practice of the period and the inherent time required for various activities to occur. Thus, all times given are essentially approximations.

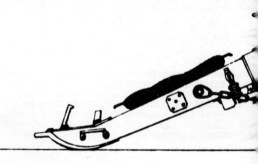

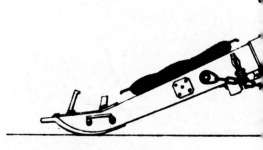

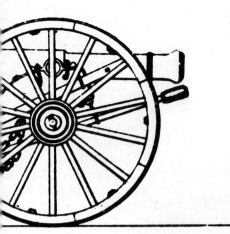

How Many Guns Did It Take?

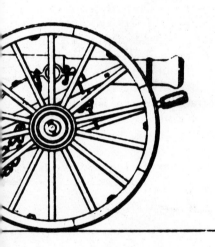

How Many Guns Bombarded Cemetery Ridge? The number of Confederate cannon which took part in the bombardment of Cemetery Ridge on 3 July is given variously as anything from 138 to 79 in accounts which are all more or less equally reliable. The figure given here is "about 150," which is basically that of Lee's chief of artillery, Rev. Brig. Gen. William N. Pendelton, who said "nearly 150." This can be reconciled rather readily with the highest number given, 179, cited by Col. Edward P. Alexander. Alexander was responsible not merely for the guns which were to conduct the bombardment, but also for about two dozen short range howitzers which were to be held in reserve and used to accompany the infantry attack. Merely deducting these from the figure of 179 brings it down into the "about 150" range. Neither is it any more difficult to reconcile this figure with the lowest estimate, 138, which is clearly too low. At least 142 guns can be definitely demonstrated to have fired during the bombardment, which is certainly within the limits of Pendleton's "nearly 150." As a result of these calculations we are left with between 142 and 155 guns. Since it is impossible to clarify the matter further, the figure "about 150" appears reasonable. On the other side of the battlefield, were apparently 106 guns deployed along Cemetery Ridge. However, only about 85 actually engaged in counter-battery fire during the bombardment, and most of these for short periods only, as Union chief of artillery Brig. Gen. Henry Hunt preferred to save ammunition for the expected infantry attack. There was room along the ridge for many more guns, but 136 or so were being held in reserve, for use once Confederate intentions became clearer.

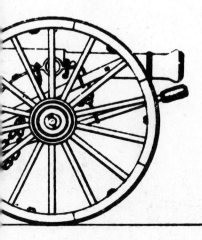

Union signalmen on Little Round Top spotted the movement almost as soon as it began. They flashed word of it to Cemetery Ridge, where the troops were already engaged in myriad activities, bringing up ammunition, fetching water, carrying off the wounded. The artillerymen were resiting the guns, cleaning and reloading them. At the sight of the advancing Confederate troops, men cried out, "Here they come! Here they come! Here comes the infantry!" Even as the Rebel line emerged from the wooded slopes of Seminary Ridge, Union commanders bolstered their line. Hays, commanding the right end of the ridge, packed both brigades of his division into his front, intermingling them so as to get the maximum number of men on the line. Alexander Webb moved most of his brigade to the stone wall along the angle, where Alonzo Cushing, already twice wounded, directed the resiting of his three remaining pieces while with one hand he attempted to keep his intestines from spilling out of a wound in his abdomen. Gibbon, their division commander, brought up additional guns and positioned two regiments closer to the front as a ready reserve. Soon, on a thousand yards of front from Zeigler's Grove southwards, there were some 5,750 infantrymen in 27 regiments, supported by about 500 artillerymen with 23 guns. Out on picket duty about 150 yards in front of the lines were the *8th Ohio*, along the

Emmitsburg Road on the right, and there were skirmishers strung out along the front in the open fields. The men were steady, if anxious, as they ignored the occasional artillery round which still came over and watched almost with admiration as the Rebels advanced. Haskell would later write, "More than half a mile their front extends, more than a thousand yards the dull gray masses deploy, man touching man, rank pressing rank, and line supporting line. The red flags wave, their horsemen gallop up and down; the arms of eighteen thousand men, barrel and bayonet, gleam in the sun, a sloping forest of flashing steel. Right on the move as with one soul, in perfect order, without impediment of ditch, or wall or stream, over ridge and slope, through orchard and meadow, and cornfield, magnificent, grim, irresistible."

The attacking brigades had not only to advance under artillery fire, but also had both to shift front and to close the considerable gap between them if they were to strike the Union lines with full force. Their peculiar deployment, angled obliquely at about 20° to the Union lines, with Pickett's men about 325 yards in advance of, and to the right, of Pettigrew's, had been dictated by the terrain. Seminary Ridge, behind which they formed ranks, was angled thusly. And right up against the eastern side of the ridge, in the middle of the ground over which they had to advance, was Spangler's Woods, a

Confederate dead, bloated from several days in the sun

small but overgrown area. These had dictated the deployment, and now the troops had to engage in various march maneuvers to correct their lines. Union Lt. Col. Edmund Rice, whose *19th Massachusetts* lay right in the path of the attack, on the left of the *II Corps* front, noted that many of his men were impressed by "the grandeur of [an] attack of so many thousand men."

As the Yankees on Cemetery Ridge looked on with amazement, Pickett's men marched directly forward for about 450 yards, and then, even as they came under artillery fire, imperturbably faced 45° to their left to advance for another 250 yards. At this point their left flank halted in a depression which offered some cover, while their right advanced some 300 yards more, pivoting some 30° to dress ranks with the left. Meanwhile, Pettigrew's men advanced, moving about 850 yards and also halted in the same depression. By this time, roughly 1515 hours, the two columns were no more than 300 yards apart. The shallow ground gave the troops some respite from the increasing volume of artillery fire, and they paused for a minute or

two to reform their ranks and dress their lines. They were but 700 yards from Cemetery Ridge. In addition to the 23 guns which were firing into their front from Cemetery Ridge, the men were being enfiladed by 29 guns from Cemetery Hill on their left. There were 43 more guns on their right, on Little Round Top and in the grand battery positioned at the lower end of the ridge, but these were as yet unable to fire effectively, for Pickett's men were partially sheltered by the berm along which ran the Emmitsburg Road. Surprisingly the troops in front took the fewest losses, for the guns on Cemetery Ridge were virtually out of long range ammunition. Those on the left flank fared less well. Subject to the attentions of the guns on Cemetery Hill, Brockenborough's small brigade was getting the worst of the pounding. Enfilading fire repeatedly tore through the ranks, killing and wounding many. The brigade was keeping together well, the men closing ranks to fill the gaps, but they had suffered grievously and morale was becoming brittle. By this time Rebel skirmishers were trading shots with their Union counter-

Above: *Dead Confederate infantryman in the wheatfield shows the devastating effects of artillery fire*

parts. The advancing rebels kept on. Pickett's men now faced somewhat leftwards, and advanced another 250 yards, emerging over the berm of the Emmitsburg Road to receive the full attentions of the batteries on the Union left, while Pettigrew's men pressed on for another 125 yards. Within minutes, at about 1520, the columns converged, with Pickett's left meeting Pettigrew's right. All through the advance Confederate officers had been keeping their men together. Longstreet, observing from the rear, had several times passed messages to Pickett and Pettigrew. Pickett decided that victory was at hand, and sent back for reinforcements to follow-up the imminent break-through. Both he and Pettigrew stayed close to their men, riding back and forth among the lines, with a steady stream of staff officers to keep them fully informed of all developments. The injured Garnett—one of the few officers to participate in the attack mounted—rode at the head of his men. Armistead, who had placed his old black hat on the end of his sword when the advance began, to hold high overhead as an improvised flag, found, much to the amusement of his men, that the point kept piercing the cloth so that he repeatedly had to put it back at the tip. Nevertheless, despite this light note the going had been grim. Many had been killed and wounded, some men had taken to the rear.

Even as the two columns converged, Union infantry began to get into action. The *8th Ohio* had formed up directly beneath Cemetery Ridge, a few yards off to the left of the flank of the attacking columns. Its commander, Lt. Col. Franklin Sawyer, had 200 of his own men, plus 75 stray skirmishers from the *125th New York*. He formed them into a single line perhaps 100 yards wide, and attacked right into the flank of over 12,000 battle hardened veterans. It was audacious—and it worked. Sawyer's men headed right for the flank of Brockenborough's already shaken brigade. The brigade broke even before contact was made, officers and men alike fleeing to the rear in disorder, losing three colors and many prisoners. As Pickett attempted to shift some regiments to cover the flank, Sawyer pulled his men back, placing them behind a fence, from whence they began laying down a large volume of rifle fire. The advance continued. At the point of convergence Pettigrew's men faced slightly left, and Pickett's right.

Side-by-side now, the two divisions plunged forward, absorbing their skirmishers. The troops began to pick up the pace as they covered the last 400 yards to the Union lines. As

CHARGE!

The Confederate Order of Attack. The deployment of the Union regiments along Cemetery Ridge has never been in doubt. Not so the precise order of the regiments within each of the attacking Confederate brigades, for no original documents survive which contain them. Several efforts have been made to reconstruct the order of battle for some brigades by means of interviews with participants and careful perusal of various memoirs. As a result there is a general consensus on the matter. What follows is a reconstruction of the order of the regiments in the brigades which constituted the attacking column, given from left to right and front to rear.

PETTIGREW'S [HETH'S] DIVISION
Brockenbrough's Brigade: 55th Va.—47th Va.—40th Va.—22nd Va. Bn
Davis's Brigade: 2nd Miss.—55th N.C.—42nd Miss.—11th Miss.
Marshall's [Pettigrew's] Brigade: 11th N.C.—26th N.C.—47th N.C.—52nd N.C.
Fry's [Archer's] Brigade: 5th Ala.—7th Tenn.—14th Tenn.—13th Ala.—1st Tenn.

TRIMBLE'S [PENDER'S] DIVISION
Lane's Brigade: 33rd N.C.—18th N.C.—28th N.C.—37th N.C.—7th N.C.
Scales' Brigade: 38th N.C.—13th N.C.—34th N.C.—22nd N.C.—16th N.C.
Pickett's Division
Garnett's Brigade: 56th Va.—28th Va.—19th Va.—18th Va.—8th Va
Kemper's Brigade: 3rd Va.—7th Va.—11th Va.—24th Va.
Armistead's Brigade: 38th Va.—57th Va.—53rd Va.—9th Va.—14th Va.

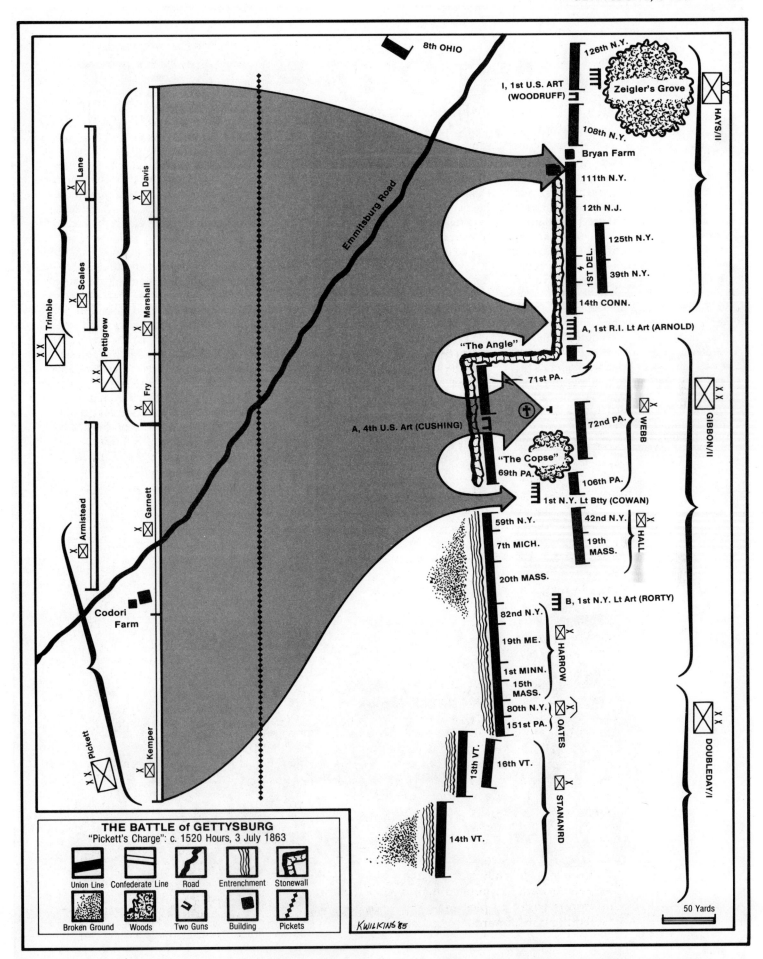

8th OHIO

126th N.Y.

Zeigler's Grove

I, 1st U.S. ART
(WOODRUFF)

HAYS/II

108th N.Y.

Bryan Farm

111th N.Y.

12th N.J.

125th N.Y.

39th N.Y.

14th CONN.

1ST DEL.

A, 1st R.I. Lt Art (ARNOLD)

"The Angle"

71st PA.

72nd PA.

WEBB

GIBBON/II

A, 4th U.S. Art (CUSHING)

"The Copse"

69th PA.

106th PA.

1st N.Y. Lt Btty (COWAN)

59th N.Y.

42nd N.Y.

19th MASS.

HALL

7th MICH.

20th MASS.

B, 1st N.Y. Lt Art (RORTY)

82nd N.Y.

19th ME.

HARROW

1st MINN.
15th MASS.

80th N.Y.

OATES

DOUBLEDAY/I

151st PA.

13th VT.

16th VT.

STANANRD

14th VT.

Emmitsburg Road

8th OHIO

Lane

Davis

Scales

Marshall

Trimble

Pettigrew

Fry

Armistead

Garnett

Codori
Farm

Pickett

Kemper

THE BATTLE of GETTYSBURG
"Pickett's Charge": c. 1520 Hours, 3 July 1863

Union Line	Confederate Line	Road	Entrenchment	Stonewall
Broken Ground	Woods	Two Guns	Building	Pickets

K.WILKINS 85

50 Yards

PICKING OUT PICKETT

Where was Pickett? After the failure of the attack on Cemetery Ridge, Maj. Gen. George Pickett came in for considerable criticism concerning his conduct during it. Much of the recriminations revolved around his location at various critical moments during the attack, most notably at the time of the final rush up the ridge. A number of hostile accounts suggested, and many flatly stated, that he deliberately avoided the post of danger, preferring to hang back rather than lead his men into the mouths of the Yankee artillery. This is hardly fair, since it was the task of brigadier generals to lead the men forward, as was ably done by Garnett, Kemper, and particularly Armistead. The post dictated by duty for a major general was in the rear, directing the advance and shifting brigades about as needed. This Pickett did well. He kept the advance going, issued the appropriate orders for dressing the lines and changing the direction of march. He also maintained contact with Longstreet and his brigadiers by a steady stream of messengers. During the final moments of the attack he was at the Codori farm, about 200 yards from Cemetery Ridge, about in the center of where his division was supposed to be, although Kemper's brigade had slipped northwards. The only fault—and that a grievous one—which can be attributed to Pickett was at the climax of the attack. Pickett stood alone near the Codori house, having dispatched all four of his aides on various missions. As the Union troops on the fringes of the area under attack streamed down the ridge to take the attackers in the flanks, he appears to have decided that the game was up. He remounted his horse and rode slowly off to the rear, leaving his men to fend for themselves in their retirement. How different the conduct of Brig. Gen. James J. Pettigrew. Pettigrew too properly remained in the rear of his division as it advanced, keeping in contact with Longstreet and his brigadiers. But when the assault faltered he remained on the field, directing the retirement, trying to get a rear guard organized. Despite a wound in the hand he stayed with the troops until the end, being among the last to regain the security of Seminary Ridge. It was against Pettigrew that Pickett's performance was measured and found wanting, though to blame him for the failure of the attack is unreasonable, for his personal failure came after the climax of the action.

the intrepid Hancock rode among them fully exposed to the enemy—who gallantly refrained from firing upon him—Union skirmishers fired off a few last rounds, forcing Garnett's brigade to halt and deliver a volley, and then scuttled for safety up the ridge. The firing from Cemetery Ridge became more intense as the artillery began to deliver canister, great shotgun-like bursts containing scores of oversized musket balls, which tore wide swathes in the ranks. As their officers exhorted them to maintain a steady pace, the Confederate infantry pressed on, now so close to the front that the batteries on Cemetery Hill and at the south end of the Ridge could no longer fire upon them. They began to receive rifle fire. Brig. Gen. George J. Stannard's brigade of 1,950 Vermonters from Doubleday's division was positioned on the Union left, a bit forward of the main lines and was the first to open fire, at about 1525 hours. Though none of the men had been in action before the previous day, they were as steady as veterans, putting out volley after volley into the front of Kemper's brigade. Unable to take the fire, the Virginians drifted to their left, narrowing the attacking front from a little more than a thousand yards to less than 600. The entire weight of the attack was directed right at the troops on either side of the conspicuous copse of trees near the angle in the stone wall atop the ridge, right in the center of which was Webb's brigade of Philadelphians and Cushing's depleted battery.

At 250 yards every infantryman II Corps who was able to do so, opened up with his rifle. At the same time, the artillerymen began firing double loads of canister. A storm of lead smashed into the face of the advancing troops. Hundreds fell. Confederate cohesion, so magnificently displayed as they advanced for nearly 20 minutes under fire, dissipated. Men broke ranks, clustering together about their officers and their flags. Some fled, but most pressed on,

The Bryan Farm on Cemetery Ridge was the scene of fighting on 3 July when Confederate troops assaulted the ridge.

giving a cheer and running up the slope. Davis' and Pettigrew's brigades, and portions of Fry's drove for the Union right, held by Hays' men. Kemper's brigade was forced further leftwards by fire from its front and flank, delivered by the Stannard's Vermonters and Gibbon's left-hand brigades, under Brig. Gen. William Harrow and Col. Norman J. Hall. Meanwhile, in the center, Garnett's men, and most of Fry's were pressed forward towards Webb and the angle, with Armistead's following behind. Kemper fell. Garnett was enveloped in a shell burst from which his bloodied horse alone emerged. Yet still the troops pressed on. Atop Cemetery Ridge the determined horde that began sweeping up the deceptively shallow-looking slope intimidated the faint hearted. Some men attempted to flee until their officers brought them to their senses, sometimes with bared steel.

On the extreme right of *II Corps'* line, in front of Zeigler's grove, Brig. Gen. Alexander Hays had intermingled several regiments from his division. Col. Sawyer's *8th Ohio* and the stray skirmishers from the *126th New York*, were still firing into the enemy flank from behind a fence in the fields, about 200 yards from Zeigler's Grove. Hays had two New York regiments directly in front of the grove, supported by Woodruff's regular army battery. To their left, there were some farm buildings belonging to Abram Bryan, a black man who had wisely fled with his wife and two teenaged sons when the Rebels invaded Pennsylvania. Among these, and along the upper reaches of the stone wall were the *111th New York* and the *12th New Jersey,* the latter armed with old smooth bore muskets which they had loaded with buckshot. To their left were the *1st Delaware* and the *14th Connecticut,* two companies of which carried Sharps breechloading rifles. The left of the division rested on Capt. William A. Arnold's battery, *A, 1st Rhode Island Light Artillery* with six 3"-rifles. Two more New York regiments were positioned immediately behind those on the line. Gallantly led by Col. J. K. Marshall, Pettigrew's own brigade struck here, with Davis' to its lefts, and Lane's, from the second line, yet further left, where Brockenborough's ought to have been. The thirteen regiments of North Carolinians and Mississippians had been reduced to small bands huddled around their colors and their officers, but they swept up the slope bravely, to receive a storm of fire full in the face. Despite the fact that they were taking fire in their flank from the *8th Ohio,* some of Lane's men managed to get among the Bryan farm buildings between Zeigler's Grove and the stone wall, only to be pinned and surrounded by the *111th New York,* the survivors eventually surrendering. The 26th North Carolina attacked into the front of Arnold's battery. It disintegrated under a wave of lead, only two men reaching the Union lines, one still bearing the colors; holding their fire, the Yankees induced the two to surrender. Some say that, before falling, a private from the 11th Mississippi planted the colors on the Federal lines; others that not a man of the regiment got within ten feet. Though not 150 men followed Lt. Col. J. A. Graves up the slope, the 47th North Carolina almost breached the lines, only to be pinned to the forward slope. Unable to

advance or withdraw, they too were soon forced to surrender. The right side of the Union line had held. As the survivors of the attack attempted to retire, they were subject once more to the withering fire which they had faced as they advanced.

The left of the front along Cemetery Ridge was that held by elements of Doubleday's division of *I Corps*, with Stannard's Vermonters and a regiment each of New Yorkers and Pennsylvanians. Their fire had driven Kemper's Brigade leftwards, toward the Union center. Thinking fast, Stannard saw a magnificent opportunity before him. If he could bring his brigade into the fields, he might take the attackers in their flank as they smashed into the center. The imperturbable Hancock saw the opportunity as well and, putting spurs to horse, rushed along the rear of the lines to issue the necessary orders. Gibbon too, sensed it, and began running towards his left, where lay the largely unscathed brigades of Harrow and Hall. But the maneuver would take time, and seconds now counted.

On Gibbon's right was Webb's brigade, holding the angle in the stone wall with two regiments—the *69th* and *71st Pennsylvania*—supported by two guns from the wounded Cushing's battery, *A, 4th Artillery*, and five 3"-rifles of Capt. Andrew Cowan's *1st Battery, New York Light Artillery*. It wasn't much, perhaps 275 rifles

A romantic — and highly innaccurate — portrait of "Pickett's Charge" as seen from Cemetery Ridge

Romanticized painting of the "High Water Mark of the Confederacy" shows Armistead with his famous hat about to fall mortally wounded.

and seven guns to hold more than 250 yards of front, though some 450 men from the *72nd* and *106th Pennsylvania* were just coming up. It was almost exactly 1530 hours when, giving the famed "Rebel yell" for the first time in the charge, fifteen regiments of the decimated but still game Virginians, Tennesseeans, and Alabamians of Fry, Garnett, and Armistead smashed right into Webb's Philadelphia Irishmen. With the mass of Rebel infantry swarming up the ridge, most of the *71st Pennsylvania* broke, fleeing 100 yards to the rear before being rallied by Lt. Haskell at sword's point, with a little help from Webb. As they fled, the Rebel infantry came over the top of the stone and rail fence.

The gallant Cushing—who had to hold some fainthearted gunners to their posts at pistol point—ran his last gun right up to the fence to fire his last round of canister right into the attacking ranks and then fell dead with his third wound of the day, a bullet through the mouth which tore through the back of his head. Hat still on the tip of his sword, Armistead reached the fence. Crying "Give them cold steel!" he led his men over it. Webb attempted to throw in the *72nd Pennsylvania*. It delivered a heavy fire but, despite both Webb and Haskell, refused to advance. As more Confederates came over the wall, Armistead's heroic band overran Cushing's guns, fighting hand to hand with the surviving gunners, under Sgt. Frederick Fuger, and some heroic holdouts of the *71st Pennsylvania*, under Sgt. Maj. John Stockton, who gradually fell back.

The issue hung in the balance. As Haskell rode to bring up Hall's brigade, Webb walked calmly across the front, passing to the right, and within yards, of Armistead, to get to the left of his brigade. There the *69th Pennsylvania*, having denied its right to the breakthrough, was calmly pouring fire into the enemy. He ordered it to fire without regard for friendly troops, and brought a hundred men of the *106th Pennsylvania* to their support. This daring measure momentarily held the growing band of Confederates in the angle. Armistead fell mortally wounded in front of an abandoned gun about 30 yards inside the Union lines. But the Rebels were in the angle in strength. Rebel infantrymen began drifting into the copse of trees. If more came over the wall and if they could break out of the angle, the entire front might split. Still more troops would be needed.

Cowan's *1st New York Light Artillery Battery*, having with the aid of Hall's men beaten off an attack from a large but disorganized group of Kemper's men, fired into the mass from the left. Hunt rode up. Shouting at Cowan to avoid hitting friendly troops, he emptied his pistol at the enemy until his mount was hit and he went down. Hall knew what to do without awaiting orders. As Haskell rode up, he wheeled three of his regiments—the *59th New York*, the *7th Michigan*, and the *20th Massachusetts*—90° to their right, and threw them into the copse of trees on the right of the *69th Pennsylvania*. Hancock came up behind the *19th Massachusetts* and the *42nd New York*. Reining in his mount, he pointed towards the copse, shouting "Forward, men! Forward! Now's your chance!" Col. Rice got his regiment moving instantly, with the New Yorkers following soon after. Minutes later, Brig. Gen. William Harrow, to Hall's left, brought his three regiments and two companies of sharpshooters into the trees as well. Soon after Col. Theodore Gates brought up his *80th New York* and the *151st Pennsylvania*, from Doubleday's front. A furious fight developed as the Confederates sought to break out of the angle. Gibbon was hit, falling unconscious. Hancock's saddle was struck and pieces of wood and leather and nail were driven into his thigh. Minutes earlier the loss of these two might have had decisive results, but no longer. The Confederacy's moment had passed.

As the Federal regiments crowded into the copse of trees sorted themselves out, an overwhelming volume of fire swept the angle. The Union line advanced. A Confederate gun near the Peach Orchard opened up, sending a shot tearing through the crowded Union ranks. Desperate hand-to-hand fighting ensued. Within minutes it was over, as hundreds of rebels surrendered in the angle and before the stone wall, and yet more hundreds fled as Meade looked on, cheering and waving to his troops. The Confederate tide had crested, and begun to ebb. The time was perhaps 1540 hours. It had taken perhaps ten minutes from the time Armistead reached the stone wall for the Union troops to smash the attack. Yet even if Armistead's daring band—which at its peak numbered perhaps 350 men—had broken through the line, it would have meant little, for nearly 13,000 men—the bulk of the Union reserve—were converging on the spot on Meade's orders.

Even as the Confederate regiments recoiled from Cemetery Ridge, they came under new pressure. Hays threw the *8th Ohio*, the *126th New York*, and a mass of skirmishers in against the left flank of the retreating Confederates, while Stannard brought the *16th* and *13th Ver-*

And His Dying Words Were...

Armstead's Last Words. As Confederate Brig. Gen. Lewis A. Armistead lay mortally wounded in the middle of "the angle" atop Cemetery Ridge he uttered a cry for help, adding the phrase "as the son of a widow." As the Rebel tide was ebbing by then, some men on the line received permission to go to his aid. A romantic tradition has it that one of them was 1st Sgt. Frederick Fuger, of Cushing's battery. Fuger had known Armistead in the pre–war army, when both had served in the *6th Infantry* and in Utah. According to one of Fuger's fellow gunners, Christopher Smith, Armistead said to Fuger, "I thought it was you sergeant. If I had known that you were in command of that battery I would never have led the charge against you." They carried out Armistead to the rear. A surgeon was summoned. When he arrived, Capt. Henry H. Bingham saw that he could do nothing for the dying man. He offered to see that his personal effects were sent to his family. Meanwhile, a messenger came up. He explained that he was from Maj. Gen. Abner Doubleday, who had heard that a Confederate general—possibly Longstreet himself—had been captured. The messenger politely inquired as to Armistead's rank. Armistead responded by saying, "Tell General Doubleday in a few minutes I shall be where there is no rank." Bingham and Armistead engaged in some small talk, and Armistead learned that his old friend Hancock had been wounded at about the same time he had been shot. Armistead, whom Bingham described as being "seriously wounded, completely exhausted, and seemingly broken spirited" gave his watch for safekeeping to one of the onlooking officers. Then he said "Say to General Hancock for me, that I have done him, and you all, a grievous injury, which I shall regret the longest day I live." Then Armistead was carried to a field hospital, where he died on 5 July.

Although many observers have attempted to discredit or place sinister connotations on them, there seems no reason to doubt the authentiticity of any of the words attributed to Armistead in his last hours. The phrase "as the son of a widow," is, of course, a Masonic password, but there is nothing mysterious in that, nor do we have to attribute Armistead's rescue to brother Masons, as he was obviously a high ranking officer. Given that grievously wounded men often utter strange phrases, the words are more likely to have been inspired by the pain from which Armistead was suffering at the time than any sinister conspiracy. The exchange of words with Sgt. Fuger is also probable, for by the end of the fighting in "the angle" the gallant sergeant was apparently on the line with the *72nd Pennsylvania*, whose troops it was that brought Armistead to the rear. Few have connected Armistead with Doubleday's account, yet it seems reasonable to do so, in as much as Armistead was the only Confederate general taken that day. The greatest controversy has been inspired by Bingham's account, for to some the words attributed to Armistead suggested that, in the hour of his death a Confederate general had denied the righteousness of the Southern cause. Northerners made much of this, sometimes embroidering upon it to make it sound stronger. Southerners, on the other hand, reacted to the statement by denying that Armistead had said any such thing. Despite this, Dr. Bingham's account has a ring of truth to it, and was reported rather casually. Indeed, after the war, when his veracity was under attack from unreconstructed Rebels, he wrote out a careful statement in which he described the circumstances and events in great detail, even noting that he was uncertain as to whether Armistead had said "regret" or "repent". This ought to have stilled all criticism, but the matter had passed beyond reason

and become part of the myth of the "Just Cause." These words, and their clumsy construction, ought to be taken for what they were, the painful utterances of a dying man who had no personal animosities towards those of his friends against whom he found himself fighting.

mont against their right. Pressed from behind by Gibbon's men, the retreating Rebels were now subject to a murderous cross-fire, even as they were pounded by artillery from Cemetery Ridge in their rear. The terrible battering was relieved only when the Confederate right flank guard brigades, those of Wilcox and Lang, tardily came up, supported by a resumption of artillery fire from Seminary Ridge. These diverted Stannard's attention briefly, and by the time he had beaten them off, the main body of the attackers had reached the safety of the Confederate lines, where Lee came forward to meet them and offer his apologies. By about 1600 hours it was all over. The great attack by means of which the Army of Northern Virginia was to smash the *Army of the Potomac* had itself been smashed.

Altogether "Pickett's Charge" had taken no more than an hour. No one kept an accurate record, but it appears that, including many hundreds of prisoners, more than 60% of the attacking force had become casualties, some 6,500 men, one of the highest loss rates in the war. There was but one uninjured officer above the grade of captain in the brigades of Kemper, Garnett, and Armistead. Some regiments had losses as high as 85%. In contrast, Union casualties had been comparatively light, totalling perhaps 1,500 men, roughly 25% of those engaged. Gibbon's division, which bore the brunt of the attack, lost about 40%, but no other major unit lost more than about 18%. In the ultimate contemporary measure of victory, Union troops had captured at least 28 Confederate battle flags—possibly as many as 33—without the loss of a single one, and had lost temporarily only two cannon. Firing continued for a while, but as the afternoon wore on the battlefield fell silent once more. As surgeons offered what help they could to the wounded, the troops began to savor the results of the day's action.

On the Union side there was great elation. It had been a hard fight, but at the moment of crisis everyone had done his duty. The troops themselves had the most praise for Hancock, who was mobbed by cheering men even as he lay in a hospital bed—game as ever, he dictated a report to Meade, in which he recommended an immediate counterattack, and then attempted to address the troops before passing out. But it was the *Army of the Potomac* itself that was the victor. A fine, skilled, professional force, Gettysburg was the first battle in which it was ably led on all levels and permitted to fight to the end. Meade, neither as brilliant a strategist, nor as able an administrator, nor as inspir-

Lee meets his returning troops in the aftermath of "Pickett's Charge," 3 July.

ing a leader as either McClellan or Hooker, was, unlike either of them, willing to fight. The troops had been greatly disappointed with the results of Chancellorsville. When Meade gave them their chance, they took it. Almost everyone had performed well, occasionally magnificently. Only one incident marred the day's success.

Brig. Gen. Judson Kilpatrick, commanding the *3rd Cavalry Division*, on picket duty covering the Union left flank, had been instructed to harass the exposed Confederate right flank. Through the afternoon, his troopers had a modest degree of success, forcing Hood to put several regiments into line to cover his flank. At about 1730 hours, Kilpatrick learned of the successful defense of Cemetery Ridge. He decided to attack. Overruling the objections of one of the most brilliant young officers in the army, Brig. Gen. Elon J. Farnsworth—whom he virtually accused of cowardice—he ordered a charge directly into the face of Hood's infantry. The result was predictable. Though nearly 100 prisoners were taken, about 20% of the 300 troopers from the *1st Vermont Cavalry* fell, and Farnsworth himself was killed, taking five wounds. In considerable compensation for the disaster, was the fact that Brig. Gen. David Gregg's *2nd Cavalry Division* had successfully clashed with Stuart's cavalry several miles east of the main action, on

the Rummel Farm, between the York Pike and the Hanover Road, beating them off and once again demonstrating that Southern superiority in the mounted arm was a thing of the past. Thus, Kilpatrick's foolhardy venture did not mar the general elation in the Union ranks. When Meade appeared on Cemetery Ridge, within minutes of the breaking of the attack, the troops cheered him.

There was no cheering in the Confederate ranks, only great dejection. Despite the skill, determination, and courage of its men, the Army of Northern Virginia had failed in its most severe test, one which it had undertaken with the greatest confidence. And that, perhaps more

The "cavalry action" at Gettysburg on 3 July, which actually occurred about a mile east of the main battlefield

Farnsworth's charge

THE THIRD DAY
Who Won?

The Third Day. The final day's fighting was clearly a Union victory. For this, Lee must ultimately bear a large share of the responsibility, perhaps all of it. Despite the heroic way in which the troops conducted it, the attack had been unwise, possibly even a foregone conclusion. The battle had been lost on the second day, when, despite horrendous losses, the *Army of the Potomac* had attained the security of Cemetery Ridge. Lee ought to have heeded Longstreet's advice and avoided a direct clash entirely. To have attempted a frontal assault against superior forces was at best foolhardy, given the numerous demonstrations of the superiority of the defense over the offense which had occurred throughout the entire war. Just eight months earlier the *Army of the Potomac* had itself essayed a frontal assault at Fredericksburg, albeit on less favorable terrain, only to be repulsed at great cost with but trivial losses to the Confederacy. On 3 July Meade held a somewhat less favorable position than Lee had held at Fredericksburg, but with substantially more men. The best course of action for 3 July would have been to pull Ewell's corps back over to the left and stand on the defense along Seminary Ridge, tempting Meade into an attack. Should Meade have made such an effort, the result could well have been a Union debacle. And if he failed to attack, or tried to engage in some fancy maneuvers, Lee could have pulled his army back across a series of readily defensible ridge-lines until he could break off contact and retire.

In the *Army of the Potomac* it seems as if everyone did well. Meade, who after all had only been in command five days, kept his head, lightly supervising his subordinates, all of whom were doing their jobs properly, and moved his reserves as he saw the need develop. The true hero of the day was undoubtedly Hancock, who was constantly at the post of danger and did exactly what had to be done to break Lee's grand attack. Alpheus Williams had done nicely in beating off Ewell's blow on Culp's Hill earlier in the day, though Slocum's ill-advised interference had caused one serious reverse. The other corps commanders had all done their part in essentially support roles. Hays, Gibbon, and Doubleday had handled their divisions well, certainly contributing to the successful outcome of the fight. Several brigade commanders—Webb, Hall, Harrow, Stannard, Greene, and Kane in particular—had performed with great resourcefulness and courage.

In the end, battles go to the side which had made the fewest mistakes. At Gettysburg, for whatever the reason, that side was the Union side. This was one reason that the battle assumed the importance which it did, for Lee's defeat at Gettysburg was not merely a tactical or strategic reverse. It was also a moral disaster. The *Army of the Potomac* had long been superior to the Army of Northern Virginia in numbers and equipment. It had several times already proven itself equal to its foe in technical skill and courage. And now it had proven equal in leadership.

Date	Action
JUNE	
5	Franklin's Crossing
9	Brandy Station
9	Stevensburg
13	Winchester
13	Berryville
14	Stephenson's Depot
14	Martinsburg
17	Aldie
17–18	Middleburg
18	Middleburg
21	Middleburg
21	Upperville
22	McConnelsburg
26	Hanover Court House
27	Mummsburg
28	Rockville
28	Mechanicsburg
28	Harrisburg
29	Westminster
30	Hanover
30	Chambersburg Pike

The Principal Battles, Engagements, and Skirmishes of the Gettysburg Campaign
1 June–26 July 1863

Various official sources list as many as 106 battles, engagements, actions, and skirmishes occurring in Virginia, West Virginia, Maryland, and Pennsylvania related to the Gettysburg Campaign. There were probably many more. Most of these were small affairs, often involving no more than a cavalry patrol on either side, and few had any major impact on the course of events. This table includes only actions in which at least 1,000 men were involved on at least one side. It should be kept in mind that many of these affairs have more than one name, and some could be considered different aspects of a single larger incident, while others could be broken down into two or more separate ones. The name used is that most commonly applied, or that of a nearby locale in the case of unnamed incidents. Figures for numbers engaged are in thousands. Casualties are given in parentheses in absolute numbers, and have had to be estimated in cases for which there is no reliable data available. An asterisk (*) is used to indicate the victor, in such cases where a clear winner emerged.

Forces Engaged				
Union	Confederate	JULY		Union	Confederate

Union	Confederate	Date	Battle	Union	Confederate
2.0 (40)	1.0 (50)	1–4	Gettysburg	88.5 (23,050)*	63.9 (28,500)
8.0 (825)	9.0 (300)	1	Carlisle	3.5 (12)	4.5 (0)
3.0 (100)*	0.5 (225)	2	Baltimore Cross Roads	6.0 (100)	2.0 (100)
7.0 (100)	14.0 (100)*	3	Fairfield	0.5 (242)	1.5 (150)*
1.8 (50)*	9.6 (50)	3	Rummel Farm	4.5 (254)*	6.0 (230)
8.8 (4500)	10.0 (150)*	3	South Anna River	10.0 (100)	2.5 (100)
1.3 (200)	9.6 (10)*	4	Fairfield	2.5 (30)*	0.7 (100)
2.1 (305)*	1.0 (120)	4	Monterey Gap	1.0 (50)	1.0 (50)
0.3 (175)	1.0 (50)*	4	Emmitsburg	0.6 (70)	1.0 (80)
2.0 (50)*	1.0 (100)	5	Fairfield Gap	2.2 (100)*	1.0 (100)
7.0 (150)*	4.0 (200)	6	Fairfield Gap	8.0 (50)*	5.0 (150)
6.8 (200)*	3.8 (300)	6	Falling Waters	2.0 (10)*	0.5 (20)
0.1 (2)	1.8 (0)*	7	Greencastle Road	2.0 (20)*	3.5 (150)
1.0 (50)*	0.6 (150)	7	Harper's Ferry	1.0 (20)	0.5 (20)
0.8 (200)	6.0 (20)*	7	Boonesborough	5.0 (50)*	2.0 (100)
0.7 (400)	1.5 (25)*	8	Williamsport	7.0 (120)*	3.5 (200)
0.5 (10)	1.8 (0)*	9	Boonesborough	6.0 (100)	5.0 (100)
1.0 (?)	1.8 (?)	11	Hagerstown	3.0 (50)	2.5 (75)
0.1 (50)	0.5 (12)*	12	Funkstown	3.0 (75)	2.5 (75)
1.5 (200)*	0.8 (150)	13	Conococacheague Line	5.0 (200)	5.0 (200)
0.5 (?)	1.0 (?)	14	Falling Waters	7.5 (300)*	3.0 (900)
		16	Sheppardstown	1.5 (104)	0.5 (100)
		21	Manassas Gap	1.8 (29)	1.0 (25)
		21	Chester Gap	2.0 (100)	1.0 (50)
		22–23	Manassas Gap	9.0 (103)	5.0 (100)
		24	Battle Mountain	1.5 (100)	1.2 (100)

than any other reason, was why it had failed. A sympathetic visiting British officer, Col. Sir Arthur J. L. Fremantle of the Coldstream Guards, would note in his diary, "It is impossible to avoid seeing that the cause of this check to the Confederate lies in the utter contempt felt for the enemy by all ranks." Col. William C. Oates of the 15th Alabama put it even more succinctly, when he wrote of Lee, "He was overconfident." The failure was a terrible blow to Lee. At one point he cried out in an agonized tone, "Too bad! *Too bad!* Oh! Too bad!" Now, with his grand attack broken, and more than two divisions in fragments, he had to face whatever Meade might have in store.

As it turned out, Meade had nothing in store. He considered making a counterattack. Even after beating off the Rebel attack Meade had available plenty of ammunition, over a dozen fresh batteries, and lots of relatively fresh troops—the virtually unscathed *VI Corps* plus the bulk of *V Corps*, the battered but rested *III Corps*, and parts of both *I Corps* and *XII Corps*. But he rightfully thought better of it. Even his uncommitted forces were tired after days of marching under the hot sun, and the army's rations had practically run out. Nor was the tactical situation suitable. His best available fresh outfits, the *VI* and *V Corps*, were over on the left, in the area of the Round Tops. To shift these troops into the center would take time, and expose them to a flank attack from Longstreet's corps. Moreover, the rebel batteries still lined Seminary Ridge, and, although they were low on shot and shell as a result of the bombardment, he knew very well that they still had plenty of canister. He essayed a probe of the Confederate right flank, only to find that Long-

street's troops were still full of fight. In addition an attack there would be over the same rugged ground on which the fighting 2 July had been. Either option seemed ill-advised. The only way Lee could still win the battle was for the *Army of the Potomac* to risk an offensive. Time was on Meade's side. If he waited he could expect reinforcements and supplies within a few days, while Lee's situation would deteriorate further. The better part of wisdom was to wait and see what Lee had in mind.

Capt. Thomas Goode Clarke, C.S.A. (above) *and his sons Albert and Jonathon* (opposite) *all three of Company F. 42nd Mississippi were all killed at Gettysburg.* (Collection of James W. Thompson)

CHAPTER VIII

THE RETREAT, 4 – 26 JULY

There were intermittent rains all during the morning of 4 July, cooling and refreshing the tired troops of both armies. By then Lee had pulled back Ewell's corps and brought it into line alongside Hill's, making a continuous front about 7,000 yards long from Oak Hill along Seminary Ridge. The last of the ammunition was served out and it was discovered that the army had enough for one more day of heavy fighting. Hoping Meade would attempt an attack, Lee had his men dig rifle pits and trenches on the western side—the reverse slope—of Seminary Ridge, under cover of the woods. Meanwhile he laid plans for retreat. That morning he sent his supply train, with its previous cargo of wounded men and booty, off under escort. One column, 17 miles long, went north-westwards through Cashtown, while a smaller one went to the southwest, through Fairfield. Lee held his troops in the trenches all day, hoping Meade would strike.

Meade refused to attack, disregarding even Lincoln's polite urgings that he do so. In the circumstances this was wise, though he might perhaps have thrust a strong column towards the mountains in an effort to canalize Lee's retreat. Instead, he confined himself to some probes with cavalry and infantry, while he spent the day resting the army. Anticipating needs over the next few days, he instructed Maj. Gen. Darius Couch, commanding the emergency volunteers and militia along the Susquehanna, and Maj. Gen. William H. French, who had 11,000 good troops available at Frederick and Maryland Heights, to be prepared to advance on short notice. Meanwhile, he arranged for rations to be brought up for the hungry troops, some of whom had not eaten in two days. The medical corps began bringing out the wounded, many of whom were found in houses and barns and cellars in Gettysburg now that the Rebels had pulled back from the town. Thousands of stragglers were returned to their units by the Provost Marshal. Ammunition was inventoried and distributed, with Hunt calculating that the average artillery piece had fired 100 rounds so far during the battle and that there remained unexpended over 100 more per gun. Then Meade waited.

By afternoon, with the rains coming down more heavily, Lee knew he would have to move. It would be a painful move, for nearly 7,000 seriously wounded men would have to be left behind, but he had no choice if he was to save the rest of the army, now reduced to not more than 45,000 men. In the evening, A. P. Hill's corps set out for Fairfield, followed after a short interval by Longstreet's, and then Ewell's, which stepped off at about 0200 hours on 5 July. The cavalry was out covering his flanks with grim determination. During the night Meade received evidence that a retreat was underway. He arranged for Gouverneur Warren to conduct a probe with Sedgwick's *VI Corps*. Meanwhile he issued orders for the army to move southwards. Warren encountered Ewell's rear guards near Fairfield at about 1500 hours. A small skirmish resulted, really an exchange of artillery at long range, and Warren and Sedgwick both came away convinced that Lee had deployed his entire army in Fairfield Gap. Meade immediately ordered the army to march to the support of Sedgwick. On Meade's instructions, Sedgwick essayed another probe on 6 July, which provoked a spirited response. Meade, who had briefly toyed with the idea of pursuing Lee through Fairfield Gap, decided that such an advance would be unprofitable if the gap was held in strength. In addition, he had received information to the effect that Lee was closing on Hagerstown, further south. Telling off a couple of brigades to follow Lee's rearguards through the gap as they withdrew, Meade put the *Army of the Potomac* on the road for Frederick. Meanwhile, Union cavalry harassed the retreating Confederate supply trains, inflicting some losses. Over the next few days Buford's and Kilpatrick's troopers, seeking to impede the Rebel retreat, traded blows with Stuart's. Particularly hot little actions occurred near Greencastle and at Hagerstown.

It was not until the morning of 7 July that Meade began a really determined pursuit, with some units pressing on as much as 34 miles despite extremely heavy rains. By 9 July the *Army of the Potomac* was drawn up on a front roughly five miles long running southwards from Boonesborough to Rohrsville, just east of the old Antietam battlefield. The army had successfully shifted its base to Frederick, less than 15 miles to the rear and in direct rail communications with Washington and Baltimore. At Frederick a great supply dump was being set up.

The retreat after the battle of Gettysburg

Nevertheless, many men needed shoes after the exhausting march, and there was a shortage of fresh horses for the cavalry and artillery. Even as the army was moving into this position, Meade effected some organizational changes. The higher officer ranks of the army had been badly depleted in the battle, with Reynolds dead and Hancock, Sickles, Gibbon, and Butterfield wounded. Maj. Gen. John Newton now had Reynolds' *I Corps,* Maj. Gen. William H. French

would take Sickles' *III Corps* from Birney, and Brig. Gen. William Hays would take over Hancock's *II Corps.* Brig. Gen. Alexander Webb took over Gibbon's division. Butterfield's loss was by no means unwelcome. Relieved on 5 July, his position as chief of staff had been cooperatively, and ably exercised temporarily by Maj. Gen. Alfred Pleasonton, the chief of cavalry, and Brig. Gen. Gouverneur K. Warren, the chief of engineers. Meade now made Brig. Gen. A. A. Humphreys his chief-of-staff, giving his division to newly arrived Brig. Gen. Henry Prince. All of the new men were competent, but none compared with Reynolds and Hancock, whose loss Meade felt deeply, both as personal friends and as brilliant commanders. Another loss of great concern to Meade was the many thousands of veteran troops who had been killed or wounded or captured. Moreover, due to peculiarities of Federal recruiting policies, he now also faced the loss of additional hundreds of men through expiration of their enlistments, including all of Stannard's fine brigade of Vermonters and several other regiments as well. Fortunately, replacements had begun to come in. The return of stragglers had brought the army up to about 65,000 men. Now 8,500 more from French's old command in western Maryland were incorporated bodily, mostly into *III Corps,* with a few going to *II Corps.* He also received about 1,500 cavalry, returning to duty after being remounted, six fresh batteries, and a single new long-service regiment, the *39th Masssachusetts.* An additional 10,500 short service men were forwarded from Baltimore and *XVIII Corps,* on the Carolina coasts. This was a net gain of about 21,500 men, but only about half of them were reliable enough, or had sufficient enlistment time left, to permit their incorporation into the army. There were other troops on hand as well, totalling over 30,000, but these were all emergency short-service men enlisted during the invasion of Pennsylvania. Meade ordered them to advance cautiously, so as to pose a potential threat to Lee's army and to restrict his foraging, but knew that they were completely overmatched by Lee's veterans. Certain political leaders, including Lincoln, failed to comprehend this essential point.

To all appearances, Meade, with over 100,000 men, was hesitating in face of an enemy with little more than half his numbers. Pressed by Washington, Meade won General-in-Chief Henry Halleck to his views. By now Meade was convinced that Lee intended to make a stand north of the Potomac, which was in flood, con-

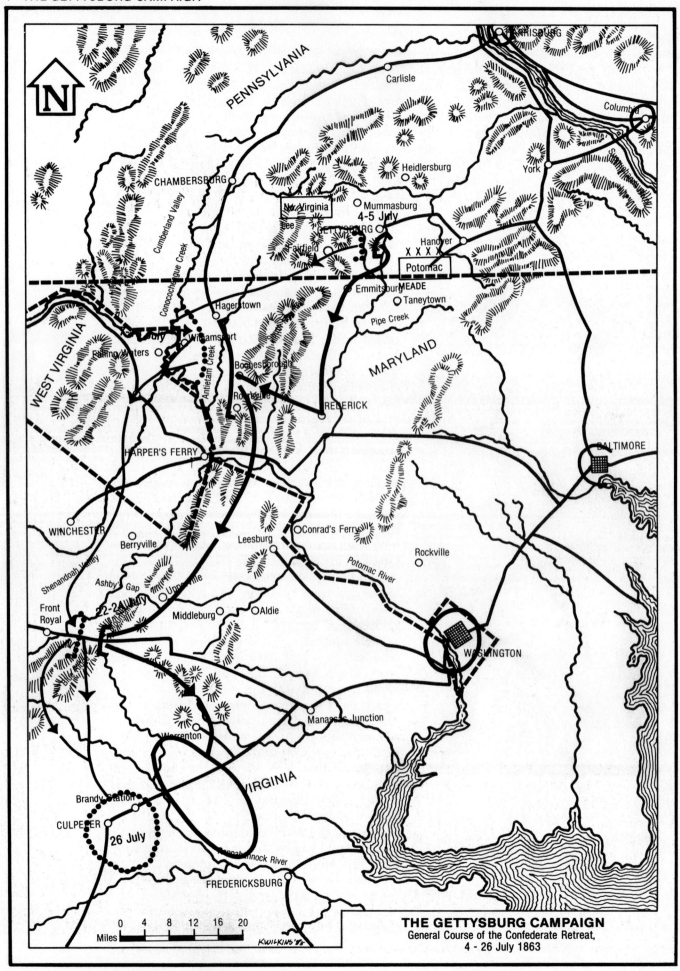

THE GETTYSBURG CAMPAIGN
General Course of the Confederate Retreat,
4 - 26 July 1863

centrating his army for battle west of the old Antietam battlefield. Meade intended to mass his entire strength before seeking a battle. Meade advanced with extreme—perhaps excessive—caution from the Boonesborough-Rohrsville line, taking three days to push on but eight miles. Lee abandoned Hagerstown on 12 July, and Meade then established himself on a broad front of about a dozen miles, from Hagerstown southwards along Antietam Creek towards the Potomac. There he was in position to seek battle with Lee. Lee, of course, had already made extensive preparations to meet him.

Lee had gotten his entire army into the Hagerstown area by 7 July. He had little inclination to effect an immediate crossing of the Potomac, which was in flood in any case, and set about preparing for battle. By 11 July he had established a sound defensive line on a seven mile front curving from Conococheague Creek on his left to the Potomac, on his right. This put water lines in his rear, making it theoretically an unfavorable position, but the terrain was good, and there were two normally good crossing points in his rear, at Falling Waters and Williamsport. He had limited communications with the other bank, permitting him to transfer his wounded and bring up some badly needed supplies, and his engineers were working on repairing a pontoon bridge damaged by Union raiders on 6 July. In addition, he fortified the entire front, and prepared a second line behind it, to cover the two towns. Aside from the cavalry, he tried to keep his troops out of contact with the enemy. Stuart's cavalry was kept busy, however, covering the flanks and keeping Union cavalry away from the main body. Skirmishes continued to occur on an almost daily basis. These were mostly small affairs, but there were occasional larger ones, notably near Hagerstown and at

Part of Camp Letterman, a vast field hospital established at Gettysburg after the battle to treat the seriously wounded.

Funkstown. By 13 July, however, his position was sufficiently secure as to permit him to pull in his cavalry as well, and it assumed a position on the flanks of the main line. Then he waited, hoping that Meade would attack him.

Meade intended to attack on 13 July, and so informed Halleck. But he was still new at his job, having assumed command only a fortnight before. Conducting a successful offensive battle was a different matter from conducting a successful defense. He convened a conference of his senior officers at about 2000 hours on 12 July. There he proposed a reconnaissance in force which could be converted into a proper attack should the opportunity present itself. Five of the corps commanders (Hays, *II*; French, *III*; Sykes, *V*; Sedgwick, *VI*; and Slocum, *XII*) expressed total opposition to the plan, two only favoring it (Wadsworth, *vice*; Newton, *I*; and Howard, *XI*),

along with Humphreys, Warren, and Pleasanton. As the bulk of his field commanders, including the two who were technically senior to him, Slocum and Sedgwick, opposed the plan, Meade felt it would be unwise to make the attempt. This went against his own judgment, for he had perhaps 75,000 men, albeit many were green, and Lee had no more than 55,000, though veterans all. He postponed the attack until he could make a personal survey of the Confederate lines. He spent 13 July doing just that in the pouring rain, accompanied only by Humphreys, against a background of heavy skirmishing between the two armies. Upon its completion, he issued orders substantially implementing his original plan for 0700 hours on the morning of 14 July. By then it was too late, for Lee had flown.

Lee had hoped that the *Army of the Potomac*

Charge of the 6th Michigan c

would attack on 13 July. When it failed to do so, and when the Federal troops began entrenching themselves, he remarked, rather unfairly in view of the reception he had prepared for them, that "They have but little courage!" He ordered a retreat. By this time his engineers had completed repairs to the Falling Waters bridge, and the Potomac had fallen to the point where it could be forded in places. The movement started just after dark, with Longstreet and Hill's men using the bridge and Ewell's the ford at Williamsport. Despite the heavy rains, the move was well executed. By noon on 14 July only two divisions, Heth's and Lane's (formerly Pender's) remained north of the river. Scouts sent out by Brig. Gen. Horatio G. Wright, of the *1st Division, VI Corps*, got wind of the movement early on 14 July. He immediately got his skirmishers forward, to discover that the enemy had evacuated their trenches. He pushed his entire division towards Williamsport. Sedgwick followed with the rest of the corps, and at 0830 hours Meade ordered a general advance.

The cavalry went in first, with Kilpatrick's division of about 3,500 sabers pushing up to Falling Waters. There he surprised Heth, with some 3,000 infantrymen, entrenched on a ridge about 2,500 yards from the town. Kilpatrick made a hasty, ill-conceived attack with but two squadrons. Though Pettigrew, actually commanding the Confederate rear-guard, received a mortal wound during it, the attack was a failure. Both squadrons were virtually eliminated as combat formations. As Kilpatrick renewed his attack in more formal style, Buford's division came up and hit the enemy on their right rear. The Rebels put up a tough rear guard fight, finally getting across the river in about an hour,

Cavalry charge at Falling Waters.

with a loss of some 700 prisoners and a few wagons. The Army of Northern Virginia had crossed the Potomac and reached the security of the Shenandoah Valley.

Both armies now began to move eastwards, Lee's to return to his former lines south of the Rappahannock and Meade's to attempt to intercept him. The *Army of the Potomac* crossed the river whose name it bore near Harper's Ferry on 17 July and began moving down the eastern side of the Blue Ridge Mountains, roughly paralleling Lee's line of march up the Shenandoah Valley about 15 to 20 miles to the west. Both armies had their cavalry out, and several small skirmishes took place. On 21 July there were larger clashes at Manasas Gap and Chester Gap. These convinced Meade that Lee's army was in the vicinity. On 22 July he ordered Maj. Gen. William French to force Manasas Gap with his *III Corps* in preparation for a general attack. Unfortunately, French proceeded in a rather lethargic fashion, allowing Confederate light forces to block his advance. As a result his corps did not get through the gap until the next day, only to find Lee deployed before Front Royal with two corps in line—Longstreet's and Hill's—and a third—Ewell's—nearby. French halted immediately. Meade began to get the balance of the *Army of the Potomac* forward, anticipating a general attack for 24 July. That night, Lee slipped away.

Manasas Gap was the last important engagement of the Gettysburg Campaign. On 24 July Ewell's corps began arriving at Culpeper Courthouse, just south of the Rappahannock River. Hill and Longstreet came up soon after. On 26 July the *Army of the Potomac* began encamping not five miles away, just north of the Rappahannock. Despite nearly two months of maneuver and battle the two armies were virtually back where they started from. The Gettysburg Campaign was over.

CHAPTER IX

THE GETTYSBURG CAMPAIGN AND THE WAR FOR THE UNION

Although it was essentially won in the Western Theater, the Gettysburg Campaign was the central event of the Civil War. These seemingly contradictory statements are both true. To seek victory in the Western Theater implied a long, hard struggle. Such a conflict was one for which neither Union nor Confederate political and military leadership was prepared or understood. Both sides thought in terms of a short war, with immediate decisive results, harking back to Napoleon's many swift victories or the war with Mexico, rather than to the more accurate model of the lengthy American Revolution. For the North, a protracted war meant unprecedented mobilization and repeated offensives to wear down the Confederacy's resistance. For the South, such a war meant a repetitive series of defensive battles designed to erode the Union's will. This was highly unpalatable to both sides. A quick win was what both were seeking, and a quick win could only be gained in the Eastern Theater. But a quick win proved elusive and by mid-1863 some perceptive individuals were beginning to understand that the war would be long. It was against this background that the Gettysburg Campaign ran its course. The greatest offensive effort of Confederate arms, the campaign represented perhaps the only opportunity that the south had to win the war by offensive means. The Confederate loss at Gettysburg meant that the war would go on. The South would never again have so fine an army as that which marched north from Culpeper Courthouse in June of 1863, while the armies of the Republic would continue to grow stronger and better, for in a protracted war, the greater material resources of the Union would inevitably triumph.

July of 1863 saw two great defeats inflicted upon the South, for Union success in the East at

Frank Haskell, a Gettysburg veteran, wrote one of the most vivid accounts of the battle.

177

Gettysburg was matched in the West by the surrender of Vicksburg to Maj. Gen. Ulysses S. Grant on 4 July. Together these two events mark the central moment of the war, in both a literal and a figurative sense. In July of 1863 the war had run nearly two years since Bull Run and had nearly two years yet to go before Appomattox. Gettysburg and Vicksburg were signals that the tide of battle had turned definitively against the South. Thus, in a very real sense, the Gettysburg Campaign was the "High Tide" of the Confederacy.

Lee's headquarters at Gettysburg

APPENDIX: AFTER GETTYSBURG

A little more than a week after Gettysburg, while the armies were still maneuvering back towards the Rappahannock line, serious riots occurred in many northern cities. The riot was once a commonplace of urban life throughout history. They were a way in which the inarticulate masses at the bottom of the social ladder could communicate their feelings to, and shake up the complacency of, those at the top. Rioting was also a form of amusement for the lower classes, and provided a useful and sage pretext for theft. Riots were by no means rare in the United States. Indeed, the death of Robert E. Lee's father, Henry Lee, a hero of the American Revolution, was a result of the long term effects of injuries received at the hands of rioters in Baltimore during the War of 1812. Riots were particularly frequent in the nineteenth century, as the population of America's cities grew faster than their ability to properly provide for their new citizens. Ethnic and religious tensions ran high. It was a far cruder and far more violent age than the present. The riots which broke out in the North during the summer of 1863 were sparked by the Enrollment Act of 3 March 1863.

The Enrollment Act instituted a military draft. This was the first that the Federal government resorted to conscription for military purposes, though such a proposal had been considered during the War 1812. Compulsory military service was, however, not new. The states had always had the authority to raise troops by compulsion, and frequently did. What made the Enrollment Act different was that the draft was to operate under direct Federal authority, bypassing the state governments. The Act was prompted by a decline in voluntary enlistments. Recruiting policy during the war left the procurement of manpower up to the states. The President fixed a quota for each state, and the governor filled it in any way he could. At first this was not difficult, for men volunteered in the hundreds of thousands. The demand for manpower was met quite adequately through the early part of 1863, though enlistment bonuses had to be offered in order to stimulate volunteering as time went on. But gradually the pool of willing volunteers began to dry up. At that point the Enrollment Act was passed. By this time the government of the Confederacy had been directly conscripting men for nearly a year, despite great resistance from state and local authorities and widespread draft evasion, including rioting.

The Enrollment Act was intended to stimulate volunteering. All able-bodied men not otherwise exempt were to be enrolled by the Provost Marshal and held liable to military service if called. As drafted men did not collect the lucrative Federal, state, city and even county bonuses, it was thought that, rather than waiting to be drafted men would voluntarily come forward. This all looked fine on paper, but there were some problems with the Enrollment Act. The Enrollment Act permitted a man to furnish a substitute: someone otherwise exempt who would volunteer to serve in the drafted man's place. And it permitted commutation. For $300.00 a man could buy himself out of the draft. Now in 1863 $300.00 was a considerable sum, representing nearly a year's income for a common laborer. Thus, the Enrollment Act seemed to many to place the burden of the war on the backs of the poor. At the same time, the Enrollment Act seemed a denial of states rights, and a foretaste of authoritarianism which did not sit well with many. This fueled rising racist sentiments among many people at the bottom of the social heap.

The Emancipation Proclamation, greeted by many as a major step on the road to Abolition, was not looked upon favorably by the lower classes of the Northern cities. Rough, ignorant men, the typical urban worker began to fear that with Emancipation the newly freed blacks would flood into the cities of the North, taking their jobs. A virulent racism was already common in America, and the immigrants imbibed of it. Thus, when actual enrollment of men for the draft began, in July of 1863, rioting broke out in many northern cities, the most widespread, bloody, and devastating riots in American history. There were disorders in Boston, Brooklyn, Baltimore, Jamaica (N.Y.), Rutland (Vt.), Portsmouth (N.H.), Wooster (Oh.), several other cities, and in the Pennsylvania coal country, but the most serious and most costly outbreak was in New York.

On Saturday, 11 July, the Provost Marshal had drawn the first names of what was to be a call for 12,500 men. That Sunday they were published in the newspapers. Crowds began to gather, but nothing untoward occurred. The next day a crowd gathered outside the Provost Marshal's office at 47th Street and Third Avenue as the drawing resumed. A brick was thrown through the window. A police officer passing by tried to restore order and was beaten. As the Provost Marshal and his staff fled out a back door, the crowd surged into the office, sacking it. Over the next four days bands of rioters 20 to 50 strong spread terror throughout the city. Badly outnumbered, the police were unable to concentrate sufficient force swiftly enough to smash the mobs. Rioting flared each day, with increasing intensity, as the uncontrollable mobs, often swelling to huge gangs of upwards of 300, including many women and even children, roved through many districts of the city, most notably throughout the midtown area, the Lower East Side, Greenwich Village, and down as far as the southern tip of Manhattan. Streetcars were overturned, police stations, recruiting offices, businesses, homes, and bordellos were sacked and burned. Many black men—though curiously few women—were beaten, some were lynched and others burned to death. Whites who attempted to interfere were given the same treatment.

With the police unable to cope with the disaster, Mayor George Opdyke called for the militia, only to find that it was on duty in Pennsylvania. Some recruits were available, some discharged veterans volunteered, and many civilians came forward to help. About a thousand men were made available from the harbor forts. These were still insufficient. Unable to sieze control of the streets on a permanent basis, Police Commissioner Thomas C. Acton and Brig. Gen. Harvey Brown disposed these forces as best they could, garrisoning city hall, police headquarters, armories, several arms factories, and the gas works, and sending flying squads of several hundred police and troops to suppress the most serious outbreaks. Some of these flying squads were ineptly handled, for no one had any training in the suppression of civil disorders. Numbers of the police and troops were injured and several killed battling the rioters, and many of the rioters were shot down.

The worst days were 14 and 15 July. The looting reached enormous proportions, tremendous fires burned out of control. Persons unwilling to join the rioters were beaten. The Colored Orphan Asylum, at Fifth Avenue and 43rd Street, was sacked and burned, though the rioters did give the staff time to evacuate the 237 children present. Several armories and arms factories were attacked. At some the rioters were successful, and they distributed arms. At others they were fought off by truncheon wielding police. At one point a huge mob marched down Broadway, heading for City Hall. Police Inspector Daniel Carpenter gave battle just below Bleeker Street. Holding the rioters in front with several hundred policemen, he hit them in the flank with several hundred more debouching from Bleeker Street. The mob disintegrated under police clubs and bullets, fleeing in all directions hotly pursued by Carpenter's men. Disorders flared in the semi-rural town of Harlem and in Brooklyn, both of which were covered by the Metropolitan Police. An attempt was made to sack the offices of *The Tribune* and lynch Horace Greeley, but it was smashed by Carpenter with 200 cops assisted by the employees and an armed squad from the staff of the rival *New York Times*. The Mayor's house was attacked, but successfully defended by a combination of oratory and a conspicuous display of force. Others, particularly prominent Republicans and blacks, were not so fortunate. The Brooks Brother store was looted and burned, losing over $50,000, but the rival Lord & Taylor, which had very good employee-management relations, was defended by its staff, who had been armed by the police.

Things began to ease late on the evening of Wednesday, 15 July, when two militia regiments, the *7th* and the *65th New York* reached the city from Harrisburg. The Roman Catholic Archbishop, John Hughes, spoke to a large crowd gathered outside his residence. And the Mayor announced that the city would pay the commutation of any drafted man, or award the $300.00 in cash as an enlistment bonus if he chose to serve. Things began to calm down a little. The next day the troops and police began to systematically suppress the rioting on a district by district basis, reinforced by several more regiments. On Friday there were no serious outbreaks reported, though tensions ran high and heavy patrolling was necessary. Maj. Gen. John Dix, arrived by steamer with 4,000 troops from his *Department of Virginia*. A few days later more troops arrived from the *Army of the Potomac*. With them on the streets the danger was passed.

The rioting had little effect on the draft, though the drawing of names was postponed for about a month, and the city's quota somewhat reduced. In the end the draft brought relatively few men directly into the army. Only about 200,000 men were actually subject to draft calls. Of those liable, 42,581 furnished substitutes—frequently in the form of a discharged veteran willing to re-up—and 82,724 paid the $300.00 commutation fee. Of the balance, only about 52,000 were actually enlisted, the others being found unfit for military service. However, the threat of the draft does seem to have done its work. Voluntary enlistments continued at a satisfactory rate.

The New York Draft Riot was, and remains, the bloodiest riot in American history. At least 105 people were killed during it, and possibly as many as 120—the normal murder rate was extraordinarily high, and there is some difficulty in determining whether certain deaths were riot-related or not. Eleven of the dead were black, three were policemen, eight were soldiers, and one was a civilian volunteer, the rest were all either innocent civilians or rioters. At least 268 people (105 policemen, 35 soldiers, and 128 citizens, including at least 23 blacks) were seriously injured and about 600 more less seriously so. As in the case of most civil disorders, the rioters suffered greater losses than the authorities. Altogether 443 people were arrested, though few were convicted. John V. Andrews, a Virginian resident in the city, received the heaviest penalty, three years on a charge of treason, having made an inflamatory speech at the onset of the riots. Most of the 60 or so other persons convicted did much less time. The total financial loss remains unclear, and estimates ranged upwards of $2,500,000, though only about $1,500,000 was paid out in claims against the city. The black population suffered most. Hundreds lost everything when their homes were destroyed, many others saw their jobs go up in smoke. A group of prominent merchants organized a committee to assist blacks in finding jobs and homes, but the blow to the black community had been devastating. By 1865 the black population of the city had fallen by nearly a quarter, from 12,581 to 9,943.

At the time there were those who said that the riot had been deliberately provoked by Confederate agents. This has proven to be unfounded, due partially to creative apologists for the Union cause, and partially to the fact that there were some outspoken Rebel sympathizers among the rioters. In addition to John V. Andrews, there was R. S. McCulloh, a Professor of Mathematics and Physics at Columbia University, who managed to elude the police and fled South. However, neither man had anything to do with the origins of the riot. Indeed, had the riot been planned it could easily have been far worse. There were literally tens of thousands of arms in the city, in factories, arsenals, and armories. Although the rioters did manage to sieze some of these, they could easily have taken far more. The rioters needed no outside agitators to stir them up. Although many professional criminals avidly took part in the riot, most of the rioters were uneducated, unskilled, impoverished workers, living in tenements in the mid-town area and in squalid huts and sheds in the semi-rural areas uptown. These were always classes that were most likely to riot. Relatively recent Irish Catholic immigrants seem to have predominated—then virtually at the bottom of the social scale—but the rioters included people from every ethnic group in the city, and from every religious group as well. The riot was frankly a phenomenon of the times. It was simultaneously an expression of unrest due to social and economic inequities, a demonstration against the draft, a racist outbreak, and an anarchic holiday. The impoverished mass at the bottom of the social ladder had rioted before, and they would do so again. It was the normal order of things.

WHICH SIDE HAD

During the Gettysburg Campaign two of the most skillful armies in the world maneuvered and fought against each other for nearly two months. One of them, the Army of Northern Virginia, had had the better of the other, the *Army of the Potomac* in virtually every encounter between the two for well over a year. Yet in this campaign, the Army of Northern Virginia suffered a devastating defeat. One reason for this was the leadership of each army. The senior officers on both sides were the products of the same military educational system, virtually everyone being a West Pointer. All had imbibed the concepts and principals of Napoleonic warfare as expounded by Henri Jomini, with its rationalistic systems. It is unlikely that any had ever heard of Karl von Clausewitz, let alone read him.

The military leadership of the Confederacy was generally superior to that of the Union for the first few years of the Civil War. There were many reasons for this. The South was essentially an aristocratic society, drawing its senior officers primarily from the landed planter class, men who were bred to command, and men whom less privileged southerners were quite willing to follow. Moreover, at the start of the war some very fine officers of the old army took service with the Confederacy. Many of these men embodied both the high technical competence of the professional soldier and the aristocratic character of the planter class. In addition, the Confederacy lacked a regular army. As a result, all of the 313 officers who had betrayed their oaths to the Union to "go South" soon attained high rank in the newly created volunteer "Provisional Army." Thus, a great deal of natural and professional leadership talent was immediately available to command the field armies. In contradistinction, the North was essentially a democratic society, with a deep suspicion of the regular officer, who was widely viewed as an aberrant character in a democracy, and a belief that war was not a technically difficult profession. In addition, the Union retained the services of the regular army. This army already had numbers of senior officers, and it was these men who led it in the initial stages of the war. However, the qualities necessary to attain high rank in peacetime are not usually those needed in war. Though there were many good men among the 767 active officers who remained loyal, most of these were left with the regular troops, rather than being spread among the volunteers. One result of this was that the younger officers who first reached high rank were those who had left the army some time before the war, and reentered it as volunteers in 1861, such as George McClellan, William Tecumseh Sherman, Henry Halleck, Ambrose Burnside, Joseph Hooker, and Ulysses S. Grant.

As the South was on the strategic defensive during the war, its generals enjoyed a considerable advantage over those of the Union, for the changing technology of war had come to greatly favor the defensive. The result was that the initial batch of Union commanders was not particularly successful, while the Confederate commanders gained a considerable reputation for competence. Of course, as time went on, and defeats accumulated, better officers rose to command the armies of the Republic. This was critically important in terms of the eventual outcome of the war, for Union leadership grew steadily better during the struggle, while Confederate leadership, good at the start, did not improve markedly. The brilliance of Robert E. Lee and several of his subordinates generally obscures the fact that most Confederate commanders were rather ordinary, deriving their reputations as much from the inherent advantage of the defensive as from any particular talent for war. By mid-1863 the differences between the military leadership on both sides had begun to disappear. Certainly there was little to choose from between Union of Confederate company and regimental officers, and probably not much difference between their brigade commanders. But the Confederacy still retained something of an advantage in the higher levels, at least in the Army of Northern Virginia.

Robert E. Lee was certainly one of the finest defensive strategists in history, and a resourceful, imaginative, and daring tactical commander. James Longstreet was one of the best tacticians in American history, being meticulous, thorough, and brave, though with no

BETTER GENERALS?

talent for independent command. Ambrose P. Hill and Richard Ewell had proven able division commanders, but during the Gettysburg Campaign were each directing a corps for the first time. This was a matter which ought to have caused Lee more concern than it would appear to have done, particularly as Ewell had an independent streak, much preferring to be left alone to do things in his own way and on his own terms. The south had its political generals too. Virginian A. P. Hill had been chosen by fellow-Virginian Lee to command III Corps over the more capable South Carolinian Daniel H. Hill since it contained but one brigade of South Carolinians to three from North Carolina and two from Virginia. Indeed, Virginians were noticeably over-represented in high places in Lee's army: only one of three lieutenant generals and four of eleven major generals were not Virginians, while Virginia supplied but 7.5 of the 37 infantry brigades and five of the seven cavalry brigades involved in the campaign, most of which were commanded by men from their native states.

Among Confederate division commanders, two of Longstreet's subordinates, Lafayette McLaws and John B. Hood, were particularly able. Jubal Early was perhaps less skillful than either of these but was certainly more aggressive, although rather insubordinate. The rest were all seasoned officers of proven ability. J. E. B. Stuart was, of course, one of the best cavalrymen in history, particularly capable when needed to screen movements or to secure information, but had an unfortunate thirst for glory. Lower ranking Confederate commanders were all generally good, some of them particularly so.

The leadership of the *Army of the Potomac* was not in the same class as that of the Army of Northern Virginia. Joe Hooker had been, and would subsequently again prove to be, a good corps commander. As an army commander he was an able administrator and a particularly brilliant strategist, but he lacked the intestinal fortitude and imagination to lead the army into action successfully. His replacement, George G. Meade, was neither as brilliant a strategist, nor as able an administrator, nor as inspiring a

leader as either McClellan or Hooker. He was, however, unlike either of them, willing to fight. Cautious and unimaginative he might have been, but he possessed a determination and dogged pugnacity which his predecessors lacked. Moreover, he had the confidence of his subordinates.

Among the Union corps commanders, both John Reynolds and Winfield Scott Hancock were excellent, being resourceful, bold and aggressive men, fully the equal of Hill or Ewell, though certainly not of Longstreet, nor of the late "Stonewall" Jackson. The others were capable, if unspectacular. Dan Sickles, the last political general left in the *Army of the Potomac*, had little professional skill, but was commendably aggressive in a command which had often lacked aggressive generals. Alfred Pleasonton was by no means as brilliant a cavalryman as Stuart, nor, indeed, as his own subordinate John Buford, but was reliable, understood his job, and did what he was supposed to do. Most of the Union division commanders were good. Several were particularly so, including James S. Wadsworth, Abner Doubleday, John Gibbon, Andrew A. Humphreys, Alpheus Williams, and John Newton. Several of these would eventually rise to command corps, though skill with a division was not necessarily a guarantee of competence with a corps. Lower ranking Union commanders were by this time quite skilled.

All of this leads to the conclusion that the leadership of the Army of Northern Virginia was still considerably better than that enjoyed by the *Army of the Potomac*. Yet in the end, it was the Army of Northern Virginia which suffered defeat. There were a number of reasons for this. Confederate strategy was certainly at fault. There was, in fact, no over-all strategic direction of the Confederate war effort. Although President Jefferson Davis was a West Point graduate with a brilliant war record in Mexico and a period of service as Secretary of War, he failed to perform as a war leader, preferring instead to immerse himself in the technical minutia of military administration rather than in the development of a grand strategy for winning the war. The result was that every Confederate

army commander was pretty much on his own. Thus Lee was able to gain approval for his plan to conduct an offensive in the Eastern Theater in the interests of relieving pressure in the Western Theater. The Union, on the other hand, had by mid-1863 begun to distinguish the military and the political aspects of warmaking, and to understand that the war was a single entity, with the needs of any one theater necessarily being understood only within the framework of the entire struggle. As a result, Lee went north into Pennsylvania with some vague notions about easing the pressure on Vicksburg and in Tennessee, and gaining supplies to carry the army through the winter, and possibly just possibly, securing foreign recognition. In contrast, Lincoln's instructions to his commander were fairly clear, his objective was the Army of Northern Virginia. Beyond this, is the fact that during the Gettysburg Campaign, Lee and his generals were performing rather poorly while their opponents were doing rather well.

A significant case in point illustrating the fact that Lee was not at his best is the careless way in which he handled Stuart's instructions, permitting the latter to go off and get lost, thus depriving Lee of his "eyes" in the middle of the most critical campaign hitherto in the war. In addition, Lee does not seem to have been overly concerned by the fact that two of his corps commanders were new at their jobs, and gave both Hill and Ewell considerable latitude right from the start of the campaign, which permitted them to spread their forces halfway across Pennsylvania by 28 June. In contrast, Meade, who was even greener at his job than either Hill or Ewell, took immediate control of his army, kept his corps closely concentrated, and moved with considerable dispatch once information as to the enemy's whereabouts began to come in.

A look at the performance of the various commanders during each of the three days of the battle is somewhat useful.

Head Quarters 1st Division, 1st A. C.
November 5th, 1863.

To the

Gov. of Pennsylvania,

Sir:

In noticing in the papers to-day an account of the proposition for a National Cemetery at Gettysburg, for the men that fell there in July last, I am reminded that I have neglected a duty which I owe to one of your Regiments,—the 56th. That Regiment is in the 2d Brigade of this Division; and was, at that time, under my command. It was my fortune to be in the advance on the morning of July 1st. When we came upon the ground in front of the enemy, Col. Hofmann's Regiment,—being the second in the column,—got into position a moment sooner than the others, the enemy now advancing in line of battle within easy musket range. The atmosphere being a little thick, I took out my glass to examine the enemy. Being a few paces in rear of Col. Hofmann, he turned to me and inquired, "is that the enemy?" My reply was "yes." Turning to his men, he commanded, "Ready,—Right-Oblique,—aim,—Fire!" and the battle of Gettysburg was opened. The fire was followed by other Regiments instantly, still that battle on the soil of Pennsylvania was opened by her own sons, and it is just that it should become a matter of history. When Col. Hofmann gave the command "aim," I doubted whether the enemy was near enough to have the fire effective, and asked him if he was within range; not hearing my question, fired, and I received my reply in a shower of Rebel bullets, by which many of the Col's. men were killed and wounded. My own horse, and those of two of my staff, were wounded at the same time.   *   *   *   *   *   *

I desire to say to your Excellency, that the 56th is one of the very best Regiments in the service.

Very respectfully, your obedient servant,

L. Cutler,
Brigadier General

A good soldier, Brig. Gen. Cutler, sets the record straight by apologizing for failing to give proper credit to a regiment.

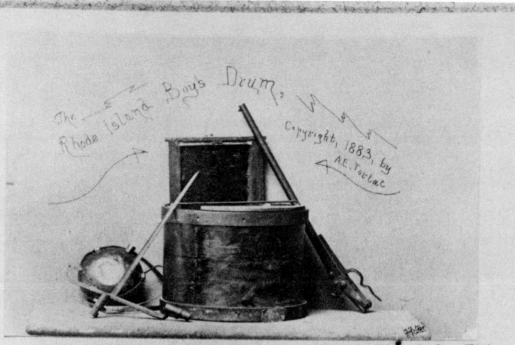

"Kiss me, before I die," said the little drummer boy to Mrs. Judge Fisher of York, as he laid at the foot of Round Top, dying far away from home and his dear mother. She kissed his pale cheeks, and tenderly held him in her arms, till his spirit had fled. His bereaved mother came several times in search of his body, but it could not be found, till 1867, when it was sent on to her home, in Providence, R. I. His broken drum was found near him, by farmer Jacob Weikert, who turned it into a bee-hive. Whittier, hearing of the peaceful work of this drum, wrote his poem upon it. The above is a photograph of the drum, with honey-combs. Its peaceful mission will be continued, and it will be exhibited in churches and Sunday-schools, willing to cast their pocket honey into it, to place a memorial of this young hero, or any of our country's dead, in the Historic Tower and Memorial Church, soon to be erected on this battle-field. We furnish cut stones, place and inscribe them at 30 cents per letter. Polished granite and marble at 50 cents per letter. Windows $100 and upwards.

Address and remit to the Memorial Church Association, Gettysburg, Pa.

N. B.—32 stereo views of this field are mailed at $1.50 per doz. This card for 25 cents, the poem and photo of drum, unmounted, for 10 cents.

BY J. G. WHITTIER.

In the old Hebrew myth, the lion's frame,*
  So terrible alive,
Bleached by the desert's sun and wind became
  The wandering wild bee's hive;
And he, who lone and naked-handed tore
  Those jaws of death apart,
In after time drew forth their honeyed store
  To strengthen his strong heart.

Dead seemed the legend; but it only slept
  To wake beneath our sky;
Just on the spot whence ravening Treason crept
  Back to its lair to die,
Bleeding and torn, from Freedom's mountain bounds,
  A stained and shattered drum
Is now the hive, where on their flow'ry rounds,
  The wild bees go and come.

Unchallenged by a ghostly sentinel,
  They wander wide and far,
Along green hill-sides, sown with shot and shell,
  Through vales, once choked with war,
The low reveille of their battle-drum
  Disturbs no morning prayer:
With deeper peace, in summer noons, their hum
  Fills all the drowsy air.

And Samson's riddle is our own to-day—
  Of sweetness from the strong,
Of Union, Peace and Freedom plucked away
  From the rent jaws of wrong.
From treason's death we draw a purer life,
  As, from the beast he slew,
A sweetness sweeter for his bitter strife,
  The old-time athlete drew!

*Judges xiv. 5–18.

Promotional flyer for one of the many hundreds of monuments and memorials on the field at Gettysburg

LINCOLN'S GETTYS

On a cool afternoon of Thursday, 19 November 1863, a little more than four months after the Battle of Gettysburg, President Abraham Lincoln delivered what is perhaps the most well known speech in American History, a model of the oratorical art. The occasion was the dedication of a portion of Cemetery Hill as a National Cemetery. Although the distinguished politician and orator Edward Everett was to be the principal speaker of the day, Lincoln had been asked to say a few words.

Contrary to widely accepted tradition, Lincoln wrote the first draft of the address at the White House, not on a train. Nor did he write it on the back of an envelope. He began it on a piece of White House stationery. As originally composed, it had but eight sentences. He subsequently added a ninth, in pencil, which ran over on to another piece of paper. This was the version he brought with him to Gettysburg on 18 November.

That night, both Lincoln and Everett were guests at the home of David Wills, a local Republican Party official. At some point during the night Lincoln revised his speech, writing a second draft on two fresh sheets of paper, and adding the final tenth sentence.

The ceremonies occupied much of the next day, which was rather overcast.

BURG ADDRESS

The 70-year old Everett spoke for two hours, delivering an address full of rhetorical flourishes and classical and historical allusions. When he was finished a patriotic ode was pronounced by a large chorus. Then Lincoln was introduced. Lincoln held his speech in his left hand, referring to it only occasionally, as he spoke slowly in his somewhat nasal, mid-western voice.

"Four score and seven years ago our fathers brought forth, upon this continent, a new nation, conceived in Liberty, and dedicated to the proposition that all men are created equal.

"Now we are engaged in a great civil war, testing whether that nation, or any nation, so conceived, and so dedicated, can long endure. We are met here on a great battlefield of that war. We have come to dedicate a portion of it as a final resting place for those who gave their lives that that nation might live. It is altogether fitting and proper that we should do this.

"But in a larger sense we can not dedicate—we can not consecrate—we can not hallow—this ground. The brave men, living and dead, who struggled here, have consecrated it, far above our poor power to add or detract. The world will little note, nor long remember, what we say here, but can never forget what they did here. It is for us, the living, rather to be dedicated here to the unfinished work which they have, thus far, so nobly carried on. It is rather for us to be here dedicated to the great task remaining before us—that from these honored dead we take increased devotion to that cause for which they gave the last full measure of devotion—that we here highly resolve that these dead shall not have died in vain; that this nation shall have a new birth of freedom; and that this government of the people, by the people, and for the people shall not perish from the earth."

Contrary to tradition, applause interrupted Lincoln five times during his brief address. At the end the crowd gave what one observer called "tremendous applause" and three cheers. Despite Lincoln's belief that the address was a "flat failure," its oratorical merit was recognized immediately. Everett put it best when he told Lincoln ". . . there was more in your twenty lines than in my twenty pages." History and popular sentiment, have proven him right. The Gettysburg Address turned the battle into a symbol of the war for the Union, and it is for that, as much as for its oratorical merits, that the speech is remembered.

Scene at the National Cemetery on 18 November, 1863, when Lincoln delivered his famous dedicatory address. Lincoln is believed to be one of the figures near the top of the crowd between the two flags in the center left.

GUIDE FOR THE INTERESTED LAYMAN

RECOMMENDED READING.

The Civil War is perhaps the most widely-written about subject in American history. There has been a steady stream of books and articles almost continuously for more than 120 years. This listing of works which have some bearing on the Gettysburg Campaign is by no means to be considered definitive. Rather, it is a short guide for further reading. The more serious student of Gettysburg should consult Richard A. Savers' *The Gettysburg Campaign, June 3—August 1, 1863: A Comprehensive, Selectively Annotated Bibliography* (Westport, CT: 1982) for a more significant guide to the literature of the battle and the campaign.

The single most valuable work on Gettysburg is undoubtedly Edwin B. Coddington's *The Gettysburg Campaign: A Study in Command* (New York: 1968 & Dayton, OH: 1979), which is exhaustively researched and meticulously detailed. All other works are essentially useful supplements to this.

OF PARTICULAR VALUE ARE:

Edward J. Stackpole, *They Met at Gettysburg* (3rd Ed., Harrisburg, PA: 1982), a classic account which remains of considerable value.

Glen Tucker, *High Tide at Gettysburg* (Indianapolis: 1958) and *Lee and Longstreet at Gettysburg* (Indianapolis; 1968). Tucker's books are both careful accounts of the battle, done from an essentially Southern point of view. The second work is notable for its discussion, and refutation, of the criticisms levelled at Longstreet and for its examination of other problems in the battle.

George R. Steward's *Pickett's Charge* (2nd Edition, Dayton, OH: 1980), is a meticulous account of the circumstances and events of the

Confederate attack on Cemetery Ridge on 3 July, done in great detail.

Fairfax Downey's *The Guns at Gettysburg* (New York: 1958) is a good account of the artillery during the battle, with considerable detail on the lives and work of artillerymen and of their service, while his *Clash of Cavalry* (New York: 1959) is the best account in English of Brandy Station. Curiously the undoubted best work on the subject is in German—and does an excellent job of illustrating the life and work of cavalrymen, their mounts, and their service.

A remarkable guide to the appearance of the battlefield may be found in William A. Frassanito's *Gettysburg: A Journey in Time* (New York: 1975), which carefully examines contemporary photographs and drawings, and which may be usefully supplemented by Vol. III of *The Images of War*, edited by William C. Davis (New York: 1983).

More general accounts of the battle within the framework of the war itself may be found in the appropriate volumes of Allan Nevins' *The War for the Union*, Bruce Catton's *The Army of the Potomac* and *The Centennial History of the Civil War*, and Shelby Foote's *The Civil War: A Narrative*, all of which are available in a number of different editions.

Douglas Southall Freeman's classic *R. E. Lee: A Biography*, available in several editions, remains unsurpassed as an account of Lee's life, though Freeman was overly respectful of his subject. His later *Lee's Lieutenants* is more balanced, and shows some sensitivity to Longstreet's views. Similar in its coverage of Federal leadership is Kenneth P. Williams', *Lincoln Finds a General* (New York: 1949–1959). Aside from Lee, biographies of most of the commanders during the campaign are few in number, but note should be taken of Freeman Cleaves, *Meade of Gettysburg* (Norman, OK: 1960), Edward J. Nichols, *Toward Gettysburg: A Biography of General John F. Reynolds* (University Park, PA 1958), Edgecomb Pinchon, *Dan Sickles* (Garden City, NY: 1945): Glenn Tucker, *Hancock the Superb* (New York: 1960); Manly Wade Wellman, *Giant in Gray: A Biography of Wade Hampton of South Carolina* (New York: 1949); Martin Scheneck, *Up Came Hill* (Harrisburg, PA: 1958); H. J. Eckenrode and Bryan Conrad, *James Longstreet* (Chapel Hill, N.C.: 1936): and Burke Davis, *Jeb Stuart, The Last Cavalier* (New York: 1957).

There are many firsthand accounts of the battle available. Perhaps the most readily accessible of these are those in Vol. III of *Battles and Leaders of the Civil War*, edited by Robert Underwood Johnson and Clarence Clough Buell, which has seen several editions. *Gettysburg* edited by Early Schenk Myers and Richard Brown (New Brunswick, NY: 1948) usefully collects a great many accounts of different incidents during the battle from a range of individuals, which includes everyone from generals down to schoolboys. Frank A. Haskell's *The Battle of Gettysburg* and Sir Arthur Fremantle's *Three Months in the Southern States* have both also been reissued with some frequency. The memoirs of many of the participants are available, among the most interesting of which are Longstreet's, *From Manasas to Appomattox*, which has seen several editions. Rarely available, but recently reissued, is William C. Oates' *The War Between the Union and the Confederacy and a History of the 15th Alabama* (Dayton, OH: 1980).

A useful guide to the military practice of the times is H.C.B. Rogers' *Confederates and Federals at War* (New York: 1983), which may be supplemented by Jack Coggins' *Arms and Equipment of the Civil War* (New York: 1962), which covers an enormous range of detail, from uniforms to tactics, and is profusely illustrated. Aside from a great deal of racial clap-trap, *Attack and Die* by

GUIDE FOR THE

Grady McWhiney and Perry Jamieson (Alabama: 1982) gives a good look at the problems of Civil War tactics. Other works of value on this subject are B. I. Wiley's two volumes, *The Life of Johnny Reb* (Indianapolis: 1943) and *The Life of Billy Yank* (Indianapolis: 1952). Mark M. Boatner III's *The Civil War Dictionary* (2nd Edition, New York: 1979) is a handy reference to all sort of information on the conduct of war during the Civil War, on the individuals involved, and on the Gettysburg Campaign in particular. Also of value as reference works are the two volumes by Ezra J. Warner, *Generals in Blue* (Baton Rouge, 1984) and *Generals in Gray* (Baton Rouge: 1983).

The subject of Lincoln at Gettysburg has been explored in Philip B. Kunhardt's *A New Birth of Freedom* (Boston: 1983)

The practice of medicine during the Civil War is discussed in Stewart Brooks' *Civil War Medicine* (Springfield, IL: 1966), George W. Adams' *Doctors in Blue* (New York: 1952), and H. H. Cunningham's *Doctors in Gray* (Baton Rouge, 1958).

The importance of music and musicians in military operations prior to the twentieth century is often overlooked. For the Civil War see Kenneth E. Olson's *Music and Muskets: Bands and Bandsmen of the American Civil War* (Westport, Ct: 1981).

On the New York draft riots, Adrian Cook's *The Armies of the Streets* (Lexington, KY: 1974) is likely to remain unsurpassed.

No student of the Campaign and Battle of Gettysburg can ignore the value work of John W. Busey and David G. Martin in elucidating the numbers of men involved, along with the numbers and types of artillery pieces and sundry other bits of information incorporated in their *Regimental Strengths at Gettysburg* (Baltimore: 1982), on which the present work relies rather heavily.

There are a number of novels which deal with Gettysburg. The most recent of any military interest—literary and historical merit aside—are John Jakes' *The Blue and the Gray* and Michael Shaara's *Killer Angels*. Tom Wicker's *Unto this Hour* has a very good picture of military life during the war, as does Jakes' *North & South*, which has a fair picture of pre-war West Point as well.

JOURNALS

There are a number of periodicals which are devoted to the Civil War, or which regularly feature Civil War articles. These include:

The Civil War Times Illustrated, a general interest magazine covering all aspects of the war, usually with articles of considerable utility and reliability, it is also of great value for its reviews of current Civil War literature.

Blue and Gray is devoted primarily to those interested in reenacting Civil War battles, and contains many articles devoted to details of equipment, uniforms, and military practice.

Military Images deals with pictures of the American military, with an emphasis on the Civil War, and frequently provides useful information on the details of military dress and the history of particular units or individuals.

Strategy & Tactics is primarily a military history journal, and regularly contains articles on Civil War topics.

CIVIL WAR INTEREST GROUPS.

Many organizations exist for persons interested in the Civil War. The most notable of such are the Civil War Round Tables. First organized in the 1940's, these exist in many cities, usually meeting monthly for dinner and a lecture on a Civil War topic. Some round tables have been meeting consistently for over 30 years.

There are also a number of re-enactment

INTERESTED LAYMAN

clubs. These are composed of people who dress up in Civil War era uniforms and attempt to recreate the feel of life in camp and in battle during the war. They provide useful "hands-on" experience in learning how muskets are loaded and used, and in how contemporary drill and tactics worked. Various round tables and re-enactment groups are regularly listed in *The Civil War Times Illustrated* and *Blue and Gray*.

SIMULATIONS AND WARGAMES.

There are a considerable number of wargames which focus on the Gettysburg Campaign in one way or another. What follows is a brief listing of some of the more notable such simulations still in print.

Gettsburg (Avalon Hill, 1964)
High Tide (Phoenix, 1982)
Killer Angels (West End Games, 1983)
Lee Moves North (Simulations Publications, 1973)
Terrible Swift Sword (Simulations Publications, 1976)

FILM.

While the Civil War has been a central theme in a number of notable motion pictures, Gettysburg has been rather neglected. The two most significant efforts to portray the battle span a period of over 75 years. D. W. Griffith, whose father was colonel of the Confederate 1st Kentucky Cavalry, included the battle in his masterful, and racist *Birth of a Nation* in 1915. The effort is, however, unrealistic and overly romanticized. More recently, the television version of John Jakes' *The Blue and the Gray* did a more ambitious job of Gettysburg, which, while inaccurate in numerous ways—including having Lincoln speak after Gettysburg but before Vicksburg—is useful for some of the technical details, most notably in terms of the artillery, as in his *North and South*. In most films uniforms are generally too uniform, and usually too clean.

DISCOGRAPHY

During the Civil War centennial a number of recordings were issued with music from the period. None are currently in press.

MUSEUMS.

There are numerous museums which contain materials related to the Civil War.

Although there is no national military museum in the United States, the U.S. Army maintains 68 separate museums devoted to a variety of particular subjects. Though none are devoted specifically to the Civil War, most have some Civil War memorabilia, even when their specific mission may deal with a completely different subject.

There is an interesting Civil War exhibit in the Museum in the Statue of Liberty. One of the best collections of Civil War materials is that in the Museum of the Confederacy in Richmond, which has a useful library associated with it. In addition, many state and local historical societies also have useful exhibits.

THE GETTYSBURG NATIONAL ★ MILITARY PARK ★

The movement to preserve the Gettysburg battlefield as a memorial park was started by the veterans themselves. After many years, their efforts resulted in the acquisition of the their lands, and adjacent land by the National Park Service. Today park land encompasses a significant portion of the original battlefield.

The Gettysburg battlefield is remarkably well preserved. Aside from the areas adjacent to the town of Gettysburg itself, and along some of the routes leading northwards from it, development has been relatively limited. There has been no significant construction or erosion on the field, save in the area immediately west of Cemetery Hill. There has, however, been a rather considerable expansion of wooded areas, so that sites which were sparsely treed in the summer of 1863 are now virtually forested. It is thus no longer possible to see clearly the area of "Pickett's" charge from Little Round Top, since a grove obscures part of the view.

The field is liberally sprinkled with memorials, markers, and guns dedicated to particular units, individuals, and states. The Pennsylvania monument is the largest, but that to Brig. Gen. Gouverneur K. Warren on Little Round Top is perhaps the most impressive. There is no monument to Longstreet. Many of the markers are properly sited and provide useful guides to the location of specific regiments, batteries, and individuals during the battle. This is particularly the case for the markers along Cemetery Ridge. In other cases, however, monuments have been placed for aesthetic reasons, and are of little use as guides to the battle. A number of the monuments are meticulously preserved and regularly decorated, notably that to the *New York Irish* brigade. Others are sadly neglected. The descendents of some of the men who fought at the battle preserve their memory, and it is moving to note that on both the Pennsylvania memorial and the New York memorial on Little Round Top, the names of individual soldiers are carefully polished by their progeny from time to time.

About 25 years after the battle several hundred cannon were placed on the field as part of the preservation program. While the exact number varies, in as much as pieces are sometimes removed for repair, there are about 225 guns marking Union positions and about 180 for Confederate ones. However, only one gun—a 3"-rifle at the foot of Buford's statue—has been positively identified as having been at the battle. Many clearly were not, for they bear 1864 foundry marks, and a number of the pieces are facsimiles, such as 6-pounders which have been drilled out to look like 12-pounder Napoleons. The most carefully sited pieces, which are in some instances accompanied by caissons, are those along Cemetery Ridge, where one may even find one with a burst barrel.

the Visitor Center, and the Cyclorama Center, provide useful exhibits on the battle, though with occasional inaccuracies and with a generally bland narrative. The cyclorama itself is rather spectacular, but not always informative. It is possible to tour the field by bus or car, but walking, bicycle, or horseback are undoubtedly the best ways for anyone seriously interested in understanding the course of events. The field can covered on foot in two full days, devoting one to the areas of the first day's battle, and to the fighting on Cemetery Hill and Culp's Hill, and the second to the area from the Peach Orchard to Little Round Top and to Cemetery Ridge and the ground before it, saving "the angle" for last.